BEYOND THE PALE

THE STORY OF SIERRA NEVADA BREWING CO.

KEN GROSSMAN

WILEY

Published by John Wiley & Sons, Inc., Hoboken, New Jersey.
Published simultaneously in Canada.

For general information about our other products and services, please contact our Customer Care Department within the United States at (800) 762-2974, outside the United States at (317) 572-3993 or fax (317) 572-4002.

Wiley publishes in a variety of print and electronic formats and by print-on-demand. Some material included with standard print versions of this book may not be included in e-books or in print-on-demand. If this book refers to media such as a CD or DVD that is not included in the version you purchased, you may download this material at http://booksupport.wiley.com. For more information about Wiley products, visit www.wiley.com.

Library of Congress Cataloging-in-Publication Data:

Grossman, Ken, 1954-
    Beyond the Pale: The Story of Sierra Nevada Brewing Co./Ken Grossman.
    Includes index.
    ISBN: 978-1-118-00736-5 (cloth); ISBN: 978-1-118-22188-4 (ebk);
    ISBN: 978-1-118-23557-7 (ebk)
        1. Sierra Nevada Brewing Co.   2. Brewing industry–California–History.
3. Beer industry–California–History   4. Grossman, Ken, 1954-
5. Brewers–California–Biography.   I. Title.
HD9397.U54
338.7'66342092–dc23
    [B]
                                                                2013020065
Printed in the United States of America
10   9   8   7   6   5

CONTENTS

PREFACE

In 2009, I was first approached by my friend and colleague Sam Calagione, founder of Dogfish Head Brewery, about being involved in a book on the dawn of American craft brewing. Sam planned on doing several long, in-depth interviews with a handful of brewers to try to capture what it was like during the early years before many people accepted or even knew what "craft beer" or being a craft brewer was all about. The marketplace was so different than it is today, and it's hard for many beer drinkers who grew up with craft beer to imagine a time when there were virtually no options other than American light lagers and a few almost indistinguishable imported lagers.

I was enthusiastically but cautiously on board and welcomed the opportunity to revisit those early years of building Sierra Nevada Brewing Co. and tell my story. Over the years several people had tried to convince me to write my own book, but I never felt I had time and put it off. When Sam asked, my time was already pretty well committed, as usual, but it seemed worthwhile. I thought I could fit it into my busy schedule since he would be doing most of the work. Sam had already written two beer books, and I thought he had the desire and energy to dig in to the story.

In the past few years, there have been several accurate and well-researched publications that have done a good job touching on the early pioneers of craft brewing and the industry's rapid growth over the past 30 years, as well as giving a good overview of the wider beer industry. Maureen Ogle's *Ambitious Brew*, Tom Acitelli's *The Audacity of Hops*, and Steve Hindy and Tom Potters' *Beer School* give readers an inside look at the craft industry. Even so, there's a lot that hasn't been written about the amazing American beer revolution that has spawned an unprecedented consumer movement and that has now spread globally with US-inspired craft breweries opening in dozens of countries around the world.

Sam planned to write a more focused book with just the handful of brewers who took a big leap of faith and decided to get into the brewing business when, based on all accounts, the odds were heavily stacked against them. He was going to start with the first generation of homebrewers who went "pro" in the late 1970s and early 1980s. Charlie Papazian's participation would weave in the role that homebrewing played and the establishment of the Association of Brewers, which became the current Brewers Association.

When Sierra Nevada took that leap, the American brewing industry had hit bottom, with scarcely 40 individual brewing companies in existence. The industry had hit a high of more than 3,000 breweries in the 1870s but declined after that as a result of Prohibition, the repeal of Prohibition, and other forces. The few small breweries that remained in the 1970s were unable to compete with a handful of aggressive national brands that capitalized on economies of scale both in lower production costs and in their ability to leverage syndicated radio, and later TV, to promote their increasingly homogenous light lagers. Most of the surviving small brewers tried to match the style and price of national brands, but with declining volumes and, in most cases, deteriorating pre-Prohibition plants, they couldn't remain competitive or sustain their companies.

Sam intended to focus on the small group of brewers who were the first to reverse that trend. In the late 1970s there were half a dozen of us who made the jump from homebrewing to establishing the first crop of micro, or craft, breweries in America. Most people in the brewing industry thought we were nuts, and the rate of brewery consolidation had some analysts predicting that there would be only two or three breweries that survived into the future. People wondered what we were thinking, opening breweries when so many had failed so recently. Even many of my closest family members and friends weren't sure it was such a great idea, but I persisted with my vision for Sierra Nevada.

I can't speak for everyone in that early group, but I think most of us had a similar vision. We wanted to make a different kind of beer; we didn't want to make what the other breweries were brewing. In most parts of the country, there really wasn't any interesting American beer on the shelves, and the majority of what you could find was light lager. As accomplished homebrewers we wanted to brew the types of beer we had grown to love, and we wanted to share *our beer*, our hoppy, dark, flavorful creations. Our friends loved our beers; certainly we could find other people who would as well. We all had modest ambitions and severely limited budgets. All of us borrowed and begged money from family and friends because no institution would loan us a penny. We cobbled together our breweries with used parts, resourcefulness, and ingenuity and proceeded to brew the beers we loved. At the time, what we were doing certainly didn't seem to be a movement and definitely didn't seem to be one that would grow for more than 30 years to become what it is today.

To get started on his book, Sam came to Chico and we spent time discussing those early years and developing the framework for what he'd write. He has a publisher interested in the book but is still in the planning stages. In the meantime, Sam's publisher (John Wiley & Sons, Inc.) was also very interested in my story and wanted to tell it, so they asked me if I wanted to write my own book. I didn't jump at the chance when they asked because my life was getting more complicated by the minute. I had been agonizing about building a second brewery and had just made the decision to move forward with looking for a location. The last thing I needed on my plate was writing a book, so I dragged my feet for several months until one day I had an uncharacteristic lapse in judgment and finally succumbed.

Looking back, it's hard to say exactly why I caved in. Still, I know that our consumers and fans are interested in the Sierra Nevada story. Only recently have we expanded Sierra Nevada's tours, and I'm still surprised by the number of people who come to Chico with the sole purpose of visiting the brewery. I'm also keenly aware that I haven't made this journey on my own. My family, friends, and employees have been there in one way or another every step of the way, and Sierra Nevada wouldn't be what it is without them. I'm not inclined to wax nostalgic, but as my children take a greater role in the company and

I contemplate my future, it seemed like a good time to look back at how we started and got to where we are today.

This book has taken much longer than anyone involved ever intended, and I owe a great debt of gratitude to all involved for their patience and persistence. Juggling my duties running my brewery in Chico and designing a new brewery in North Carolina coupled with frequent travel the past few years has made focusing on a book difficult. This project would not have been possible without all of the help I received from my daughter, Sierra Grossman, and Melissa Cafferata, who took my ramblings and musings and turned them into an organized story.

As much as I have grumbled about this undertaking and additional burden to my already full schedule, the process has been both enlightening and very rewarding. Thankfully, I squirreled away a good stash of historical information about Sierra Nevada (there are also many people who accuse me of being a pack rat). While writing this book, I came upon a lot of great memories and some anguish rereading and looking at thousands of old articles, photographs, and correspondences. Sierra and Melissa have joked that their next project will be a museum full of my mementos from the last 30-some years.

I am often asked how it feels now to have built this successful company. My first response is usually that I didn't build it on my own; legions of people have contributed to Sierra Nevada's success. Of course, watching your seemingly impossible dream grow into a successful reality is great. And to do it in beer is even better. The craft brewing community is a wonderful place to work, and I'm proud to have been part of the craft revolution in this country. It's been a long slog at times and a lot of hard work for the past 30-plus years, but I've always found that being persistent and staying true to my values has paid off. I hope you enjoy the ride as much as I have.

ACKNOWLEDGMENTS

This book is dedicated to the unfathomable number of people who have contributed to the success of Sierra Nevada Brewing Co., both those who have helped craft our amazing beers and our fans—brewery visitors, Pub regulars, and loyal drinkers. We've all played a part in the American craft brewing revolution that forever changed the beer industry.

Beyond the Pale would not have been possible without all the effort of my daughter, Sierra Grossman, and her partner in crime, Melissa Cafferata, who acted as my editors, bringing life to my often disjointed stream of thoughts and weaving them into a cohesive story.

My mother, Eleanor Guy, put up with my harebrained ideas and, although it caused her great anxiety over the years, always supported me.

Initially the brewery was only a pipe dream with a scant chance of success, but almost from the beginning it took on a life of its own, too often becoming a demanding and all-consuming force that nearly overwhelmed me. Building the brewery over the past 35 years has brought me a great deal of joy and satisfaction, but I am also keenly aware of the sacrifices that others have made to support my dream. I want to thank my family—Katie, Sierra, Carrie, and Brian—and acknowledge what they endured. For me, the balance of work and home life was often severely tilted, and many times I was so involved with the brewery that I neglected my very special and amazing family.

I would especially like to thank my wife, Katie, who has stuck with me all these years through this often tumultuous and challenging voyage. Katie bore the brunt of raising our family and keeping some semblance of normality at our home when I was totally absorbed in some challenging phase of the brewery's growth (and there have been many). To Katie: It's been a hell of a journey so far, and I know it's not been an easy one, but thanks for sticking with me.

1

A TOASTER, A DRYER, AND A GLIMPSE OF THINGS TO COME

Blessed is the mother who gives birth to a brewer.

—Czech saying

When I was two years old, I inserted a pair of tweezers into an electrical outlet. I vaporized them, gave myself quite a jolt, blew a fuse, and scared the wits out of my mother. Blowing a fuse was new, but I was already a dedicated student of electrical theory and this was not the first experiment that had unexpected results. It was this type of outcome that taught me to hide my experimentation from my mother; however, it's hard to hide a blown fuse. She knew that I loved to take things apart, but she didn't know the extent of my curiosity or how much it would shape the course of my life. The fact that I've survived to write this story is either incredible luck or a true testament to man's (or a boy's) ability to survive against amazing odds.

SETTING THE STAGE

I grew up in a typical, middle-class family in the 1950s. My mom was a housewife, raising three kids with a husband who was rarely around. My father was a partner in a small law firm that specialized in an obscure and now mostly obsolete aspect of the law related to interstate trucking; he had clients around the country and traveled a lot. He practiced law during the time when a three-martini lunch was the norm, and he fully embraced the program. I can recall visiting his office when I was young, but only a few times. I remember being fascinated by their now-antique phone switchboard with all the plugs and sockets that the receptionist used to route calls. On one occasion, I swapped a few of the plugs while playing with it and probably disconnected a few important calls. He didn't bring us kids to the office very often after that.

My brother, Steve, is two years older than I am; like most younger brothers, I tagged along with him and his friends much of the time. We enjoyed each other's company and were always close. My sister, Diane, is four years younger than I am. Being the youngest and only girl of the family, she didn't always fit into our gang of neighborhood boys.

My parents lived in an apartment in downtown Los Angeles, but they wanted to move out of the busy city. In 1959, my father got a promotion, and we moved to Woodland Hills in the San Fernando Valley when I was four and a half. Our two-bedroom, two-bathroom middle-class corner house was in a nice neighborhood but nothing fancy. The area had been an old walnut orchard, probably remnants of the Otis Chandler–Owens River water and land grab. We had just over half an acre with several big old walnut trees, so we had lots of room for building forts, tree houses, and go-kart tracks. We even had chickens for a little while until the rooster attacked and chased one of the neighborhood kids, who ran through a closed sliding glass door in terror. His injuries and the damage put an end to our livestock.

My parents divorced when I was 10, but since my dad had rarely been around before that, it wasn't that dramatic of a shift in our family dynamic. After my parents divorced, my mother worked for the Head Start program as a teacher and later went back to school to get her master's degree in guidance and counseling with the hope of getting a better-paying job. In the absence of my father the position of a male role model fell mostly to my mother's father, Lewis Drucker, a generally soft-spoken and kind father, Superior Court Judge, and family patriarch. He had been born and raised in New York City in a family with limited financial resources, and as a young teenager he hitched and rode the rails out to California, where he later put himself through law school.

Even though my grandfather was a respected and successful judge, he often seemed most contented with a paintbrush in hand or when trimming oleanders around my mom's house. Much like him, I have always had the need to keep busy, not just physically but also mentally. Even while relaxing, I've always felt the need to be working on a project or accomplish something, whether it's tearing apart a stove or rebuilding the shower in a vacation house. One of the strongest memories and life lessons I got from my grandfather was his mantra, "Waste not, want not." I can't count the number of times I heard him say that to us kids or, for that matter, to anyone else who'd listen. Even though I didn't have his experience of living through the Depression, I developed a penchant for resourcefulness, frugality, and collecting because of his influence.

TODDLER TINKERING

My early years marked the beginning of many years of dangerous and foolhardy behavior. I remember always enjoying taking things apart and figuring out how they worked. In the beginning, this usually meant a one-way trip for the devices because they were rarely restored to their original condition. I was regularly reprimanded for dismantling the household appliances. My mother tells stories of me still in diapers taking apart the toaster, the washing machine, electrical outlet covers, and anything within my reach, using kitchen knives, tweezers, or whatever I could turn into a rudimentary tool. The way my mother tells it, if I was left alone for a few minutes she would find me by following the trail of screws, washers, and bits of deconstructed devices. These stories became family lore, and like many things often repeated were also embellished; the extent of what actually transpired is hard to know. These early experiments were an indication of what would be a constant quest to understand how things work, and although it took a little longer to figure out how to put things back together, I learned a lot in those early years and soon started to invent and design my own devices and creations. My first invention came about when I was four years old. After watching my mom stoop to pick up clothes and hang them on the clothesline, I fastened a pulley to the laundry basket with a rope to hoist it to hip level, eliminating the need for her to bend over repeatedly.

My mom's older brother, Bob, helped encourage my growing interest in science and technology. When I was just starting to read, he introduced me to the *New Tom Swift Jr. Adventures* series. In the books, Tom invented all sorts of devices, fought for justice, and explored space. Although I wasn't much of a reader at that time, I was captivated by Tom and all his adventures. I had most of the series, but *Tom Swift and His Megascope Space Prober* was one of my favorites. Tom was a young, handsome, accomplished scientist and a brilliant inventor. He drove a sports car, had a beautiful girlfriend, and traveled through space solving all manner of critical issues while thwarting evil forces. What part of that wouldn't be inspiring to a young boy? After I started reading the series, I got more serious about inventing and building gadgets. Tom's inventions also helped give shape to some of my own projects.

Just before they separated my parents decided to add on to our two-bedroom house. I had the opportunity and a plan to wire my room and ran some small wires under the sheetrock for built-in stereo speakers and other projects I was contemplating. I built my own crude electronic door lock by removing the outside knob on my bedroom door and coupling an electrical switch to a standard key cylinder. I hid the contraption in a linen closet down the hall. I had salvaged parts from our old washing machine and mounted the solenoid that had held the gearbox in the spin cycle on the door with a lever arm to actuate the lock. The only way to get the door open was to use the switch in the closet; it was crude, but it worked (most of the time) and kept unwanted intruders out of my bedroom.

According to my brother, Steve, who also read the books, my inventions were nothing to talk about and I didn't hold a candle to Tom Swift because he was a *real* inventor. I felt deflated by his assessment of my skills but was undeterred. Even though I came to see Tom's adventures as farfetched and unrealistic, I was never able to part with the books. They played such an important role in my early fascination with science and physics, as well as demonstrating what a young person can accomplish, even if none of it was true or even realistic. Years later, I had a few of my more artistic friends draw an 8-foot-wide, black-light rendition of Tom perilously floating in space after his tether had been mysteriously severed. To this day, I still have most of the series intact on a bookshelf in my living room, as well as the drawing of Tom (although it's not in the house).

CAST OF CHARACTERS

Our neighborhood was full of young families with a number of boys close in age to my brother and me, and over the years we grew to be a tight gang. Most of us attended Calvert Elementary, which was close enough that we were able to ride our bicycles to school from an early age. In kindergarten I started to meet some of the other neighborhood kids and developed strong friendships that have lasted all these years. These friendships became a bright spot in an otherwise dreary school experience for me. My recollections of my first day of school remain with me today. School sucked—I couldn't stand the confinement, rules, and authority. All the freedom I'd experienced until then suddenly went away and bells, schedules, and lessons provided unwanted structure. I didn't understand why I couldn't go out to play when I felt like it or why I had to spend the day with a bunch of kids my own age. The first few days were rough, for both my teacher and me, and set the stage for many parent-teacher conferences to come.

In second grade, through my lack of attention, indifference, or early nonconformity, my teacher suggested to my mom that I needed an IQ test. My teacher equated my lack of attention and constant disruptive behavior with some kind of learning disability. I have some memory of the ordeal—trying to find patterns of numbers and trying to describe inkblots and free associations—but maybe I have just seen that in so many movies that it seems like a memory. Although my teacher probably didn't believe it, the results were well above average. The IQ test marked the beginning of my disconnect with conventional educational methods. Even at that young age I recognized that there was a price to be paid for nonconformity. Staying true to who I was set me on a path outside the norm. Although frequently labeled a troublemaker, I was lucky to have the support of my mother and many friends along the way.

The family that moved into the house across the street from our new home had four children—a daughter, Deborah, and three boys. Bill was slightly younger than me, and Thumper and Tommy were a couple of years older. Because my dad was rarely around, I quickly adopted the Hungerfords as a second family and spent a lot of time with them. The father, John, or Big John as he was usually called since one of his sons was named John (Thumper), quickly became an important figure in my life. One of my early mentors, Big John had one of those inquisitive minds that was never satiated. He had a well-equipped shop that doubled as a playground for us kids, probably much to his dismay, with a welding machine, an air compressor, and many cabinets full of wrenches, screwdrivers, and almost any other tool you could think of. He couldn't resist a sale on tools, and even if he didn't need anything, rather than buying one of something, he'd get six. His passion and at times compulsive habits touched every aspect of his life and everyone who knew him. His collections combined with his meticulous ways occasionally came at the expense of others—along with many other chores, his children were required to wash and wax his slightly eclectic fleet of cars every week until he realized the regular cleaning and buffing regime had started to remove much of the paint.

Big John's obsession with cars was a source of amazement and intrigue for the other neighborhood friends and fathers. He installed and modified his vehicles to contain every conceivable aftermarket gadget and upgrade he could get his hands on. Some of these modifications come standard in automobiles today, but in the 1960s he was ahead of the curve. He had air shocks and an onboard compressor that he could activate from the dash to check and inflate his tires at will. The list of gadgets and improvements was never-ending, and weekends were spent finding real estate under the hood for the next innovation. Big John also outfitted each vehicle with its own spare parts; in the event you needed a replacement part, you could find it in the trunk inventoried, sealed, and labeled. I remember being off on some adventure, somewhere we weren't supposed to be, with one of his newly licensed sons when the water pump in his Peugeot failed. We pulled into a service station, assessed the problem, and, sure enough, found the new part, labeled and stored with all the tools needed for the repair neatly organized in a container in the trunk.

Another one of Big John's traits that rubbed off on me was his thirst for knowledge. He was an educator by occupation, and after teaching school for several years he became a principal and later held a senior position on the Los Angeles Board of Education. Besides spending time tinkering in the shop and working on his cars and house, he devoured information. Anything was fair game—science, technology, history, food. Piles of periodicals, pages torn out of magazines, and drawers full of folders crowded his library.

Although as kids we spent many hours working on projects in Big John's shop, we were not necessarily a welcome group, and at times were forced to sneak in when the parents were at work or away. We had the tendency not to clean up after ourselves and would occasionally lose our access to the shop as punishment. I was generally blamed for most of the disarray, probably with good reason because I spent the most time there and wasn't the neatest child. We tackled many diverse projects ranging from bicycle repair and modification to building go-karts and minibikes at the beginning of our motor sports phase. I recall removing the two-stroke engine from a neighbor's lawnmower and modifying and mounting it on a go-kart we were building. We were proud of the invention, but the neighbor wasn't too happy when he found the mower missing its motor in the spring.

The Moellers were another neighborhood family that came to play a big role in my life. Greg Moeller was about a year older than me; he had a brilliant mind and wry sense of humor. He had an older sister, Ann, and a younger brother, Kurt. Their parents, Cal and Jean, loved to entertain, and they hosted many memorable parties. Cal had spent his career in aerospace, working on the Minuteman missile and later on various projects at Rocketdyne. Before he retired, he helped design and test space shuttle engines. Cal was active in the Sierra Club and was an avid hiker and mountaineer; he took the neighborhood kids on many of their first treks. He was an ardent cyclist and often rode with us and helped expose us to outdoor activities.

Cal was also a devoted homebrewer, winemaker, audiophile, rocket scientist, and foodie. He started brewing in the 1950s at college, where he studied to become a metallurgist. This was during the dark ages of homebrewing, well before any quality ingredients or sound information was available, so whether he started brewing to save money or because of his fascination with science and the alchemy involved in brewing will never be known. The Moellers had rows of carboys in their service porch with air locks bubbling away. On weekends the kitchen stove held large boiling pots of malt and hops.

Cal thought that kids should be exposed to science at a young age, so he converted a wooden shed in the backyard into a "laboratory" that he equipped with a range of chemicals and reagents, many of which are now regulated or found only in advanced college chemistry classes. We had metallic sodium that ignited when added to water and jars of mercury that we unwisely played with, coating dimes and filling our shoes to shuffle around like Frankenstein. We also had all the compounds to make really great rockets and explosives. Although Cal gave us some rudimentary safety training, I don't recall having much direct supervision, and other than some books of experiments, we were pretty much left to learn on our own. From one of our young science geek friends we learned the recipe for a compound we called Super Flash, which I later learned was similar to the formula used in plastic explosives and ammunition. It was supposedly 10 times as powerful as gunpowder and had the added benefit that it could be triggered to explode when it came into contact with a strong acid, which enabled us to develop delayed fuses. A few of us decided to blow up every mailbox on the next block, and when suspicion arose that we were behind the prank, we blew up a few more closer to home to confuse our parents' investigation. Our smokescreen worked, and although our parents suspected us, they were never able to prove conclusively that we were the culprits. I don't think Cal intended to for us to use our scientific knowledge for destructive purposes, but we were teenaged boys with boundless curiosity.

Another early entrant into our high-spirited gang was Dave Sheetz, who lived on the next block over and often lent his support to our antics. His father had been employed in marketing at a local brewery but passed away at a young age, just shortly before we met, and our shared fatherless existence forged a bond between us. Sheetz earned the respect of many of the neighborhood youth with his wheelie prowess on his Sting Ray bicycle and being able to travel the length of the block on his rear wheel, but even more for his ability to compress enough air into his stomach to recite long passages while burping and popping a wheelie.

YOUTHFUL ADVENTURES

Cal was also interested in early high-fidelity audio equipment and upgraded his sound system regularly. Stereo FM radio was a fairly new concept; the first stations had only begun broadcasting in 1961. When he replaced his old mono radio with a newer one, he gave the old one to Greg and me to play with. We found a circuit diagram to build a multiplex converter to receive stereo signals and set about building the modified circuitry. There was a Radio Shack a few miles away, so we made regular trips on our bikes to buy diodes, capacitors, and resistors. Although it wasn't a terribly large sum of money, all of my allowance, less than $2 a week, regularly went toward buying components for the conversion. With my mom struggling to make ends meet, and my grandfather helping her out, I was reluctant to ask for money.

On our last trip for supplies, without enough money to get the last needed pieces, I slipped a small bag of circuit board clips into my pants, casually strolled out of the store, and climbed on my sister's pink banana-seat bike (mine had a flat tire that day) to make my escape. I guess I wasn't quite as discreet as I thought, and the manager, who'd seen me slip the parts into my pocket, followed us out of the store and yanked me off my bike as Greg hightailed it home. It was bad enough to be caught but worse to be apprehended on a pink getaway bike. It was my first encounter with the law, and they threw the book at me as far as I was concerned. It was the day before my twelfth birthday, and my mom grounded me; the police notified the school that I had been caught shoplifting, so the principal called me into his office to reprimand me. A small bag of circuit board clips turned into a triple humiliation.

After my run-in with the law, I realized that I needed a regular source of income. I was in junior high and needed money to fund my many hobbies and vices, not to mention my growing interest in girls. In eighth grade I made the decision to get a steady job. I had been working for the next-door neighbor shoveling manure from their two horses, but it was neither steady work nor my cup of tea. The only perk was that he owned a bar and would occasionally leave some beer lying around. To find a job, I walked down Ventura Boulevard and knocked on every shop door that looked like a possibility. I was finally offered a job at a furniture store doing odd jobs, moving things around, cleaning up, and assembling furniture. When the owner ran out of things for me to do at the store, he would take me to his daughter's house, where I did everything from dishwashing to babysitting. They liked me and paid me pretty well, but in my teenage mind, it wasn't a grown-up job. I applied for and got a job at a small bicycle shop that opened close to home. I started working there after school and on weekends assembling bicycles, which suited me much better. I continued working part-time at bicycle shops, increasing my skills and knowledge, for the next several years.

Although I now had a job, Greg's and my interest in electronics continued to evolve, and we began doing TV and stereo repair for friends and family. Back in those days most problems were related to bad tubes, a failed capacitor, or a burned-out coil, so troubleshooting was not nearly as complex as it would be with today's microchip technology. Although I didn't master circuit theory at a very high level or totally grasp the complexity of the devices I worked on, I had a decent rate of restoring dead televisions and radios. I had picked up a cast-off radio tube testing center that was commonplace in many stores at that time, so my work area in the garage looked fairly professional for a teenager.

Because of my limited income, I got into the habit of scrounging bits and pieces for my many projects. As luck would have it, a treasure trove of material, liberated by the passing of the elderly man who lived directly across the street, provided a nearby source of parts and tools. He had owned a hardware store, and when it closed, he moved much of the inventory home. When he passed away, his wife had a yard sale that I took advantage of, and then she started putting whatever was left of the old inventory in the garbage. My friends and I made a habit of digging through the trash until his wife reprimanded us, so we started scoping out the take in the afternoon and pouncing after dark. This charade went on sporadically for months. I don't know why our neighbor wouldn't give us the leftovers; maybe she felt guilty for throwing away things that had value. In the end, I had collected a lot of transformers, electrical hardware, and all sorts of junk to incorporate into my ongoing projects.

Our interest in mechanics extended to bicycles, which we adopted as our preferred mode of transportation around the neighborhood. The banana-seat Sting Ray was the hot ride back then and I wanted one badly. Schwinn made the original Sting Ray, which was built to be very beefy and designed to take abuse from rowdy kids like us. I tried to convince my father that I had to have a Schwinn, but to no avail; he bought me an imitation built by Steyr Puch, which was a lightweight copy imported from Austria. Whether it was because he had to drive across town to buy the Schwinn or because the knockoff cost $20 less I don't know, but the excitement of getting a new bike was dampened by the realization my dad had bought the imitation. I almost immediately started to take apart, modify, and customize the bike. I installed a smaller front wheel in an attempt to make it look like a chopper. Once I had it all set up like I wanted, I went with some of the bigger kids across the boulevard where there was a terraced hillside for a new housing project. The steep hillside provided the perfect ramp for high-speed jumps, and being the young daredevil that I was, I decided to go down without using my brakes. It was a quick descent, and the small front wheel didn't help my trajectory or the landing. I did multiple somersaults, breaking my arm in seven places, but even that didn't dampen my enthusiasm for cycling.

When I was 14 years old, I convinced my mom that I needed my own space and got her permission to build an outbuilding to live in. Little did she know I had already built a hideaway, dubbed The Hole, in our backyard. Above ground it was shaped like an igloo made from walnut branches covered in dirt that camouflaged a series of tunnels and underground rooms that we dug one summer. Accessed through a trapdoor in the igloo, The Hole was a mushroom-shaped room that we reached by climbing down a rope ladder through a narrow tunnel. It had lights, stereo, and air provided by a contraband evacuation system that vented into the neighbors' yard. We also built side tunnels called torpedo tubes that were large enough for two people to fit into, and we slept down there from time to time. My mom knew about the igloo but not about the trapdoor or the space underneath.

The Hole caved in eventually, prompting the need for a new space. Greg and Sheetz had already built their own backhouses, giving me ideas for improvements to make mine superior. Greg's had been converted from the now unused "science lab," and Sheetz had transformed his sister's kid-sized dollhouse in the backyard. I approached my Uncle Bob, an architect, to draw up the plans before going to the county office to apply for a building permit. I was probably the youngest person ever to do that. Permit in hand, I became the foreman on the project. I did all the wiring myself and enlisted Thumper, Bill, Steve, Sheetz, and Greg to help with framing and roofing the split-level structure. I had never poured concrete before and had no tools, but I dug the footings to code and ordered a truck to deliver concrete for the slab. The driver was shocked to pull up and find a bunch of kids with no tools, experience, or adults to help, but he graciously agreed to provide the tools and stayed to help us lay the slab. Because I had obtained a permit the county building inspector came back to sign off on the completed project. Aside from some incorrectly wired boxes that were easily remedied, my self-taught construction skills were enough to earn me a pass.

EDUCATION MY WAY

Even though I would have preferred to spend my time riding bikes and tinkering on my projects, I grudgingly went to school. By the time I started junior high, I saw school as a place to see friends, goof off, and have fun. Other than the shop classes and PE, my most memorable moment was receiving a grade of A-U-U in a science class, the first ever in the history of the school. I achieved an A grade, but the two unsatisfactories were for work habits and behavior.[1] My mom was furious and didn't understand why I was so pleased. She didn't see any reason to be impressed. In junior high, my love of science and my mischievous bent got me into more serious trouble. One of my wilder friends told me about a pretty fantastic formula for making stink bombs that didn't involve any combustion and could be dispersed very discreetly, only needing to be dropped in water to release large quantities of hydrogen sulfide. One rainy day he and I decided to test

---

[1]If my grandchildren read this, know that it's not something I'm proud of now, although at the time I thought it was pretty cool.

our formulation, so I tossed some pellets in the sinks, toilets, and puddles around the school grounds. It worked better than we could have imagined and, once unleashed, there was no stopping the stench. The entire school was evacuated, and because of my friend's earlier bragging about the recipe, he was identified as the culprit; I was deemed guilty by association. We were both suspended for a week. I thought it was funny at the time but was grateful not to have been punished more severely.

My creativity and curiosity finally started to find adult-sanctioned outlets in junior high shop classes. My school offered a wide range of industrial technology classes, including wood shop, small engine repair, crafts, drafting, and, my favorite, a fully equipped metal shop with a small foundry. I developed a great interest in creating metal objects and made the obligatory, but now politically incorrect, hand-peened ashtray in seventh grade when I was 12. My metal shop teacher, Mr. Benson, had the distinction of being an ex–prison guard and ran class as such. He was a tall, tough-looking man and had no problem keeping his students under control. I connected with him, and he gave me a lot of attention and freedom. I was able to take his class as an elective for a second semester, and it seemed like I had achieved a teacher's pet status and was granted special privileges. Subsequent projects were more complicated, and I eventually tackled making a screwdriver from scratch. It doesn't sound too hard, but it involved designing, melting, and casting a sturdy aluminum handle over a hand-ground tip of tool steel that I heat-treated myself. To finish the project I turned the handle on a lathe and knurled the grip. The challenge of building something with my own hands, the skills I developed, and the satisfaction I felt were monumental.

In addition to channeling my energy into practical skills, Mr. Benson also played an important role in how I learned to deal with grief. In junior high one of my best friends was killed in a tragic car accident that also critically injured another one of my friends. I was supposed to go to the movies with the gang that day, but my mom wouldn't let me go with the newly licensed driver. Mr. Benson was one of the more sensitive people who stepped up and helped all of us handle the loss.

Unfortunately, this was the first of several of my close friends who passed away early in life. Greg Moeller died in his late 20s, unable to pull himself out of a downward spiral fueled by alcohol and loss of direction in his life. Another friend from my television repair days died a sad and painful death as an early sufferer of AIDS. Losing friends while young taught me the importance of lasting relationships. Many members of the neighborhood gang were early supporters of the brewery and are still in my life today.

A Central Character Enters the Scene

In the late 1960s, I met Steve Harrison. Although his family moved into the house next door to the Moellers, our paths didn't cross for the first few years because he went to a different junior high than the rest of the kids in the neighborhood. He was a few years older than I was and hung out with a circle of wild friends from his old neighborhood. In the beginning, my mom warned me not to associate with him. Then she and his mother became friends, and we started to have more opportunities to hang out. For the first few years, our circles of friends still didn't mesh because his group was much rowdier than my gang. Harrison started to settle down a bit, or at least abandoned some of his more self-destructive habits, after getting into a serious car accident after partying. He retained a wild streak but soon integrated into our group, and his outgoing personality and sense of humor were ongoing sources of amusement for us. Our gang already had a Steve (my brother), so we called him Harrison. Because he had his driver's license and a car, he often served as the driver on our escapades. Harrison went through cars like they were worn-out shoes—totally expendable and not worthy of care or repair. He sought out and bought large, old, American cars. Among many others, he had a Studebaker President and a 1960s era Pontiac Bonneville. Harrison took his cars on adventures and seemed not to care if they made it back. One time, he attempted motorcycle hill climbs in the Bonneville, much to the shock and chagrin of the dirt bikers he scared off the course.[2] Although he later got very serious about road cycling, in his teens Harrison was notoriously lazy and, at one point, would drive whatever clunker he had at the time miles down Ventura Boulevard to a drive-through store to get cigarettes so he wouldn't have to get out of the car.

Aside from being ingenuous, Harrison was also highly intelligent, passionate and impulsive. When he embraced something he was very focused and committed, but when he got bored, he was done with it and would move on without looking back. Harrison and I became good friends; he ultimately moved to Chico shortly after I did and became the first employee at Sierra Nevada. Harrison was a vital part of our early success; his passion and dedication to the brewery motivated everyone around him.

I hit the peak of my rebellious phase right about the time Harrison came onto the scene, and my behavior was pretty reckless by the time I started high school. Other than my shop classes, I didn't enjoy school nor did I do particularly well in my classes. I rebelled against any and all authority figures. I came of age at the end of the 1960s and embraced the culture of the time, including engaging in activities that got me into trouble but ultimately also helped expand my worldview. By that time, the neighborhood gang had solidified,

---

[2]In hindsight, the neighborhood streets were full of oddball cars, none of which was considered a classic back then. Cal had an English Rover Sedan, couple of Studebakers, a Hawk, and a Lark that ended up being Greg's first cars. The Hungerfords had a Peugeot, as did my father. The families across from the Hungerfords collected Packard Patricians, and at the end of the street, there was an Edsel and Renault Dauphine. Eventually, they both came up for sale, and my brother almost ended up with the Edsel as his first car. He settled for the cheaper Dauphine, instead, which I was later, probably accurately, credited with lighting on fire. I started smoking cigars in high school and had a penchant for a morning Hav-A-Tampa Jewel, a small, lone-wood-tipped slim cigar. The Renault seats had lost much of their fabric, and the fine wood excelsior that was used as stuffing made the ideal fire starter. Presumably an ember from my morning smoke smoldered in the school parking lot until the car finally exploded into flames during first period. Sheetz was in a class on the school's second floor and witnessed the flames and fire engines; upon hearing it was a red Renault, he knew it was Steve's car.

and I was one of the youngest members. Most of the others were closer to my brother's age, so they had more freedom, which I benefitted from. By then most of them were driving, giving us the ability to explore new pursuits and the world outside our neighborhood.

NEW HOBBIES

Even though I had been exposed to photography as a child, it wasn't until later that my interest peaked. My Grandpa Lew had an old darkroom in his basement that we played hide-and-seek in as kids. We got a thrill out of running around the pitch-black darkroom. Both of my mother's brothers had a fascination with photography and had given me a quality, hand-me-down box camera. In high school Big John introduced Thumper and me to his old photography equipment, including some movie cameras, prompting me to buy my first 35-mm camera to take photographs and build a darkroom in my mother's garage.

Photography marked the beginning of our group's artistic pursuits. Although Harrison had lost interest in it, Sheetz, Thumper, Dan Young (another neighborhood friend), and I took a lot of pictures and started staging and filming movies. Being near Hollywood, we had access to great props left over from movies and musicals. At one point, MGM auctioned off costumes from *The Wizard of Oz*, and we managed to get hold of some of them. We briefly used them in films but found that we could have a bigger impact and more fun with our new treasures by donning the costumes and wearing them around town. We went to a local mall wearing horned hats and outrageous outfits, and Sheetz wore a big black cape and a black face shield. We strolled through the center of the mall, side by side in a row. We also took our performance art to school and were considered outlandish oddballs by the majority of students. Our outrageous actions confused our classmates, but we were pretty pleased with ourselves and didn't care what others thought. Some of our inspiration came from the Firesign Theatre, a well-known performance group that we had been listening to on records and had recently seen perform at Pierce College. Their antics fit well with our craziness and inspired many stunts.

We also listened to KPFK, an alternative station in Los Angeles that had an all-night show that played music and live recordings from Jimi Hendrix to Buffalo Springfield. Some in our extended gang were into a more eclectic music scene and influenced us to listen to divergent recordings from to Captain Beefheart to Gustav Holst's "The Planets." We also regularly snuck into shows at the Valley Music Theater near our neighborhood, where we saw great bands, including Buffalo Springfield, Spirit, and Ike and Tina Turner, among others. We were also lucky that our friend Amir's mother's boyfriend owned a recording studio and let us hang out there after school. On one occasion, we were allowed to sit in the studio while Led Zeppelin recorded. Fortunately, I had my camera with me and took lots of pictures while they recorded the song "Whole Lotta Love."

As we were exploring new hobbies, Cal took a bunch of neighborhood kids on a trip to the High Sierra. After that I started going on extended backpacking trips with my brother and a group of friends. It didn't take much to convince my mom that we were probably less likely to get into trouble in the mountains than in the city. We usually trekked on the East Side of the Sierra, driving up Highway 395 to destinations like Bishop or Lone Pine to enter the Sierras at trailheads starting above 9,000 feet; the terrain became alpine very quickly. We hiked stretches of the popular John Muir Trail or went cross-country on knapsack trails, typically covering 10 to 15 miles a day, making camp wherever we saw fit. We usually spent a week to 10 days away, and because we had limited financial resources we discovered we could cheaply provision in Chinatown, stocking up on dried shrimp, noodles, and rice. With our Asian food discovery, we budgeted just over a dollar a day for food and generally ate pretty well. Freeze-dried backpacking food had recently been introduced. We would occasionally splurge on an item like a special dessert, but it generally remained well out of our price range. I made many trips to the High Sierra over the next several years with various members of our ever-expanding, eclectic group of friends. I loved the beauty and freedom of the mountains as well as the physical exercise. I was tired of living in Los Angeles and very much at home in the mountains.

Although most of our early excursions consisted of trail hiking and mountaineering, we did more rock climbing as time went on and occasionally climbed moderately challenging peaks. On one trip, I suffered a deep gash while descending a peak on the morning of the second day of a two-week trip. A thin flake of granite cut my calf muscle to the bone, deep enough that a finger fit in the gash. I had to hike out many miles and go to the emergency room in Bishop. It took hours to hike out and a few more before the doctor could see me and deal with the gaping wound. After the doctor stitched me up, I agreed to his request to rest for a few days before rejoining my friends on the trail. When I returned to the trailhead, I met up with a family who cared for me while my leg healed. They let me camp with them and had two daughters close to my age who took pity on me and took care of me while I recuperated. After a few days I felt ready to return to the trail; I was still a little sore, so the daughters carried my pack as I hobbled along. When I met up with my group a few days later, they were impressed with my traveling companions. It was a warm summer afternoon in the Sierra, and the two attractive girls had taken advantage of the remoteness and taken off their tops to work on their tans. When we arrived at camp, my buddies enjoyed my good fortune.

MY HOMEBREWING BEGINNINGS

Between hiking trips, I started dabbling in another hobby. I don't remember the exact day I made my first batch of homebrew, but it was sometime in the summer of 1969, between junior and senior high, when Cal became a little miffed by the regular disappearance of his homebrew and, for that matter, all of the other beverages we snuck out of his liquor cabinet. I wasn't 21 and couldn't yet buy beer, but older friends regularly stocked up on Spring Beer, a "fine" Pilsner brewed by the Maier Brewing Company of Los Angeles. It regularly sold for 89 cents a six-pack, but on sale it could be had for around $2 a case in cans—much less than a case of soda at the time.

My first experiment in fermentation involved a batch of Welch's grape juice in a gallon jug in the closet with the intention of producing wine, but it tasted terrible. I was fortunate that one of the nation's best homebrew supply stores was only a few miles from my house. I purchased a rudimentary brewing kit with an open top plastic fermenter (really just a white plastic trash can), 5-gallon glass carboy, hydrometer, short length of plastic tube to fill the bottles, and a crude bottle capper. I spent less than $25 for everything, but it was a big financial commitment for what was still an experiment for someone making $1.35 an hour.

For my first attempt I used a simple recipe that called for malt extract, a small brick of hops, and packaged generic top-fermenting yeast (that's about all you could get at the time). I used Blue Ribbon Malt and a generous amount of cane sugar. Most of my early batches were strong because in the beginning, I focused my efforts on the Prohibition brewing mentality of alcohol production rather than brewing the highest quality beers. I did what any teenager would and hid my equipment in my closet. Of course my mother found it, but I managed to convince her that it was just an experiment and I wouldn't drink it. She was working long hours, taking care of three kids by herself, and was probably relieved that I was keeping myself busy. She was relatively accepting of my new hobby because it harnessed my energy and kept me out of the trouble I tended to find myself in. Plus, it made me happy, and she always supported my creative interests. Brewing allowed me to combine my interest in science and the natural world with my growing sense of nonconformity. I began brewing multiple batches at once, allowing time for aging rather than consuming them before they were ready. I moved my brewing operation out to the backhouse. Although my friends knew what I was up to (and were enthusiastic judges of my work), I did most of the brewing myself. My brother wasn't involved early on, but Greg Shubin, a friend and classmate of my brother and a member of our expanding gang, and Moeller would come over and help with some of the batches.

Even though homebrewing was technically illegal in the United States at the time, no one was aware of anyone ever being arrested. The law that made it illegal was passed during Prohibition, and although home winemakers had their rights restored when the Volstead Act was repealed, no one had addressed the needs of homebrewers. US homebrewing supplies came mainly out of England because in the 1960s the British government made a big push to raise beer taxes and the British, being both frugal and fond of their pint, turned en masse to homebrewing. British drugstore chains got into the act and sold kits meant to duplicate popular styles and common brands aimed at average beer drinkers. The Canadian Wine Art franchise had also penetrated the US market, and stores popped up around the country that offered a range of ingredients and supplies for home winemaking and brewing. Lower-quality ingredients such as Blue Ribbon Malt Extract could be purchased at grocery stores, drugstores, and hardware stores when I first started brewing.[3] Information about homebrewing was scarce, and only a few homebrew books were available in the US market; most had been written for brewers in the United Kingdom, where homebrewing had made more headway. The books were relatively simplistic and didn't offer much science or practical techniques to produce consistent homebrew.

On one of my visits to a homebrew shop, I stumbled across new books, Fred Eckhardt's *Treatise of Lager Beer* and Dave Line's *Big Book of Brewing*. I devoured both of them and learned a lot about European traditional lager brewing and techniques like dry hopping, the procedure for adding additional hop flavor and aroma to the beer as it ages in the fermenter. Line's book was eye opening about the science of mashing and brewing; until that point, little information had been

---

[3]The fact that grocery stores stocked malt extract had to have been a carryover from Prohibition. Many breweries tried to ride out the "noble experiment" by producing a wide range of ingredients in their otherwise shuttered breweries. Some turned to malt products that could be efficiently produced in their idled brewhouses, whereas others developed drinks that could run on their bottling and canning lines. Brewers marketed and advertised an array of syrups that were supposedly intended to be used in producing breads and sweetened baked goods; they were condensed pale malt similar in consistency to honey or molasses. Other products were closer to condensed brewers wort with the bitter hops added. I have to wonder how many cans of hopped malt extract actually made it into a loaf of bread during Prohibition.

available to novice brewers. These books prompted my foray into all-grain brewing in 1970. I kept of a log of all my brews, although I lost track of the records of many of my early experiments. With the tacit approval of my mom and help from my friends who were all willing tasters, I continued homebrewing through high school.

MOVING ON

The day I graduated from high school, I took off on a backpacking trip and skipped the actual ceremony. It seemed more fitting to celebrate by doing something I loved—hiking in the Sierra.

Shortly after my graduation, Greg Moeller and Greg Shubin were heading up to Northern California to check out the state college in Chico, and I asked them if I could catch a ride to the Bay Area to join some friends on a bicycle tour. I really hadn't decided what I was going to do after high school; I knew I wanted some time to explore the world and was sure I didn't want to start college immediately. I had nothing keeping me in Southern California and had some extra time, so I went along to check out Chico. Four of us (Moeller's girlfriend, Betty, also came) traveled in Shubin's VW Microbus. The trip was 500 miles and took almost 10 hours. We arrived late that night, but it was still as hot as hell, even in early June. It turns out that the almost unbearable summer heat is common—a trait that almost ended my desire to make Chico my home.

We found the cheapest hotel we could, and the four of us shared a room. The La Grande Hotel was right downtown, had no air-conditioning, and boasted only one bathroom down the hall. Betty flipped out when she found blood splattered all over the bathtub and toilet. No one slept much, if at all, and out of a sense of place, we drank warm beer and whiskey and laughed and complained our way through the night. Most of the La Grande's tenants were permanent residents; shouting, fights, and commotion went on all night. Checkout was at six in the morning because they rerented the rooms to the night shift railroad crew.[4]

The next day we had a great tour of the community, and I fell in love with the small city. The population was around 30,000 people at the time, and when school was in it added almost 10,000 people, which certainly changed the feel from a small, sleepy town to one with a fun and wild side. Chico seemed like a much better home base than Los Angeles while I figured out what I wanted to do for the next phase of my life. So that day I decided to move to Chico with my friends and set off to try to find a job. I rode my bike to the three bike shops listed in the phonebook and got a job offer at the Schwinn Bicycle shop. They were looking for a mechanic, and I could start as soon as I wanted. With that settled, Shubin, Moeller, and I started looking for a house the same day. We found a five-bedroom house at the south end of town with two other roommates.

Having secured a house and a job, my friends dropped me off in Novato to start my next adventure—a bike tour with Bill Hungerford that would take us from the Bay Area up to Ukiah, over to the coast and down Highway 1, over the Golden Gate Bridge and down to Santa Cruz, from where I had arranged a car ride back home to the San Fernando Valley. The two of us planned to start out alone in Novato and connect with some other friends along the way. I called home and told my mother that I was moving out in two weeks when I returned from my bike tour. She was sad, but she knew she had to let me go. Some people objected to the fact that I wasn't even 18, but my mom believed I should be allowed to make my own choices.

Bill and I had a fun and challenging ride north to Ukiah. Even though I was only 17, I had a full beard and looked a bit older. We took advantage of that and stopped at several wineries along the way. On our way along Highway 1, we stopped for lunch at a small restaurant

---

[4]Back in those days train tracks went through downtown Chico in the middle of Main Street. I was shocked the first time I saw a train go through town. We tried to play a brief game of chicken on our bicycles but realized how easily the tire could get stuck in the tracks; the odds wouldn't have been in our favor had we fallen.

along the coast, where I saw my first bottle of Anchor Steam Beer. Anchor's owner, Fritz Maytag, had only recently started bottling and distributing his beer. When he purchased Anchor Brewing Company, it had been producing a very limited amount of draught and had never previously bottled. It took Fritz several years to upgrade the brewery and refine and improve the beers' stability, let alone purchase and install a packaging line. I got into a conversation with the bar owner about homebrewing because he was a homebrewer himself and had just started carrying Anchor Steam Beer. I was excited when he offered me a bottle because I had heard about it from Cal Moeller but hadn't had the opportunity to try it yet. My first sip was memorable and an inspiration for any aspiring homebrewer. It was a style of beer I loved—lots of hops and malt, and unlike any commercial beer I had ever tasted. It was close in style to the type of beer I liked to brew; it was good to discover that there was interesting American beer out there.

2

CHICO

You can't be a real country unless you have a beer and an airline—it helps if you have some kind of a football team, or some nuclear weapons, but at the very least you need a beer.

—Frank Zappa

At the end of our bike trip, I started to make plans for my move to Chico. I bought a blue 1961 VW bus from a friend. The bus fit my style and needs because I would be hauling bikes, tools, backpacking gear, homebrewing supplies, and all my furniture and essential belongings in one trip to Chico. After heading up I-5 once again, I had only a few days to settle in before I started work at the bicycle shop. I spent my first weeks in Chico, swimming in the creek, and exploring many great roads and trails on my bicycle. While exploring I met other cyclists, and we formed a small group to organize rides. We were the beginning of what was later called Chico Velo and the less serious offshoot called Mello Velo, which incorporated beer and other social activities into their rides.

Within a few weeks at the bike shop, I realized that the owners' family dynamic made for an unhealthy working environment. With the father still at the helm and his two sons constantly bickering, working in the shop was no fun. At $1.85 an hour, I was making a little more than minimum wage. After working for a couple of months as a mechanic, I had a run-in with one of the owner's sons and quit the bike shop on the spot. The other mechanic at the shop had also had enough of the family politics, so we walked out together. I had always prided myself on being a good employee and wasn't proud about leaving them stranded, but considering the circumstances, I didn't see another solution. I swore that if I ever owned a business I would run it differently.

After quitting the shop, I started to question my decision not to go to college. By then it was too late to enroll in Chico State, but Butte Community College was nearby. I was able to start the next quarter the following month. I had not been very academically oriented in high school and quickly realized that I had some catching up to do if I wanted to do well in college. I knew I wanted to focus on science, so I enrolled in algebra and chemistry courses along with some other required classes that I needed to transfer to Chico State. The chemistry class was challenging, but it reminded me of the days spent in Cal Moeller's makeshift lab, concocting Super Flash and other compounds. I was captivated. The instructor, Dr. George Boggs, was a brilliant and talented educator who reignited and reinforced my love of the sciences.[1] While I was at Butte, the Southern California exodus continued, and many of my high school friends visited and decided to transfer to Chico State. They were drawn by the opportunity to go to school and take advantage of the fun social scene that Chico offered.

---

[1] I wasn't surprised when George's talents were recognized by the college administration and others and his career quickly progressed. He went on to become president of Palomar College and later moved to Washington, DC, to be president of the American Association of Community Colleges (AACC), representing 1,100 community colleges throughout the United States.

MAKING ENDS MEET

In the fall of 1973, I met Katie Gonser; she was the roommate of one of my friends from back home who had enrolled at Chico State. I was instantly attracted to her. We hit it off and almost immediately started to spend a lot of time together. A couple of months after we met, we decided to go camping and hiking overnight at Deer Creek. Even though I had a car, we were so broke that we hitchhiked up Highway 32. It was October and very cold, so we ended up sharing a sleeping bag; after that we were inseparable. Katie spent so much time at my house that we soon decided to move in together and shared a house in Chico with Greg Moeller and a couple of other roommates. We were both living on almost nothing. My dad, when he remembered, would send me $100 a month while I was attending school. Katie received $110 a month from Social Security because her mother had passed away when she was a young child. We also signed up for the food stamp program, which helped a bit. Money was tight, but with my grandfather's "waste not, want not" mantra and my innate frugality we managed to scrape by.

I got a part-time job at a different bike shop, Pullins Cyclery, to help make ends meet. I had applied there when I was first looking for a job in town, but they didn't have any openings at the time. My boss was the son-in-law of Vern Pullins, who founded the shop in 1918 and ran the business continually into the early 1970s. His wife and daughter decided he should retire and masterminded the transfer of the business to his son-in-law, much against Vern's will. I learned many lessons about business while working for them, particularly what not to do. It was somewhat horrifying watching what transpired, both the unhealthy family dynamics and the son-in-law's lack of sensibilities and work ethic. The son-in-law had big aspirations and purchased a small, established bicycle shop in the nearby town of Oroville in an attempt to expand the business. After I had worked for them for a few months in Chico, he offered me a job managing the shop in Oroville. Although it was a small shop, I would be completely in charge of all aspects of running the business and would be my own boss. I was already seeing the rapid destruction of the historic Chico shop under the son-in-law's poor management and welcomed the opportunity to distance myself from the situation.

The job in Oroville paid $500 per month with no benefits, but after living on $100 a month, it represented a huge increase. Until then, I had been taking classes at Chico State as a chemistry major. Katie wanted to be a nurse and was getting some of her undergraduate classes out of the way. Our attendance that year was terrible because it seemed like there was always something more fun to do, and I started to struggle in some of my classes. When I took the job in Oroville, I dropped out of school and commuted the 30 minutes to Oroville every day. After a few months of that, Katie and I found a one-room house on a little creek in the foothills above Oroville and moved, even though it was uninsulated and had no heat source. When it got very cold, we put flowerpots in the oven and then opened the oven door to heat the house.

The son-in-law's management style was such that he gave me the keys to the shop, told me to open a bank account, and left me to figure out the rest. That was it—no training, no bookkeeping system, and no oversight at all. I sometimes wouldn't see or talk to him for weeks or what seemed like months at a time. I thrived on being my own boss and being able to make business decisions, and I became a shrewd businessman. It was essentially a one-man show, as I handled every aspect of the business. I had sold bikes while working at the big bike shop in Los Angeles and had a little experience ordering parts and bikes. I had also been wrenching on bikes for years, so the mechanical aspect and repairs were easy for me. Because I was a careful businessman, my shop was doing well and was fully stocked and profitable. The Chico shop was slowly failing, even though the son-in-law took the surplus money from my store's account as he pleased. Later, he started to raid my inventory because he had ruined his credit and couldn't make the payments to his suppliers. I had been operating independently, so my shop's credit was still good and I had a full stock of bikes and spare parts. I read the writing on the wall, so I made plans to leave the business and go back to school. I again enrolled in Butte College because I still had some undergraduate classes to complete, and it was more flexible and cheaper than going to Chico State. Plus, Butte had built a brand-new campus much closer to Oroville. I resumed my chemistry classes, added physics and calculus classes, and got a job on campus tutoring chemistry and working in the chemistry lab preparing experiments.

OPENING THE HOMEBREW SHOP

Between classes and working, I continued to be a serious homebrewer. We were into a lot of homesteading activities, so making my own beer was a natural fit for our way of life. We raised poultry, Katie raised goats for fun and a source of milk, and we made cheese from the milk as well. It was during this time that I realized that brewing truly was my passion. I started doing a little home malting for fun, making my own ingredients, such as wheat malt, and roasting my own grains in the oven. Quality homebrewing ingredients weren't available locally, and I enjoyed the science of turning barley into malt that I could brew with. I was sharing my homebrew with my next-door neighbor, Ron, and he convinced me that we should open a homebrew store in Chico to supply what we perceived to be the ever-growing needs of home-brewers and winemakers. We found a vacant shop space on the second floor of a building downtown at 336 Broadway, a block down from the La Grande Hotel. The rent was $57 dollars a month, and when money was tight, we were able to negotiate with the owners and do the jan-itorial services for the building in exchange for paying our rent. Ron was a carpenter and did most of the work to turn the plain, bare space into an attractive little shop as I went around and started lining up and ordering inventory from other homebrew shops kind enough to help me. Because I had such a small operation, I couldn't afford to buy the minimum quantities of many supplies and ingredients required by most wholesalers, so these shops helped me out by selling me supplies at a minimal markup. I was also able to buy directly from a few of the smaller wholesalers. John Daume at the Homebrew and Wine Shop in Los Angeles that I used to frequent let me buy supplies from him.

Wine and The People and Oak Barrel Wine Craft in Berkeley were also particularly generous.

We chose a straightforward name for our venture and opened The Homebrew Shop in 1976, with Ron and me dividing the management duties. Sales were meager in the beginning, so I juggled a few different jobs so that we had income coming in. I went back to work at Pullins Cyclery's Chico store after the founder, Vern, now in his late 70s, stepped back in to restore his credit and try to repair the damage that was done to the business that he had spent his life building. The son-in-law had run the business into the ground, and the Oroville shop that I had successfully run was closed. Vern and I had a great rapport, and he gave me a lot of flexibility to work around my homebrew shop demands.

THE HOMEBREW SHOP GROWS

Katie and I got married in the spring of 1977, and our first child, Sierra, was born at home in the middle of July. Earlier that summer, Ron and I realized that the homebrew business wasn't able to support both of us with an income stream, let alone one of us comfortably, and, besides, he was becoming bored with retail. He also didn't necessarily have the passion for brewing that I did, so we amicably decided to part ways and I bought him out. Ron had agreed to work through July, but with no one else to help out, Katie began filling in at the Homebrew Shop with three-week-old Sierra in tow. Katie wasn't thrilled at the notion, but money was tight and I had to continue working at the bike shop at least three days a week for a steady paycheck. We had made friends with another shopkeeper who ran an antique store across the hall from The Homebrew Shop; her husband farmed a 100-acre orchard that had a vacant ranch house that she said we could live in. Our growing family was happy to move out of our 450-square-foot, one-room house in Oroville that no longer seemed practical now that we had a newborn. Living in a sprawling, ranch-style home was quite a change. We were still broke; even though she gave us a great deal and we didn't pay much rent, we couldn't afford to run the electric heat.

Living in an orchard provided us with abundant firewood, so we often camped in the living room in front of the fireplace.

The Homebrew Shop continued to grow. I offered classes and walked customers through the steps of making their first batch of beer. By teaching many of the customers how to homebrew, I sold hundreds of starter kits, generally as gifts for the holidays. Although most people who started brewing beer at home didn't continue past the first batch or two, I cultivated a good group of avid hobbyists and customers. To fill the gaps I branched out and brokered wine grapes to help generate additional cash flow. With this additional revenue stream, I was finally able to stop working a second job. I traded my 1961 VW bus for a 1957 Chevy previously used by the phone company and later turned into a camper by an old friend who mounted a small travel trailer directly onto the bare frame and cut a hole through the back of the cab. I removed the camper and replaced it with a flatbed I made from scrap lumber scrounged out of the dumpster behind a wood shop (the dumpster was also the source of the wood for the crude home-built furniture in our modest house). I used it to make pilgrimages to the Alhambra glass plant in Southern California to pick up 5-gallon glass water jugs or, as they were known in the trade, fermentation carboys, to sell in the shop. I would drive the 500 miles there and buy 200 at a time, stacking them bottle to bottle like cordwood on my crude wooden flatbed. Over the years I had several high-pucker trips. On one trip in particular when I hit a bump in the road, breaking a few bottles on the bottom, I watched helplessly through my mirrors as the load shifted and the chain reaction consumed many more.

When I first started homebrewing, finding quality hops was nearly impossible because the homebrew trade consumed an insignificant amount of hops and, apparently, in the eyes of hop growers and merchants, wasn't worth pursuing. Most supply shops either stocked samples of poorly cared for British hops or small compressed blocks of aged or rejected Cluster, an old American workhorse variety of hops. When I opened The Homebrew Shop, I started traveling to Yakima, Washington, to select my own hops. Katie had a sister who lived in that area, so we had a good excuse to make the trip. On my first visit to Yakima in the mid-1970s, I was able to visit merchants and found a few who were willing to sell me an assortment of samples called brewers' cuts. These were 1-pound core samples cut out of the bale and used by breweries to judge the quality and aroma of the lot. I was such a small customer with my tiny homebrew shop that purchasing an entire 200-pound bale of a single variety of hops was out of the question, so I was grateful to be able to buy several hundred of these 1-pound brewers' cuts and get an assortment of every variety currently being grown. Hops are a little like the spice drawer when you are cooking—the different varieties all have their own unique flavor. Different quality of soils and local growing conditions also contribute to the character. I loaded my station wagon with these very aromatic samples and drove directly to Chico. I soon tracked down a European hop dealer who specialized in smaller lots of prized hops from countries such as Slovenia, Germany, and Czechoslovakia. Running my home-brew shop gave me the opportunity to brew and sample dozens of hops from around the world that had been nearly impossible to obtain before.

THE TURNING POINT

By the late 1970s the American brewing industry was consolidating at a rapid rate, and the national brands were much more effective at marketing and securing widespread distribution. Sadly, the remaining small American breweries that had originally been rooted in European brewing traditions were reaching the end of their era. As they fought for survival they tried to emulate the beer and marketing efforts of the national brands but lacked the financial and operational resources to compete. Whether some of them could have survived by changing their business model, focusing on marketing smaller amounts of more interesting and distinctive styles of beer and charging a premium price, rather than following the rapidly growing trends for lighter, high-volume, popularly priced beer, is hard to say. Even if they had made the conscious decision to move away from where the mainstream of American beer was headed, the marketplace might not have been receptive yet, and most of the small breweries' infrastructures were too costly to support the inevitable drop in volume of such a dramatic shift in philosophy and customer base. Only a few legacy American brewers, such as Yuengling, August Schell, and Matt, made the transition, essentially rebranding and repositioning their brands, while still capitalizing on their history and heritage. Not surprisingly, the American brewing industry was on the cusp of a revolution at the end of the 1970s. Fritz Maytag led the way with his purchase of Anchor Brewing and subsequent revival of older, more interesting styles of American beer and the reintroduction and reinterpretation of classic European styles.

In 1978, I attended the first combined Home Wine Making and Brewing trade show in Oakland, California. Homebrewing had been legalized the same year by a bill championed by California Congressman Alan Cranston and later signed into law by Jimmy Carter. Although homebrewing had been illegal since Prohibition, lax enforcement allowed the movement to grow; once it was legitimized more people took up the hobby. The change in the brewing landscape and the growth of my shop made this trip to the Bay Area a pivotal point in my life, sparking my interest and setting the stage for taking my homebrewing hobby to the next level. Until then, I had been somewhat isolated running my small shop in Chico. Out of necessity I had connected with the owners of several Bay Area homebrew supply stores and had stayed in touch with John Daume, who ran the Home Wine Shop in Southern California where I purchased most of my first supplies. The meeting in Oakland was one of the first industry trade shows specifically for the hobbyist homebrewer and winemaker, and it allowed me to connect with many other suppliers and shop owners.

At this conference I also finally met Fred Eckhardt, author of the first American homebrew book that really focused on brewing quality beer at home and was one of my early resources. His book opened my eyes to the wide diversity of beer styles and the importance of quality and how to achieve it, even on a small scale. Although I had not previously met Fred, I had written to him in care of his book publishing company in Portland and he had written back. We occasionally corresponded by mail because he was one of the few knowledgeable resources that I was aware of at the time in the homebrewing community.

During the trade show a group of us took a trip to the Anchor Brewery, which was then located in a small warehouse district almost under the freeway as it passed through San Francisco. Owner Fritz

Maytag was our tour guide; I don't know if he usually led tours, but as a courtesy to the homebrewing group he showed us around. I had read about Fritz and his purchase and investment in Anchor in several newspaper and magazine articles but had never met him. Ever since I had tasted Anchor Steam on my postgraduation bike tour, I had been impressed with Fritz's beer; it was one of the few commercial American beers available at the time that was truly interesting and memorable.

My first impression of the brewery was that it was old and funky with a fairly crude brewhouse and small, cramped bottling line. It had only a few open fermenters and a handful of newer looking storage tanks in a dank cellar. Even though Fritz had been in the business for 13 years and invested a lot of time and money to improve the faltering operation that he'd bought, when he had taken it over, it was in shambles; he was still working with a lot of old equipment. It was obvious that he had slowly been modernizing the operation. I thought the brewery was amazing. I was excited to tour it with the passionate and visionary owner and hear his stories of the struggles he had gone through to get it to this point. At the end of the tour, we purchased cases of beer, among them a special unavailable bottling of the first packaging of Old Foghorn. I was overwhelmed by the beer's intensity and balance; I hadn't tasted anything quite like it before.

Fritz had realized that the business model that most small regional breweries had been following was not viable and that he needed to create a different model to succeed. His vision relied on premium, higher priced, unique styles of beer that ran counter to the light lager styles that most other small breweries produced. I walked away from the tour impressed by the direction Fritz was taking away from conventional beer business, and I started to think about starting my own brewery. Before that, the only other brewery I had toured was the Van Nuys Anheuser-Busch plant, where I went as a child with my father and grandfather. We visited the brewery for the free tour, and even then I remember loving the smells of the brewhouse and fermentation cellars. At the time it boasted the opulent Busch Gardens, next to a massive marvel of polished stainless, shiny tile, and lush grounds. After the tour the adults drank free beer in the tasting room, and I have a fuzzy memory of my grandfather giving my brother and me small samples to taste.

GOING PRO

While running my homebrew store, I got to taste and sample many beers—both good and problematic homebrews. Some customers would also bring me commercial beers they had obtained on travels both in the United States and abroad, so I had tasted some European beers in good shape and knew there were great beers available in other parts of the world, although at that time I hadn't traveled to Europe and tasted them at their best. The flavorful beers that I enjoyed drinking and brewing had their roots in Europe and were brought to life by immigrants who made them widely available in America. I had previously marveled at and appreciated a few of these older beer styles that were still being brewed in very limited releases by the now dwindling US brewing industry, the most notable being Ballantine's India Pale Ale, which at one time boasted on the label that it was aged in wood for one full year. It had disappeared by the 1970s, but I remember that when I was a teenager, Cal Moeller was astounded when he could occasionally find it in Los Angeles for just pennies per bottle more than regular beer. I had the opportunity to sneak a sample or two of this old gem from Cal when it was fresh, but without a very sophisticated palate, I only knew it was a unique and strong beer.[2]

---

[2]Ballantine was actually a fairly progressive large brewery. It produced vintage Burton Ale, supposedly aged in wood for 10 years, that was not sold but given as gifts to employees and distributors for many years. Even its more common beers had a notable hop character because the company had pioneered the use of hop oil stills. Its beer featured a very distinctive hop variety, Bullion, which, although pungent, was not typically known for a refined hop note. Highly aromatic and assertive hop aromas are now common with craft brewers, but Ballantine's use of Bullion may have led to its decline from the nation's third largest brewer in 1950 to being sold in 1969 for a small sum and finally to their liquidation in 1972. The brand was brewed under contract and later went through a succession of owners and production plants. The label and brand lived on and is now being brewed by Miller for limited distribution, mainly to eastern markets, but its pioneering ways have ceased.

After the homebrewing conference in Oakland, I made plans to visit the recently founded New Albion Brewery in Sonoma, California. Owner Jack McAuliffe wasn't all that enthusiastic about having visitors, so tours were offered on a very limited basis; we tagged along with another group of homebrewers. By this time I had evolved into a serious homebrewer and had built a big refrigerated cabinet in our covered porch where I was regularly brewing 15-gallon batches of homebrew. My brother, Steve, had introduced me to Paul Camusi, a fellow homebrewer and cyclist. I had sold him brewing supplies, and we became friends during a few visits he made from Southern California to my Homebrew Shop. We started talking about the feasibility of opening our own brewery and saw the trip to New Albion as the start of our research. Jack designed his brewery to produce 1½ barrels[3] per batch, or about three times as much as my homebrew setup. After seeing his clever approach to fabricating his own equipment and the operation's simplistic level of technology, we realized that it was feasible to go from homebrewing to production brewing with limited financial or industry knowledge. We left with several cases of beer that we bought from Jack. His beers were closer to homebrew in style than Fritz's, but he made a bigger impression because his operation was essentially a glorified home brewery. I came to the conclusion that I could take my passion and talent for homebrewing and brew the kind of beer I wanted to drink.

Paul and I decided to pursue the possibility of opening our own brewery. With a young family to support, I considered what that would mean for us. I didn't know if our venture would provide financial security in the long run. At the same time, Pullins Cyclery, back in the hands of Vern, who was now more than 80 years old, was going to be sold by the family. He had become too frail to run the shop. His son-in-law had burned too many bridges, so taking over again wasn't an option. Vern's wife decided that the shop had to be sold, and, as it played out, Vern really had no say in the outcome. With the future of the bike shop hanging by a thread, I started to second-guess my intention to open a brewery. Would buying the

---

[3] A barrel is a standardized unit of measurement for breweries equivalent to 31 gallons.

bike shop be a better, safer choice? Several other local mechanics were vying for the shop, but I had a longstanding friendship with Vern; I might have been able to prevail if I had wanted to purchase his business. I was pretty sure I would have been approved for a loan and was confident that I would have been successful running Pullins. Money was still tight and I had a family to support. Running a bicycle shop in a college town would have ensured a steady income, whereas opening a small brewery promised to be a tremendous challenge with little chance of succeeding. I agonized for a few days and came to the conclusion that the safe option probably wouldn't be as rewarding. Although I enjoyed running the bike shop, I feared I would eventually become bored and lose interest. The thought of brewing beer for my livelihood was much more appealing than fixing flats and lubing chains.

Katie said that she would support my decision—whatever it was. I worried that if I didn't pursue my dream and focus on taking my homebrewing hobby to the next level and going pro, I would probably regret it for the rest of my life. We decided to sell The Homebrew Shop, and I would focus my attention on opening a brewery. It was also difficult and not very rewarding for Katie to work so many hours in The Homebrew Shop while raising Sierra. Katie really didn't like being cooped up in the small space with a baby and didn't like the retail aspect of the work. On top of that, she didn't, and still doesn't, drink. That presented a problem when novice homebrewers would bring in problematic beers and ask for advice. She did the best she could without letting on that she wasn't an experienced brewer or drinker because she thought all beer tasted awful.

One of my good customers, Bill, a Chico State psychology professor, expressed interest in buying the shop. He was a fun-loving, somewhat accomplished homebrewer and thought it would be an enjoyable side business that he and his wife could run while he kept teaching. The business had grown since I had first opened it in 1976 but still couldn't be considered a truly viable operation that could afford to hire staff and make any return. The sale price for my homebrew shop was $3,000, so it certainly wasn't a big barrier for entry. Although this was

Bill's plan, I don't think his wife was that enthralled with the notion; Bill and his wife soon split up. Later, Bill's girlfriend, Dawn, ended up running the store. Unfortunately, Bill passed away several years after he bought the business. Thirty-five years later, The Homebrew Shop is still open and operated by Dawn, a testament to her business skills and the enduring allure of homebrewing.

3

PIONEER DAYS

Beer makes you feel the way you ought to feel without beer.
—Henry Lawson

With my decision made and the business sold, Paul and I started to plot our course. He moved into the ranch house with Katie, Sierra, and me. I had been working for the ranch owner to help offset our rent, doing some tractor and engine rebuilding and maintenance, which gave me access to the equipment and workspace that would end up being helpful as I started assembling and working on brewing equipment. While I was running my store and working at Pullins Cyclery, another opportunity came up to work in a new bicycle shop and make a little more money. I had helped my good friend, Dave Morrison, get a job at Pullins Cyclery some years earlier, and when he decided to open his own bicycle shop, he asked me to help out. At that point I had worked at four different bicycle shops and had a fair amount of experience. Dave had purchased a small and somewhat faltering bicycle shop in Chico and was remodeling and upgrading it.

Working for Dave allowed me a little more flexibility and the opportunity to work for him on both Saturdays and Sundays and whenever I could pick up a few extra hours between Pullins and The Homebrew Shop.

We excitedly ramped up our brewing trials and began testing recipes that we thought we might want to produce at our brewery. We were buoyed by the sense that consumers wanted something other than mass-produced, lightly flavored beer. Imports were starting to gain momentum, and New Albion was looking for capital to expand. I think we also had a bit of luck on our side, and the time was right for the brewing industry to turn a corner. We knew we only needed to find a small market niche, just a fraction of 1 percent of the roughly 150-million-barrel US brewing industry, to make our brewery successful. We started to work on developing a business plan and researching what we would need to do to design and build our brewery.

As Paul and I worked, we realized that we had more in-depth questions for Jack, so we made another trip to New Albion. We planned to follow Jack's tactic of building everything from scratch, and although we were fairly accomplished homebrewers, we knew we had a lot to learn about production brewing and running a licensed commercial brewery. Upon closer inspection, it became obvious that Jack's modest 1½-barrel batch size that amounted to just three kegs a day, or 45 gallons per batch, presented a huge impediment for him. With that small of a daily output and therefore limited sales, he had barely enough cash flow to make ends meet, let alone fund any expansion. Like me, Jack had a working partner, Susie Stern, who helped him run the brewery. The two of them did all the brewing, marketing, sales, and distributing, as well as the multitude of chores required to run a multifaceted and complicated business. Jack impressed upon on us the need for self-sufficiency and resourcefulness. He had almost single-handedly built, converted, or adapted every piece of equipment in his brewery, from the malt mill to the homemade bottle filler.

Brewing involves sensitive biological reactions with many pitfalls and requires constant vigilance to ensure quality and success. Although

Jack's small batch size was easy to manage, larger batches wouldn't require much more labor. After some discussion Paul and I decided on a 10-barrel batch (310 gallons) size for our brewery, giving us a good balance between labor and a manageable brew size that would still be profitable.

We knew we would have a very limited budget and personnel to work with and would have to learn and master every aspect of the operation. We planned to borrow the funds necessary to build a brewery similar to what Jack had built at New Albion, but on a larger scale—big enough to generate the cash flow that would support my family and Paul. Even if we had been aware that some small-scale commercial brewing equipment was being fabricated in Europe, it would have been totally out of our reach financially. I felt I had a fair amount of fabrication and mechanical aptitude, but if I was going to build the entire plant myself, I knew I would need to hone my skills further.

I immediately checked out the classes available at Butte College that I thought would provide the training and education I needed. I also looked for classes that would give me access to fabrication equipment. The farm had some basic maintenance equipment and I had a variety of hand tools, but I didn't have the machinery or space I would need to weld, shape, and fabricate the equipment we needed for the brewery. I signed up for every available welding, fabrication, or agriculture class that got me access to the well-equipped college shop. At the time Butte College also offered a wide range of programs in the construction and manufacturing trades, so I took classes on refrigeration repair and electrical wiring. It didn't take me too long to master enough of the basics to perform all of the refrigeration, plumbing, and wiring that were required to build the brewery. I took day and evening classes, as many as I could fit in. I was still working at the bicycle shop, too, just barely making enough to cover living expenses. Katie got a job as dairy herd inspector and would head off to the dairies in the middle of the night to collect milk samples and measure the herd's milk production. Paul didn't have a job, so he started reading, researching, and working on our business plan. Our lives became consumed with bringing our dream to fruition; everything we did was with that goal in mind.

THE PLAN

At this point, I was intimately aware of only a few American craft brewers, and besides Fritz Maytag at Anchor and Jack McAuliffe at New Albion, I heard of several other homebrewers who were slightly ahead or behind my stage of planning. But I hadn't studied the history of the US brewing industry until now. I wasn't too familiar with many of the other established commercial breweries because most were located in the Midwest or East, and I didn't have any firsthand knowledge of many of these faltering brands because they rarely got to the West Coast. As I read more about the industry, I found most of the older, established American legacy small brewers were having troubles, and their brands were disappearing from the shelves or were purchased by the likes of the G. Heileman Brewing Company and Paul Kalmanovitz. I sought out as many unique and interesting beers as I could find on my travels and made a point to visit some of the more progressive and better-stocked liquor stores in search of different beers. Although there was a period of time starting in the 1970s, when you could find dozens of different beers at some of the larger specialty liquor stores, few were American and they were generally not very good representations. Most were likely handled unrefrigerated and sold as single bottles. They probably didn't turn over very fast, so they were typically very old.

Along with the practical skills needed to build a brewery, we knew we needed a business plan, but neither Paul nor I had ever written one. The Homebrew Shop was such a small venture that it really hadn't necessitated one. Luckily, when it came time to write the first business plan for the brewery, we had a resource we could turn to. I had a good friend, Jean Harvey, who had adopted many wayward souls, including several members of my Southern California clan. The Harveys took us into their household from the moment we met and acted as surrogate parents for our lively group. Jean was married to Chuck, an intellectual Chico State history professor and, under Jean's direction, a farm laborer. She was the driving force in their household and engaged in all sorts of animal husbandry pursuits. She maintained a large herd of

Nubian goats and, at times, dozens of rabbits, sheep, and anything else that she thought could be a source of income or food for her children and the ever-expanding adopted family. Partly because of Jean's influence, Katie and I set up our own small farming operation and for many years raised chickens and goats as a source of meat and milk for our family. We often ate dinner at their house, which typically comprised stews, soups, or casseroles of rabbit, goat, or often an unruly boar that was past its prime and overly ripe. Jean had four kids of her own but typically cooked for eight to twelve people every night. She was also an outstanding typist and editor; she specialized in typing dissertations for college professors and master's students and was the obvious choice to help write our business plan. We spent many days writing and rewriting our plan with Jean in front her IBM Selectric typewriter. Years later Jean went on to help start another brewery where she became a significant shareholder.

As we started to do research in preparation for writing our business plan, I began to gain insight into the plight of the US brewing industry. Other than a few large and more aggressive breweries, most of the family breweries that had reopened after Prohibition had been struggling to survive or were disappearing at a frightening rate. America once boasted around 3,000 breweries, and almost all were regional and distributed in small, local geographic areas. As product quality and technology slowly improved with the growing use of and, eventually reliance on, pasteurization, their beer could be stabilized and shipped long distances. Pasteurization was required partially as a crutch to deal with less than pristine plants and hygienic brewing methods and the trend of lighter, less hoppy styles that were subject to more microbiological problems. The more aggressive brewers started to expand their distribution footprints with the advent of national rail, an improving road system, and mass marketing in magazines, radio, and later, TV, which greatly aided big brewers' ability to sell their beer nationwide. Small local brewers had to compete with larger, more efficient production plants that could increasingly justify better and faster equipment.

As brewers tried to achieve mass production and wider distribution, and with the desire to appeal to an ever-expanding consumer base, beers became increasingly milder, lighter, and somewhat more insipid, as if the mantra of the company was not to make beer with distinctive character or flavor attributes, but beers that would not offend anybody's taste sensibilities. This trend has continued to the present time, although the quest for blandness may have hit bottom in the past few years since the bitterness levels in modern American beer seems to have stabilized a little above the mid-single digits in bitterness units (IBUs).[1]

---

[1]Hops have been added to beer for centuries; records indicate at least since the eleventh century, when they replaced other herbs as flavoring to help counter the sweet malt sugars provided by the barley. They play many important roles in brewing, providing significant antibacterial qualities during the fermenting process that help keep unwanted bacteria from thriving during fermentation and help protect the finished beer from developing off flavors. Hops are probably best known for the pleasant bitter flavor and aroma they provide. This bitterness can be measured in finished beer in the standard referred to as International Bitterness Units (IBUs). One part per million of the primary bitter resin called Isohumulone, or Alpha acid, in beer is equivalent to one IBU. These bittering compounds are primarily composed of Alpha and, to a much lesser extent, Beta acids, and are analyzed in the raw hops at harvest to give an indication of the level of bitterness they will contribute to the beer. To impart the correct balance of bitterness, most brewers base their usage on Alpha acid content when formulating a recipe. Hops are also responsible for much of the aroma of beer. Historically aroma hops were used in small quantities for a mild spice or floral note, as more of a subtle background to the malt and yeast aromas. But craft brewers have seriously pushed the envelope, and many India Pale Ales now have intense hop aroma that dominates the overall aroma. Hops are a very complex plant and contain a wide range of resins and oils that contribute a great deal to the overall complexity of beer and can vary greatly by variety, harvest year, and growing conditions. Breeding programs have focused on increasing the Alpha acid content and have more than doubled the content from about 7 percent to almost 20 percent of the dried-cone weight of hops. Many small breweries lack the laboratory equipment to analyze each batch of beer and therefore make estimates as to the level of IBUs. As the amount of hops added increases, the extraction efficiencies decrease, resulting in less than expected levels. We have rarely seen beers advertised as having extreme hop levels live up to their claims. The IBU number doesn't necessarily tell the whole story about the perceived bitterness of a particular beer but is currently the best tool to analyze and compare beer bitterness. Most domestic lagers are currently around 10 IBUs or less. The craft industry has been pushing the boundaries of hops usage. When we started out with our Pale Ale in 1980 at 37 IBUs, it was one of the hoppiest beers on the market. Now some of the hoppier beers may be in the 70s or even higher.

Of course, large brewers were keeping an eye on each other's beer and regularly analyzed the competition. An upper-level manager at a large brewery told me it was almost like clockwork—they would drop their hopping rate down ½ to 1 IBU every year, and soon they would see the competition drop theirs. It became as if it were a tit for tat competition to see who could produce the least distinctive beer. During the 1980s some popular, widely distributed national lagers dropped somewhere around 1 IBU per year. Brands that used to be close to or above 20 IBUs reduced their bitterness to 7 or 8 IBUs. Some brewers seemed to believe that the closer beer was to water the better—it was easier for more people to consume and less of anything to object to. Besides, lighter beer costs less to brew.

During this depressing and soulless era of the US brewing industry, many struggling smaller breweries must have felt that in order to compete they had to change their beer styles to emulate the lighter, homogenous style of beer that the national brewers were producing. Unfortunately, mass-produced, lightly hopped beers are less forgiving and show processing flaws, including oxygen pickup from a less-than-state-of-the-art bottling line or the detrimental effects of copper and iron that were still commonplace in many older breweries, much more readily. So besides being challenged by smaller, less efficient plants and lower productivity, they also had additional trouble consistently producing these styles of beers. Ultimately, few small brewers could hold on, and sadly many followed this flawed business model to their ends.

The year I started, 1980, represented the low point for the US brewing industry, with a mere 40 legacy breweries in existence. Only a few of them are still in existence today. A few have sold out to bigger breweries, a few survive as a brand name only with no bricks or mortar, and a few are run by entirely new entities or investment groups. By the time I started, most of the proud legacies built by generations of brewing families had disappeared from the communities in which they had played pivotal roles.

Most of what we learned about our new industry was both exciting and disheartening. On one hand, I viewed the lack of competition from other breweries as a possible benefit. The dominance of what was for all intents and purposes a single style of beer being brewed in the United States offered an opening and a niche for us. The fact that so many small brewers had struggled to compete and failed wasn't a good omen, though. The hundreds of failed breweries littering recent history didn't make borrowing from banks or finding investors easy. It was hard to ignore the facts: There were numerous small brewery failures and only a few success stories.

Our business plan covered every aspect of our business, or at least as much as we had thought through by late 1979, including the marketing strategies we would use to promote the brewery. The marketing section began with the statement that quality would be the most important sales draw of our beer. We also promised to capitalize on our local origins by focusing our marketing in the Chico area, at least to start. Our local identification and low distribution costs would help us avoid expensive advertising, allowing us to spend more on quality ingredients. The initial volume was slated to be 1,500 cases per month. We planned for $13 to $15 per case or $0.50 to $0.60 per bottle at wholesale, giving us a retail price of $0.85 to situate us in between the $0.70 to $0.90 range for imports, which we saw as our primary competition. The financial part of the plan was more detailed and included a summary of investment to date, a breakdown of monthly costs, and several pages of photocopies of painstakingly recorded purchases, but all of the detail couldn't hide the fact that we needed money.

We started to put together what we thought was a sound budget, but we didn't have a clue what we were getting into. The only existing model for a start-up brewery was New Albion, and although Jack had helped us with technical matters, we weren't privy to the financial details of his business. We had heard that Jack started with $25,000 and tried to use that figure to estimate how much we'd need. We knew our larger batch size was going to cost more, but the fixed costs for things like lab equipment and label printing weren't going to increase. We estimated that we could build and equip our new brewery for $50,000.

Paul and I were suitably pleased with our 41-page document that seemed to lend legitimacy and weight to our undertaking, but we still had some crucial decisions to make. After determining how much money we'd need, we had to find the location where we would build the brewery before approaching a bank. We knew we wanted to be in a small, rural area in California, which gave us many options. Chico was obviously a possibility, but we considered other locations as well. Finding somewhere relatively close to mountains for climbing and nature at our back door was important to me. We started looking at cities from San Luis Obispo to Nevada City. It wasn't just a matter of finding a location that we liked for aesthetic reasons; we also had to take into account a city's infrastructure and services. Water and wastewater treatment capacity would be important for our operations. We also had to think about the shipping cost of supplies and distribution of beer from the facility. One by one we eliminated every city except Chico, conveniently situated at the foot the Sierra Nevada Mountain range, and finalized our prospectus. Now we needed a name for our brewery. We had discussed several names, but with Katie's and my love of the mountains (we had even named our first daughter Sierra), we chose Sierra Nevada Brewing Co.

With our business plan in hand, Paul and I headed to the local banks to pitch our concept. I had had a good track record of paying my bills when I owned The Homebrew Shop, but I had established credit with only small, nonmainstream vendors who sold supplies to the specialized market, and I'm sure most of them were below the radar of any credit rating agency. I had never applied for or received a personal credit card, didn't own a house, and had never owed any conventional institution a penny, so I had absolutely no personal credit. Paul's credit wasn't much more established, but he at least had a gas card to his name. Predictably, the response from the banks was a resounding no. Aside from our lack of credit history, if they did a little research on the state of the American brewing industry, they'd have found that we were looking to go into a business that had a long history of failures. One of the most respected and often quoted brewing industry analysts of the time, Bob Weinberg, had recently published an article in trade magazines predicting that there would be only two or three operating American breweries by the year 2000.

It was against this backdrop that we were looking for a loan and pitching our prospectus. To compound our challenge, we couldn't have picked a worse economy to try to borrow money in. The country was in the midst of terrible economic turmoil, with inflation close to 12 percent and the prime interest rate starting to soar; it eventually reached the staggering rate of 21.5 percent in 1982.

No bank was willing to loan us money, which was possibly a godsend to our company's survival in the long run. If we had gotten a loan, it would most likely have been tied to the current market; we would have been smothered by soaring interest rates. It was a bleak landscape for starting a new business, but we were undeterred.

The Scavenger Hunt

Neither Paul nor I had much money, but we pooled what we had so that we could begin construction of the brewery. I had always been frugal and tried to put a little money away when I could, so even though Katie and I were almost always just scraping along, we had accumulated a few thousand dollars in savings. With the money I received from the sale of The Homebrew Shop, we had enough to start assembling a few pieces of equipment. We had to be very careful and limit what we spent, but even before we completed our business plan, we began to gather a few things. I almost immediately started fabricating a malt mill because it was the first piece of equipment that I knew we would need to start the brewing process. I started by building a heavy wooden frame similar to the one that Jack had used in his brewery at New Albion. I wanted to design a more sophisticated mill with four rollers like I had seen in commercial brewing books, but my woodworking skills weren't as advanced as my metalworking skills.

After a few incorrectly drilled holes, I scrapped the wood and started on a metal frame. Trying to build a fairly elaborate mill with minimal financial resources and equipment after only seeing one in a picture and a crude drawing was an eye-opening challenge. To fabricate the rollers I purchased some 8-inch well casing, the least expensive pipe I could find, at a steel yard, welded the ends and shafts in place, and turned them on a lathe; it was a fairly crude, marginally engineered first attempt at building a mill, but after several modifications it finally worked well enough to get us brewing.

In the beginning, I spent what little free time I had scouring the West Coast, visiting small, defunct dairies and salvage yards looking for stainless steel tanks, pumps, and pipe. I stumbled upon a fairly large scrap and salvage operation in Keyes, California, near Modesto, that had acres of every conceivable scrapped item. Being in the heart of the fertile agricultural valley, it was close to many food processors, wineries, and dairy processors and had a large selection of cast-off stainless steel equipment. I made many trips down to the yard with my 1957 Chevy-turned-flatbed and spent days rummaging around, picking up bits and pieces of pipe, valves, and tanks. The colorful owner, George Besone, was at once a philosopher, political commentator, and observer of the human condition as well as a masterful horse trader. Often as I was anxious to head home with my bounty, he would spend hours talking politics with me as I tried to load up my truck. I think he took a liking to me, and I often had to make my escape politely so that I could make the long trek back to Chico with my loot. He was somewhat enamored with my pursuit and gave me special consideration on pricing. He would occasionally call me even years after the brewery was up and running when he came across something he thought might be of value for my growing brewery. His scrap yard supplied the tank that I would ultimately turn into my first brew kettle, mash tun, and several other key components that I repurposed into brewing equipment.

Another tactic I had was going to small agricultural communities and checking in at the local feed stores or farm equipment dealers to inquire if they knew about any dairies that had closed in the area.

Although hundreds of small family dairy operations used to pepper the West Coast, they too were no longer able to compete with larger operations. Just as the economics of operating a small brewery in a growing and consolidating industry drove many weaker brands out of business, smaller family dairies also shut down around that time.[2] Once I got a lead, I would often discover a few more by talking to the dairymen because they had a good pulse on the local farm happenings. These decommissioned dairies provided many pieces of equipment to the brewery for pennies on the dollar, supplying the fermenters (the tanks where the yeast is first added to the cooled, hopped wort), refrigeration equipment, and all the stainless pipes and pumps. Although the dairymen were usually frugal, I became a good negotiator, typically paying no more than a dollar per gallon for the tanks and a few dollars for the pumps, pipes, and fittings. Dairy equipment is designed to meet rigorous hygiene standards, far in excess of what would have been found at a typical winery or older-era brewery.

For the bottling equipment, Paul and I went to the phone company and thumbed through stacks of phonebooks (before the Internet we had no other choice), looking for soft drink bottlers on the West Coast. Our operation was going to be smaller than other breweries in the country, so even though a closing brewery may have had the equipment we needed, we assumed it would be too large for our operation. I thought we could find some small bottling equipment in a soda bottler's boneyard for pennies on the dollar.[3] New Albion's small

---

[2]Artisan cheese has recently experienced a renaissance similar to what craft brewing experienced in the late 1980s. Ironically, Fritz Maytag's father was well ahead of this curve, having pioneered blue cheese production on his small family farm decades ahead of the recent movement.

[3]Regional soda bottlers in America had a similar trajectory to breweries but were a few years behind. Most towns had a small bottling operation serving the local market with returnable bottles. When aluminum cans and plastic bottles were introduced for soda, the small local bottlers couldn't upgrade and compete and generally closed down their packaging operations and resorted to purchasing their products from a central bottler. Often the warehouse and distribution facility was kept intact, and that part of the business operated as before. As I discovered, many of the old bottling lines were still in the warehouses and had little value to the bottlers or anyone else.

production afforded Jack the ability to hand-bottle his beer, and although it was a lot of work, he needed to wash and fill only about 20 cases per batch. We needed to figure out how to bottle a lot more beer per day if we were going to execute our business plan.

After some research we located a shuttered soft drink plant in Needles, California, and because Paul was down visiting his family, he agreed to go inspect it. He was not particularly mechanically inclined and hadn't had the same experience with mechanics, fabrication, and rebuilding engines and transmissions that I had had growing up. He called me from the plant and said they were willing to sell the entire operation for $1,500, which seemed like a reasonably good price to me, so I told Paul to go ahead and buy it. Of course I had no idea what bottling lines sold for, but that sounded like a bargain, even if it needed a little work. Paul said it was a complete plant and included a refrigerated water carbonator, a bottle washer, a filler, and the conveyors to handle the bottles. I was pretty sure we could figure out how to make it work for us, even sight unseen. Paul returned to Chico with some pictures; it looked a bit rusty and rough to me, but I didn't know what I was looking at anyway. I would have to await its arrival to get a real sense of what we bought. We hired a local trucking firm from Chico to make the torturous drive. They charged $700, almost half as much as we had paid for the equipment, but we didn't have any other way to get it from Needles.

When the truck showed up at my house with the equipment, I was heartbroken; it looked like a pile of scrap, which in reality it was. The bottle washer was corroded and full of rust, and the conveyers were twisted and useless. I had some hope that maybe the bottle filler would be able to be resurrected, but what did I know? I had seen only a couple of bottle fillers in my life. The trucking company left the trailer overnight at my house. We rented a forklift and got the truck unloaded, one of the first of many of high-pucker equipment moves. The laws of physics, large machinery, and a small forklift coupled with the fact that Paul and I possessed only rudimentary forklift skills made for a long night with many close calls. Still, somehow we managed to get the bottling line unloaded and piled up in the barn.

On further inspection I thought the likelihood of using the filler to bottle beer was questionable at best. I tracked down the manufacturer; luckily, they were still in business. After reviewing the operation manual and describing what we had purchased to the sales engineer, we discovered what we had bought was a vintage Dixie piston-operated soda filler built sometime in the 1940s. After the person on the phone had a good chuckle, he strongly advised me against using it to bottle beer. It was probably one of the last of its kind left in existence; he thought maybe a bottler's museum would want it because it was such a unique and historic machine. It was made entirely of brass and copper, and although those materials are common in older breweries, they are not ideal for handling beer after fermentation. Beer is acidic by nature and can pick up metallic flavor. Exposure to metal also decreases shelf life, but I was aware of brass parts still being used in breweries and thought it would be good enough to start out with. Many of the original gaskets and seals were made out of leather, but I figured I could replace them with modern materials. The bigger issue was that it was all assembled with lead solder, and I knew enough to know that lead was out of the question. I spent the next week taking it apart and hauling the hundreds of pounds of brass it yielded to the scrap yard. Eventually I ended up getting about a third of my original investment back in payment for scrap.[4] In the end only a few pieces from Needles were of value, but I was able to fix the refrigeration compressor and use it to supply chilled water for cooling the hot wort

---

[4]Ironically, soon after we opened I got a call from Jim Schlueter, who was trying to open a small brewery in Sacramento called River City. He had also purchased one of these gems that required the operator to wear a raincoat because it spit liquid everywhere. I relayed to him my conversation with the manufacturer and concerns about quality. Jim was obstinate and determined to make the Dixie work for him. A short time after our conversation, I heard that he donated it to the brewing program at University of California, Davis, and took a big tax deduction (admittedly a smarter move than I had made). His brewery was short-lived, in most part because of the marginal and varying quality of his product. The University of California, Davis, realized the Dixie wasn't going to function for them either, and I eventually got it from Davis with the hope that someday I would find the time to restore it and put it on display. (Somehow I haven't found time yet, but it's still in storage at the brewery.)

before fermentation.[5] The bottle washer was rusted beyond repair and had the unique distinction of having been fabricated from surplus ship decking left over from World War II. Jack had the same model of washer at New Albion. Mine still had some usable gearboxes and other parts, so I sold him the salvage rights; he came over and scavenged what he could use before I cut it up and hauled it off to the scrap yard.

FRIENDS AND RESOURCES

As we worked on securing equipment, Jack pointed us toward a great resource for more practical brewing information at the University of California, Davis (UC Davis), located just down the road outside Sacramento. Among all the outstanding educational opportunities UC Davis provides, it has a long history of offering food science programs. In this regard, UC Davis is generally recognized for its contribution to winemaking, but it has for many years offered classes and degrees on the biochemistry and science of brewing. In the early 1960s, British-educated Dr. Michael Lewis spearheaded a comprehensive brewing science program that produced dozens of talented brewmasters. UC Davis continues to offer one of the few technical and practical brewing programs in the United States, now under the direction of another British-educated, highly energetic, talented, and often humorous professor, Dr. Charles Bamforth. Even in the 1970s, the brewing library at UC Davis was filled with an extensive assortment of US and European brewing journals and books. The United States once

---

[5]Beer, at least what most of us in America call beer, is primarily or exclusively produced from a natural extract of malted barley (and often some other source of sugar or starch), but it's not called beer until the fermentation process. The brewery collects the extract, a sugary solution, in a fashion not unlike extraction of maple sap from a tree. As the malt sugar runs from the grains, this sweet wort is collected and sent to the brewing kettle, where hops are added. With the addition of hops, the brewer now refers to this liquid as bitter wort. After roughly an hour of boiling, the bitter wort is cooled, aerated, and dosed with yeast, at which point the brewer can say he has a tank full of fermenting beer!

had several brewing institutes and research laboratories that published numerous technical books and periodicals. Paul and I had purchased all the commercial brewing texts we could find, but many were out of print; so we started to make regular trips to UC Davis to read and photocopy things that we thought would be useful to us.

Michael was a colorful and opinionated British-born and British-educated brewing scientist, and when we visited the brewing library, we regularly spent time talking about our progress toward opening the brewery. He was keenly aware of the fledgling craft brewing industry, having spent time with Jack when he was getting New Albion off the ground, as well as apprenticing one of his students, Don Barclay, there (a fellow veteran of the craft revolution with a long career in the industry). We also took advantage of spending time with some of Michael's graduate-level brewing students, who advised us on the various technical challenges we thought we might face. Ironically, one of those students and early advisors was Doug Muhleman, who eventually went on to hold the top technical and leadership position at Anheuser-Busch. Doug wisely suggested that with our limited funding and technology we would probably be smart to keep our brewing process simple and focus on brewing a top-fermented ale rather than a lager beer.

As homebrewers, Paul and I had a fairly vast repertoire of beer styles that we liked brewing, and we had perfected many types, including a wide range of European-style lagers. At first we thought that was the direction we would take at our brewery because New Albion had been focusing on ales. We wanted to do something different, and our research showed that American ale was a dying style. Even though we could take advantage of all the modern hygiene and microbiology knowledge, we knew that with our small capital we would have to think almost like a turn-of-the-century brewery lacking modern equipment and process technology. With this understanding and reality, we settled on producing a range of top-fermented beers. Besides requiring a little quicker fermentation process, ale, or top-fermenting, yeast is generally much more robust, and if good hygiene is maintained, the yeast can be harvested and serially reused (or repitched, in brewing terms) from batch to batch, minimizing the need for ongoing yeast propagation. Ale yeast is more robust and less prone to mutating during successive fermentations and has less demanding refrigeration needs during fermentation and maturation, making it easier to manage. Ales generally also have a more robust and pronounced flavor profile, which we preferred, and we believed it would also probably help distinguish us in the marketplace.

Because of our lack of equipment and technology, we decided to use the time-honored, but rarely commercially practiced, process of bottle conditioning. None of our tanks would be designed to hold sufficient pressure to allow beer to carbonate in the storage tanks. We didn't want to artificially carbonate our beer, so we had to add live yeast and fermentable extract to the bottle. Many brewers used some form of artificial or added carbonation, which meant injecting either CO_2 they had collected from the fermentation process or purchased CO_2, which was often a by-product of petrochemical refineries or fertilizer production. That wasn't the direction we wanted to go, so we had no other choice than to figure out how to master bottle conditioning on a production level.

Back in Chico we pored over the dozens of excerpts and articles copied at UC Davis and rated and classified them as to their relevance in building and running our brewery. Paul and I developed our own evaluation scale, flagging the articles with one to three stars based on how helpful we thought they would be before sorting and filing them in folders based on which area in the operation they would be most applicable. I spent hours reading and rereading the handful of brewing texts that were available. I read *Malting and Brewing Science*, the most current and complete industry text available, cover to cover several times and tried to absorb the practical and arcane ideas it delved into. My chemistry and physics background proved invaluable, but my lack of biochemistry training made a few of the in-depth chapters on detailed biological concepts a little more challenging to master.

With some equipment and knowledge under our belts, we went looking for a place to call home. We eventually found what we thought was a suitable building; it was a 3,000-square-foot metal warehouse on Gilman Way, a small industrial street on the south side of Chico. By city code a brewery needed to be located in an M, or manufacturing, zone, and M zones were in limited supply in Chico. We had been looking for a while and were happy to locate in what we thought was an ideal place to start. The warehouse was just a wide, open metal shell with a small bathroom and no insulation or other improvements, but it had plenty of potential for the infrastructure we'd need.

Having operated a homebrew shop and being asked to taste countless batches of off beer, we were painfully aware of the importance of sanitation, so we were prepared to build the required framework, including drains and separate production areas to house the brewing, fermentation, packaging, and warehousing in their own isolated and defined rooms. We were aware that there was a real hazard of cross contamination by malt dust, which can contain lactic acid bacteria, so we tried to be very careful with our layout and design. We had recently heard about problems at another small brewer who had rushed into the market ahead of us but hadn't invested in the infrastructure to isolate the malt room, resulting in microbiological issues. During the malting process, maltsters steep the barley grain in water to allow it to germinate. Since barley is a living, growing organism, it can harbor harmless bacteria that sometimes survive the kilning process. Although some strains of lactic acid bacteria are great for producing yogurt, if they get into the fermentation process, they produce sour and undesirable flavors that can ruin beer. Although making these modifications to isolate our malt room was an expensive and time-consuming process, especially because we did all the construction ourselves, we knew that if we compromised on this critical groundwork, our chances of producing consistent and defect-free beer were limited.

As we began outfitting the space and building the brewery, we met a few other homebrewers who were also trying to enter the ranks of commercial brewing and were putting together small breweries. When we could find time, we would talk with them to compare notes. In Boulder, Colorado, David Hummer and Stick Ware, two college professors and friends, decided to open a brewery and still keep their day jobs. Stick visited us and told us about their progress—they had retrofitted an old goat barn that they thought would be suitable for a brewery. In Novato, California, Tom DeBakker, a homebrewer and firefighter, opened a small brewery that he ran with his wife. He brewed on his days off, and his wife took care of the other chores. We tried to visit or talk to as many of these aspiring brewers as we could to compare notes and get some insight into their plans. This first wave of craft brewers pretty much all had the same drive as we did and wanted to try to make a living on what had been their hobby. Paul and I observed some of the other brewery start-ups cutting what we felt were important corners, which they ultimately regretted; all but one of the breweries that started with us during that first wave of the craft industry went out of business, in large part because of their inability to produce consistent beers.

We paid a price for our diligence, though. Several new breweries had already opened their doors, even though we had started planning before most, if not all, of them. In many ways our brewery was larger and more sophisticated, but our lack of adequate funds and the extended construction and fabrication that we were undertaking on our own delayed our opening for well over a year. It was agonizing to watch other start-ups get into the marketplace while we were still trying to find enough money to keep going, on top of handling the construction and fabrication of our own equipment, as well as scrounging and rebuilding all the other pieces we needed.

AN EXPENSIVE LESSON

Still without a functioning bottling line, we finally located another one in Mount Vernon, Washington, at another soft drink bottler. Again, it was an antique, not quite as old as the Dixie, but still from the era when flavored sugar syrup was added to soda in one step and carbonated water in the next. I did a little research this time, and although it was not an ideal filler for beer because it was designed to handle only carbonated water, the manufacturer thought it could probably be retrofitted for our purposes but gave no guarantee it would work. The biggest concern was about oxygen pickup; soft drinks aren't nearly so sensitive to the effects of oxygen, and this generation of filler was not designed very well to exclude it. Because our beer was going to be bottle conditioned, it would be fairly low in carbonation when bottled and contain active yeast that would help mop up any surplus oxygen. Jack had bought a similar vintage soda machine but never got it in condition to fill beer. I was probably the first person to attempt retrofitting a soda filler into a beer filler, but Paul and I decided that we were unlikely to find an affordable small filler designed for beer. We took our chances and agreed to buy it.

We hired a truck and headed to the old soda plant to inspect the equipment. There we met the owner of the plant and the used equipment dealer he had enlisted to help him sell the equipment. The filler looked to be in decent shape from what I could tell, but again, what did I know? The dealer had quoted a price of $3,000 for the filler, $2,000 for a bottle washer, and $250 each for two labelers. I had hoped we could do a little negotiating and get it for less, but when we went to pay for it, we realized that the equipment dealer had led the owner to believe that we had agreed to pay much more than we had. Apparently the owner couldn't read the dealer's writing, or the dealer intentionally misled him and added the labelers up to $5,000 instead of the $500 he had quoted us. At first the owner was going to back out of the deal but then agreed to sell the equipment at the price that had been offered to us. Any hope of negotiating a better price was lost. Because I thought we needed only one labeler, I took one of the two machines for a total price of $5,250. On the drive back from Washington, I felt like I might have made a big mistake deciding to open a brewery. The realization that I'd just spent almost everything I had left to my name to buy this bottling equipment when we still hadn't secured all the money we needed for the rest of the operation was terrifying, and I knew we'd encounter more unexpected costs along the way.

Our new bottling line was much larger than we had envisioned when we designed our brewery. We realized that there was no way it would fit in the Gilman Way building, so we decided we would add on. My uncle Bob was an architect in Santa Barbara, and I asked him to draw up the necessary extension. We got permission from our landlord to add on roughly 800 square feet that would accommodate the equipment. I went to the city with my plans and met with the building official, who told me that any addition more than 500 square feet would trigger significant additional fees that I knew we couldn't afford. I made the decision that I would figure out how to shrink the footprint of the addition down to 495 square feet and changed the blueprints on the spot to avoid paying the extra fees.

Paul and I unloaded the bottling equipment at a storage yard down the road from the brewery and found someone to help us pour the slab for the new bottleshop. We borrowed four forklifts from a used equipment dealer, who had been a Homebrew Shop customer and had befriended me, and moved our new bottling line. The space was so tight that we had to construct the building around our newly acquired bottling equipment. After we moved the bottling line onto the slab, I found a local metal building contractor who would sell me scrap sheets of siding at half price. We decided to frame the building ourselves and piece the siding and roof together on the cheap. The only downside was that because we bought scrap we ended up with a colorful quilt-like pattern on our walls. With the reduced footprint, the equipment came within inches of the building, and we essentially had to load the bottles into the bottle washer from outside of the building; we had big doors that swung open, and I built an awning to cover the operator from the elements. Still, it was essentially an open-air affair.

Next I had the task of trying to convert the soda filler to a beer filler. Upon closer inspection after I dismantled it, I realized that the filler was in terrible internal condition, having been regularly left full of chlorine, which had been used to sanitize it. All the internal piping was corroded and needed to be replaced. As it turned out, it had also been assembled with what I presumed was lead solder, which I had to remove completely. The base of the bowl was a thick bronze casting, and after removing all the corroded tubes, I polished the bronze base and silver soldered it back together. I had no other option; I needed it to work, and it took me weeks to rebuild. When we went to put everything together, we discovered that some of the vital parts that we had been told were included with the filler were missing, and we needed them to run the line. We contacted the equipment broker, who turned out to be a shyster who said he didn't know what happened to those parts, but he could supply me with what I needed for only $500. We knew we were being held hostage for our parts and came unglued at the extortion attempt, but it seemed like we had no other option available. When he arrived at the brewery with the missing parts, we made him acknowledge that the paint on the parts matched the paint on the filler exactly, showing they had been repainted with the rest of our machine and belonged to it, so he had no right to ask us to pay again. I was eventually able to put the machine together and hoped it would work when we would finally have beer to put in the bottles.

By the summer of 1980, Paul and I were fully committed but rapidly running out of our personal funds. We had started with a little more than $15,000 between us and had borrowed the balance in small increments from our families up to about the $50,000 we had originally budgeted. That had now dwindled down to nothing, and we still needed more equipment. We had already exceeded our budget with some miscellaneous, but necessary, purchases and realized that our prospectus wasn't as thorough as we thought, so we updated it. The problem was that we didn't have much to show for what we'd already spent. Building a brewery was our dream, but we needed to secure even more money for our newly modified budget. We may have been naïve, but we believed that we'd somehow get what we needed and forged ahead. Originally we thought we could open with a total of $50,000, but our revised prospectus called for an additional $50,000. In the end, our inability to borrow from banks left us no alternative other than again reaching out to family and friends, who were all well aware of our plans, to try to borrow the money. Our families were skeptical of our venture. I am sure they thought it was harebrained, but we were eventually able to convince them that we had a solid business plan and were committed to making it work. Both families decided to support us and managed to come up with the additional money we needed. Paul's father, my father, my grandfather, Paul's father's law partner, and Paul's mother invested the remaining $50,000 in a way that maintained an even stake for our families.

Originally, Paul and I had established a C corporation with the help of an attorney at my father's office. At the time a C corporation was the typical structure that larger companies with many shareholders typically chose. Although it gives good insulation from liability, this structure has some negative tax implications for the shareholders as far as treating business losses. Even before we opened, the attorneys decided to change the structure from a C corporation to a limited partnership to allow our families to claim the inevitable losses on their taxes. I remember the attorneys counseling us that a 50/50 partnership was just like a marriage, and we both had to work hard to make it successful.

While building the brewery and scraping together money and equipment, I was still taking welding, agriculture, and refrigeration classes at Butte. Having access to their shop gave me the necessary forklifts and fabrication tools that I needed for refurbishing and modifying the brewing equipment I was steadily assembling. I still remember shearing and drilling out the bottom of the mash tun. This part was for a critical part of the brewing process when the crushed malted barley is mixed with water to convert the starch into sugar and the resulting sweet wort is then separated from the grain. The tank was an old milk vat that I added a perforated floor to; we were so low on funds that I decided it would be cheaper to drill the roughly 4,000 holes required to perforate the bottom rather than buy a pre-perforated stainless sheet. I spent days on a drill press with a bag of drill bits, painstakingly drilling. Everyone who came by to check on our progress thought I was crazy. The building construction was proceeding slowly but steadily because we were doing all the framing, sheetrocking, and other construction ourselves. Paul had some experience taping and texturizing and did most of the painting while I was putting together the equipment, but we still needed some crucial parts and pieces that I couldn't scrounge up.

I had found enough open dairy tanks to use as primary fermenters, but I couldn't come up with any suitable closed aging tanks (where the beer would finish fermenting and spend approximately an additional two weeks aging and maturing). I went to a company south of Chico that made small, stainless tanks designed for mounting on tractors for fertilizing and agricultural spraying. They couldn't manufacture and polish the tanks to the hygiene standards we required, so I decided I would have the tanks prefabricated and tack them together so that

I could do the welding and sanitary polishing myself. It was a terrible chore that involved being inside the tanks for days on end, welding and then grinding and polishing the seams so that they would be crevice-free and easy to clean. I convinced Paul to help, but on his first day, the grinder got away from him, giving him a deep gash that required stitches. I was on my own after that and spent several dirty, cramped weeks welding and finishing the six aging tanks. After more than a year of construction, we had most of the main equipment together, but we still had a lot to figure out.

PUTTING THE PUZZLE TOGETHER

By September 1980, we had been working on the project for more than two years, continually running out of money and having to ask our small group of shareholders to put in additional funds. Psychologically we were starting to break down; it had been such a long, hard struggle, and I started to question my decision to put everything on the line. There was still a lot to do, and it was slowly starting to grind me down. Between the weekend bicycle shop work to provide some income to live on, construction, welding, and fabrication classes, and road trips looking for parts, it was a seven-day-a-week effort with few days less than 10 hours long and many more than 12. My family life was suffering—Katie was questioning our decision, but to give up at this point wasn't something I thought I could do. I knew if I quit now, everything I had worked so hard on would be lost and there would be no salvaging most of our investment. We were getting close to being able to brew, but it seemed like the challenges just kept coming. I couldn't see cutting corners after all the hard work that we had already put in, so we decided to stay the course and keep grinding away.

I remember one particularly brutal day that almost derailed me. I thought I had taken enough refrigeration classes to allow me to design and install the refrigeration system from the equipment I had been able to scrounge. Most of the compressors used to cool the fermenters came from old milk tanks I found in dairies. With a little input from my refrigeration instructor, I was able to adapt them to operate at the warmer temperatures we needed for our ale fermentation. We still needed a cooler to put in our aging cellar, but we were so low on funds at that point that I couldn't afford to buy a new compressor or coil. My friend, Jean Harvey, located an old walk-in cooler at a closed, clandestine, backyard butcher shop located just north of the brewery in Chapman Town, an offbeat old Chico neighborhood. The owner used to raise livestock and perform butchering for his needs as well as for others in this unsanctioned operation. His business had been shut down by the Health Department, and I was able to purchase the compressor and coil out of the walk-in cooler for almost nothing. I had to remove, clean, and completely rebuild it before I could use it, though. When I got it back to the brewery, I realized that it was corroded and totally repulsive inside, covered in years of dried blood and feathers. I spent hours scrubbing fat and blood off it, getting covered by the gore in the process. I started to question what I was doing, but after the most disgusting and disheartening day I'd had yet, I finally got the cooler running and my sense of purpose back together.

I had also finally got the bottling line rebuilt, but I could test it only with water because we hadn't yet brewed a batch of beer. Still, I was pretty pleased with myself when I finally got it to run and fill and cap a few bottles. The labeler was another story. I thought, how hard could it be to fix up the one machine and get it running? We had been given the opportunity to buy a second labeling machine for $250, but we were so cost conscious at that point. We were spending what little bit of savings I had left, so we didn't want to waste the money. With the slow speed we were planning on running, we thought one labeler would be able to handle our planned speed of 50 bottles per minute. It didn't look too complicated. I had never operated any automated bottling equipment, but being fairly mechanical, I was pretty sure I could figure it out. The first labeler we acquired with the soda line was built by the Economic Machinery Company of Worcester, Massachusetts, and as far as I could tell from the limited available historical information, it was designed in the 1920s and manufactured in the 1930s. Referred to as the World Rotary, this model was the predecessor of the much superior World Tandem labeler, which replaced it sometime in the 1940s. (Some World Tandem labelers still remain in operation today at modern American small breweries.) As it turned out, few parts were available for the Rotary, so I had to fix or make what was broken or needed. I had no operation or parts manual, so I just had to figure out how it was supposed to work. Luckily we still had two small soft drink bottling companies operating in Chico at the time, and I started picking their brains regularly. The very experienced production foreman at the tiny 7UP bottling plant was extremely helpful, having operated very similar equipment. For the first year of operation, both of the local bottlers would regularly let me have their almost empty glue buckets to scrape the bottom for the few cups of label glue that we required to label our 100-case runs. Because we had decided to use a returnable longneck bar bottle, and the soft drink bottlers I had purchased didn't have a similarly shaped bottle, I had to modify the parts to handle the tall, skinny bottle. Luckily the old soda company had run a 7-ounce bottle at some point, and because I had grabbed all the spare parts I could find, I was able to carve out and modify the required pieces from those parts. The longneck beer bottles would prove to be another challenge because they have a high center of gravity and fall over easily. With the crude level of technology my vintage labeler employed, we had huge losses in our early production days.

4

MATERIALS AND INGREDIENTS

Not all chemicals are bad. Without chemicals such as hydrogen and oxygen, for example, there would be no way to make water, a vital ingredient in beer.

—Dave Barry

I n the beginning we planned to offer beer only in bottles because we couldn't afford keg-filling equipment, and they seemed to offer more sales opportunities in a time before the advent of multitap accounts. In those days draught beer was generally sold as somewhat of a loss leader and didn't have the same profit potential as bottles. At first, we chose returnable bottles because we couldn't afford to buy new glass; we naïvely thought they would be cheaper than buying new bottles, but it meant constantly searching for sources of used bottles. Paul had found several thousand cases of longneck beer bottles at the Maier Brewing Company in Los Angeles, one of Paul Kalmanovitz's first forays into the brewing world and the first of many breweries he would wring the last drop of beer out of before gutting and shuttering them. Although I never met him, I visited many of his breweries both before and after he closed them and was the recipient of many artifacts and cast-off equipment from the breweries he shut down. By all reports he was a very shrewd, colorful, extremely successful businessman and real estate tycoon.[1] My partner Paul had gained access to the shuttered Maier Brewery after Mr. Paul, as he was often referred to, had closed it in 1974. The warehouse contained thousands of cases of empty returnable beer bottles, with labels still on them and packed in heavy cardboard returnable cases. Most of the bottles bore labels of long-extinct classics such as Light and Mellow, Alpineglow, Golden Glow, Lucky Bankers Ale, and dozens of other more obscure marketing failures. Over the years vandals had rummaged, trashed, and knocked over thousands of cases; Paul had to spend hours restacking them so that

---

[1]Paul Kalmanovitz purchased the Maier Brewing Company in 1950. Like many smaller regional breweries, it had been struggling to compete against the national brands and was a takeover target of the then-aspiring Falstaff brewery. Maier's flagship brand at the time was Brew 102, and the company had been losing money. Under the ownership of the cost-cutting Kalmanovitz, Maier Brewing turned the operation around and started to make a profit, marking the start of his domination of the flailing US regional brewing industry. With the successful turnaround of Maier Brewing, he then acquired the Lucky Lager Brewery in 1970 and picked up plants in California, Washington, and Rhode Island, merging them into his newly formed S&P holding company. He soon closed the Southern California plant, merging its production into Maier Brewing. This would be his tactic for years to come, slashing costs, which often resulted in the letting go of entire departments, often days after he took control. He was also known for moving brands and rationalizing production. When the breweries no longer made a profit, he closed them, distributed the usable assets to one of his other operating breweries, and was left with a valuable piece of real estate. Many breweries were typically located in a central or light industrial section of the city or in former outskirts, and property values often outstripped the worth of the failing brewery enterprise. Although I have some limited memories of drinking Brew 102, a favorite of our group was Spring Beer, which was one of the dozens of labels that was being marketed in the late 1960s and early 1970s by Maier Brewing. I assume that most of the beer Maier Brewing was selling was the same but marketed under a multitude of names. Spring Beer could be found at $0.69 a six-pack or could be had on sale for $1.99 a case. I remember marveling even then at how you could make beer and sell it for less than soda!

we could get them on a truck. Because we didn't yet have anywhere to stack them in Chico, he transferred them to his mother's backyard in Southern California, much to her chagrin, where they spent months waiting for us to finish our brewery.

When I purchased the bottling equipment, I really didn't understand its limitations, but the bottle washer had been designed to wash only Applied Ceramic Label (ACL) bottles like the old painted Coke or Pepsi bottles. Our washer, although capable of cleaning and sterilizing dirty bottles, didn't have the additional filters or screens needed for handling the paper and pulp created when the old labels are removed in the cleaning process. It was a bottle washer as far as I was concerned, and being undeterred, we moved forward with the plan of using returnable bottles with the idea that I could either modify the washer or just operate by more frequently cleaning the limited screens and filters. I started the process of washing the labels off the bottles that had been in the warehouse for 30 years or more. I assume that as they were returned to the brewery from people's garages in their heavy, branded cases, they were sorted and stored with the thought that maybe one day the marketing department would breathe new life into them or they would be transferred to another brewery and get relaunched. In hindsight, the value of some of the thousands of classic labels I washed off might have funded the entire construction of the brewery. I ended up having to wash all the bottles once to remove the majority of the soil and old labels and then spent hours cleaning out the washer the day before the actual bottling run so that we could have good confidence of removing all the old beer and remaining bits of label.

As Paul and I were developing the recipe for our Pale Ale, we did a lot of test brewing, trying to decide exactly what flavor and aroma profile our flagship beer should have. We knew we needed to create our own style of beer that would stand out as being unique and distinctive. Now that we had almost completed construction of the brewery, we decided that we were close enough to start getting the raw materials to begin brewing our first batch of beer.

WATER

We had chosen to stay and build our brewery in Chico in part because of the abundant deep-water aquifer called the Tuscan formation, located under Chico and the surrounding North Valley area. Although slightly higher in some minerals than would be ideal for lighter types of beer, it is well suited for hoppy and darker, stronger styles. Currently, with what is understood about brewing science, the interaction and impact that minerals have on flavor, and of equal importance, the role they play in everything from enzyme reactions in the mash tun to the clarity of the finished beer, brewers are now able to manipulate the water to suit their purposes for the styles of beer they want to brew.

This was not always the case; early brewers didn't understand the concept of water chemistry, but certainly as they experimented with their recipes, they learned the importance that unique water sources played in producing different styles of beer. Without knowing why, early brewing centers developed that specialized in beer styles that worked well with their local water supply, years ahead of having the technology to understand the underlying science to remove or alter its mineral composition. For example, London has slightly salty, alkaline water, resulting in a shift of the mash pH upward, above the optimal level for the action of the natural malt enzymes to produce the optimum balance of sugars during the mashing process. They must have stumbled on the fact that the addition of roasted dark grains increased the acidity and buffered the mash, allowing a much better beer to be brewed and spawning porters and stouts as local styles. The higher chloride levels also went well with the sweeter style of beer, helping improve the roundness and mouth feel, which improved the overall drinkability.

In Burton on Trent in the English Midlands, the natural water supplies were loaded with not only some of the minerals that caused the high alkalinity found in London but also high levels of calcium sulphate, which acted to counter the effect of the alkalinity in the mash and allow for the production of a lighter colored ale that also accentuated the flavor of hops. This area soon became famous for the production of pale ales and spawned another now-famous brewing center. Many of the original European brewing centers—Pilsen, Dortmund, Munich, Vienna, Dublin—also had their own unique water chemistry and became famous for the styles of beer that evolved as they refined their brewing skills and adjusted their recipes to work with their local ingredients. Today, we understand the relationship that water chemistry plays in brewing, and brewers adjust the water to suit the style of beer to be brewed through various treatment methods, such as pH adjustment to counter the effects of high alkalinity or reverse osmosis filtration to remove some or all of the unwanted ions. Such treatments coupled with the addition of naturally occurring minerals, such as gypsum (calcium sulphate), or the addition of salts, such as calcium chloride or sodium chloride, can make any water suitable for brewing any style of beer. This practice is sometimes referred to as Burtonizing to pay homage to the very hard water in Burton.

MALT

I had a friend who worked at a company that handled seeds and grains, and he gave me a few old bins that I thought I could use to transport malt to the brewery. We were fortunate that there was still an operating malt house in San Francisco, the Bauer-Schweitzer Malting Company. They had been operating continuously since the 1870s and had been shut down only for a short time after the 1906 earthquake. San Francisco had at one time been a vibrant brewing city with dozens of small breweries opening and closing before and after Prohibition. The city also boasted several major breweries, including Burgermeister (later acquired by Falstaff) and Lucky Lager (brewed by General Brewing Co.), but when the last of them closed in the late 1970s, it left only Anchor and later the minuscule New Albion as local brewery custo-mers. I got in touch with Bauer-Schweitzer and arranged to go down and get a load of malt. I had never been to a malt house before and didn't know what to expect. It marked a big day for me—we were finally getting close to being able to brew our first batch. I asked my friend and now financial supporter, Jean Harvey, to go along to help navigate the city in my 1-ton 1957 Chevy truck. Jean and Chuck had loaned us $10,000 to help finish up the brewery, so they now had a vested interest in helping me keep the project on track. The trip down was uneventful. The malt house was located several blocks from Fisherman's Wharf, and we had planned to stop and have a nice lunch after picking up the malt. I was not very worldly, and because I had never had any money to speak of, I had rarely visited San Francisco up to that point, making the whole trip an adventure for me.

We arrived at the malt house just before lunch and had a chance to take a tour before we loaded the truck. The malt house had been renovated after the earthquake, and the kiln doors had 1906 cast into them, the story being that they had been replaced later that year. The malt house was out of place with residential buildings intruding into what had certainly been an industrial area in the distant past. It occupied many floors with equipment designed to clean and size the barley and all sorts of conveyors and storage elevators. I was very impressed with the operation; of course I had nothing to compare it to because commercial malting was something I had only read about. Bauer-Schweitzer still used the old and labor-intensive design with small-batch rotating drums for germinating the barley. This method of producing malt has mostly been abandoned around the world because of its high maintenance and operational costs. I didn't realize it at the time, but it produced an ideal malt for the style of beer we would brew, fully modified, lower in protein, and easy to convert in the simple one-temperature infusion mash that we had settled on because of the financial and technical constraints in our old-world-style brewery.[2]

---

[2]This method had evolved in Europe and was still widely practiced in England, where the availability of plump and fully germinated, or modified, barley malt was still the norm. As the grain modifies or grows in the malt house, it respires and consequently loses weight and extract potential, requiring more malt to be used per barrel. Other areas in Europe historically couldn't produce barley with as high of an extract and chose to undermodify the grain to retain more of its brewing value. Undermodified malt, although retaining more extract, requires a more complex mashing and heating process to render its sugars. Fully modified malted barley is now the norm with the improvements in plant breeding and agronomy.

Bauer-Schweitzer welcomed new customers, even as small as we were. I suspect that we got special treatment and possibly their nicest malt because it always tasted great and performed well in our brewhouse. After the tour I pulled my 1-ton flatbed truck over to their scale to get the empty weight and then pulled under the giant grain spout to get loaded. The spouts were designed for quickly loading large trucks and train cars, so it only took a few seconds to fill one of my two bins. I should have calculated what the two full bins of malt would weigh. If I had, I would have realized that one bin was probably the limit of my truck because the malt weighed over a ton per bin. I proceeded to pull forward and fill the second bin and could tell I was in trouble as the truck sank down past the overload springs and the tires almost flattened. When I drove back to the scale, I had a gross weight of more than 10,200 pounds—they had loaded more than 2½ tons of malt. I told them I couldn't handle that much and drive safely home. They couldn't, or wouldn't, take any back; they said it was my problem now, and I should have known it would be too much weight before I asked them to load my second bin. We were a cash-only customer, so I paid my bill and got behind the wheel. The front end of the truck was a foot higher than the rear. I had single tires in the rear, and I knew the load was well above their weight limit. They were so flattened as I crept out of the driveway that I thought the truck might bottom out or blow a tire. The rear end was fishtailing around as I tried to drive straight and I couldn't stop. Navigating through Fisherman's Wharf was out of the question, so I headed straight for the Bay Bridge. The truck was so overloaded that when I started up the ramp, the truck could barely reach 40 miles per hour, besides the fact that it was next to impossible to stay in my lane. I drove straight back to Chico, not stopping for anything. I was pulled over by the police when we were almost home, but thankfully the officer didn't have a scale, and he must have pitied me because he let me go without a ticket. It was late afternoon when we finally got to Chico, and we still had to unload the bins.

I had built a plywood storage container just inside the small room we'd designated for my homebuilt malt mill. We planned to use an auger I had bought to unload most of the bin, but it proved a slow and difficult process the first time. The 2½ tons of malt would last us about a month because we calculated we would need about 500 to 600 pounds per brew for our 10-barrel batch size. With only two fermenters, we projected that we would start out with a schedule of three brews one week and two the following week, or about ten brews per month. If all went well and we could find enough customers, we thought we could get up to 12 batches per month, or around 1,500 barrels per year.

Early on we decided to brew with 100 percent malted barley, and our full-bodied recipe would require almost 2 pounds of malt per gallon. Most American beer is brewed with a combination of malted barley and varying percentages of nonmalted, less expensive sources of starch, commonly referred to in the brewing industry as adjuncts. In the United States, nonmalted corn, rice, corn syrup, or whatever is cheapest is commonly used and added at percentages as high as 50 percent of the total carbohydrate component. Barley is ideally suited for brewing beer because it possesses the physical properties necessary for the natural conversion of starch into sugar. It also provides all the nutrients for healthy yeast fermentation, producing alcohol, CO_2, and a myriad of flavorful compounds that all contribute to the wonder of great beer. Although many grains can be malted, including wheat or rye, and are used in specialty styles, the base grain is almost always barley malt. In countries where barley doesn't grow successfully, grains such as sorghum may constitute the primary grain, but the beer produced is generally inferior or certainly much different in taste. Our recipe was going to comprise a blend of low-protein two-row pale malt and a smaller percentage of specially produced roasted barley malt. *Two row* refers to the number of kernels growing on the head of the barley plant; the lower number per stalk allows for plumper grain with fewer husks.

Most brewers in the United States use the less expensive, higher-protein six-row varieties that have been bred with higher levels of the enzymes that are necessary to convert the starch from adjuncts. We also wanted to use a proportion of caramelized, or Crystal, malt. In addition to adding a little bit of natural amber color to the beer, the caramelized sugars have lower fermentability that adds complexity and body to the finished beer. These specialty malts were produced by only a few maltsters in North America, and we ordered several bags to experiment with in our test brews. We chose moderately roasted malt produced by a small maltster in Wisconsin and ordered what we thought we would need to get started.

YEAST

As part of our preparation process, Paul and I ordered a range of yeast strains from several brewing laboratories. In our homebrew trials, we found one that we really liked, but the lab couldn't tell us much about where they had isolated the cultures from. They would tell us only that they had had the yeast for many years, and it or a variant had been used by a closed American ale brewery. There are only a handful of yeast families used to brew beer, but there are thousands or possibly millions of variants because they adapt and mutate, being influenced by their physical surroundings, their food, their age, and a multitude of other factors.

Brewer's yeast is a unicellular fungus that is generally classified into two broad families and is categorized by their fermentation behavior, their temperature profile, and the style of beer being produced. Although the malted barley and hops provide the soul and spice of the beer, the yeast is what provides the alchemy that turns these unique ingredients into the precious product we know as beer. Before Louis Pasteur discovered yeast, brewers and bakers realized that some force was at work that allowed the conversion of grains but didn't understand it was a living organism that was responsible. Several families and a wide multitude of strains of yeast are harnessed to perform the magic of breaking down a range of complex malt-derived sugars into almost equal percentages of CO_2 and alcohol.

Brewing strains have to have a wide range of traits, first and foremost the ability to produce good flavor and aroma compounds as the yeast digests the malt sugars and excretes alcohol and other fermentation by-products. Its ability to tolerate alcohol, a by-product of the conversion of sugars, is important because some strains will suffer and slow under the constant influence. The brewer can control many of these environmental factors by ensuring that the wort provides an adequate complement of amino acids, minerals, vitamins, and a host of other nutrients along with the sugar. Also, yeast can survive in anaerobic (oxygen-free) environments, but when it's starved for oxygen, it stops reproducing and gets down to the business of converting the sugar into alcohol and CO_2. Managing this balance and timing of adding oxygen is critical to having reproducible fermentations and healthy yeast. The brewer has to introduce enough oxygen to produce fresh, healthy yeast for the next batch but not so much that it creates an excess of yeast that has to be discarded. Oxygen has also been a great focal point in the brewing industry for the past half century as one of the largest contributors to beer staling, so brewers now typically focus on minimizing beer's exposure to air and oxygen, which is beneficial only at the start of fermentation.

Modern brewing methods have blurred some of the distinctions between yeast varieties because some brewers use lager strains and produce products marketed as ale, and others use ale strains that behave more like lagers in modern tanks. Every strain has its own characteristic properties and flavor profile, and brewers carefully select strains to impart the qualities and performance they're looking for. Yeast cells are small, very small, usually around 5 to 10 microns in diameter, and it takes a lot of them working together to convert the wort into beer. Most reasonably adept brewers propagate their own yeast from a few cells maintained in a test tube culture into many millions of cells that are then added, or as brewers say, pitched, into the cooled bitter wort. The yeast cells rapidly multiply and can double their population in hours if they are provided food, oxygen, and the proper temperature to thrive. At the height of fermentation, the yeast will have grown to 50,000,000 cells per milliliter, or the equivalent of 2,750,000,000 cells in a 12-ounce bottle of beer. I told you they were small!

HOPS

With our grain bill and yeast strain settled, Paul and I turned our attention to hops, an interesting and vital component of beer. Our plan for Sierra Nevada beer had always been to emphasize hops and their delightfully piney, citrusy, bitter flavor. Not only do hops have varying amounts of essential oils that contribute to the spicy and floral character and aroma of beer, but they also contain bittering resins that help balance out the malt's sweetness. They also provide significant antimicrobial compounds that help protect and stabilize beer. Because of these attributes, hops won out over many other herbs and spices often used in early beer making and first came into wide use around the tenth century. Their handling from the farm to the warehouse has changed very little. Hops are now mechanically harvested rather than laboriously handpicked, but the dried cones are still compacted and pressed into 200-pound bales as they have been for hundreds of years. Hops are somewhat fragile, easily degraded by light, heat, and air; keeping them in good condition requires storage below 30 degrees Fahrenheit. Early homebrewers most often had to make do with marginal quality hops that were provided as compressed bricks. Originally destined for export,[3] they were produced from the remnants of the crop that remained after the brewers had made their selections and at times may have been several years old. Because hops are best used fresh and start to age and degrade after harvest, surplus hops lose their market value, and in years when supply greatly exceeds demand, the spot price (the price paid for surplus hops bought on the spot rather than on contract) can be a fraction of the growing costs. The hops compressed into the bricks most likely primarily comprised the Cluster variety, which at the time made up the majority of US acreage.

---

[3]Although the primary use of hops is in beer, there was a small global demand for hops used in bread, particularly in Africa and other hot climates. How these alternative uses first developed remains a bit of a mystery. I assume it wasn't driven by the flavor that hops contributed to the bread but because their antiseptic properties help keep the yeast culture or starter pure in warm climates that often lacked refrigeration. In later years I tracked down the supplier of these compressed blocks, and he filled me in on their history. He told me a story about how one year there had been no surplus hops from previous harvests, so they had to supply fresh hops for their overseas customers; they were rejected because they smelled. The solution was to break open the fresh bales and leave them in the sun for a few weeks until they had been sufficiently degraded and had little aroma.

In reality, the bricks probably contained anything left over after selection and had almost no value for the brewing industry, so they could be had for pennies a pound. These hops, with marginal brewing value, were often all that was available at many homebrew shops and hardware stores that sold rudimentary supplies, so it's no wonder that most homebrewed beer had a bad rap!

From my trials as a homebrewer I was very familiar with all the attributes each hop variety contributed and had experimented with the full range of domestic hops. Although there was a growing list of new varieties being cultivated in the United States, most were being developed for their bittering value, or Alpha acid content, the analytic metric used to classify the percentage by weight of their bitter resin. Alpha and beta acids are analyzed and reported as a percentage that indicates the weight of the bitter resin to the dry weight of the hop cone. Most hops are classified into two general families—aroma or bittering. During the brewing process hops are added several times; the first hops are added at the beginning of the wort boiling process and need to be boiled for a period of time in order to extract the bittering and preservative properties. The hops typically selected for this first addition are higher in bitter resin or Alpha acid content, and some varieties may have a somewhat coarse or pungent aroma. The prolonged boiling drives out most of the volatile aroma compounds, so the choice of bittering hops has less of an influence on the character of the beer than does the later addition of finishing, or aroma, hops.

We decided to focus on one of the few new American-bred aroma hops and the first new hop variety released by the US Department of Agriculture since Prohibition. It was named the Cascade after the mountain range and had been developed at Oregon State University by Al Haunold in the 1960s as a replacement for European aroma hops. Cascade had a higher oil content than most of the European varieties and a unique pine and citrus aroma profile. For several years the Cascade languished due to a reluctance of most major breweries to experiment with aroma varieties from the United States because most brewers in America had European roots and viewed US-grown hops as adequate to use for bittering but unrefined compared to the noble aroma hops from Europe. When Cascade was finally released into commercial production in 1972, it took a few years to start gaining acceptance, but in part due to our prominent use of this hop in our flagship, Pale Ale, it is now the number one American hop used by craft brewers in the United States. Our selection and generous use of Cascade hops gave our beer the characteristic flavor it is still known for today.

Because hops are the hallmark of our product, we've always kept an eye on the hop market, which, like the beer industry, has greatly evolved over the past 30 years. Hops are very much a single-market commodity, and until recently they were almost exclusively used to brew beer.[4] If they weren't needed or wanted by a brewery, they had no other market value. Hops are typically used up in the year or two after harvest and ideally not stored for many years, particularly in their raw form, because they lose aroma and bitterness, which degrade with time. Ideally the amount grown annually is in balance with or just slightly exceeds demand. Many brewers engage in futures contracts with hop growers or dealers for future years' purchases to ensure that an adequate supply of hops are planted and can be purchased at a guaranteed price. Like any agricultural product, there's some uncertainty in predicting the crop yield, but ideally adequate stocks are available in hop handlers' and brewers' warehouses to ride out a short crop year with little disruption to the brewer's recipes. Some brewers stockpile a year or more of hops so that they can ride out a crop disaster or disruption without affecting their recipe or being forced to take inferior hops. In recent years some very large brewers have been caught short when the various aspects of hop buying worked against them—they didn't have sufficient contracts to cover their

---

[4]In recent years hop merchants and researchers have been working on other uses of hops by capitalizing on the powerful antiseptic properties of the Alpha acids. They've found a market in the ethanol fuel-distillation industry. Having a pure rapid fermentation results in higher yields of alcohol produced from the feedstock. Past practices used antibiotics in the fermentation to ward off bacterial infections, but the hop resins have been able to accomplish similar results. Another growing use for hops is in nutraceuticals, where they show promise for the relief of joint pain and as an additive in cattle feed to help digestion. The resins can also be added to toothpaste to inhibit bacteria in the mouth.

needs, they hadn't carried over enough hops for the year's production, and poor harvests resulted in few surplus hops to fill in the gaps. Hops are now very much a global crop, with growing regions in China, Germany, France, the Czech Republic, New Zealand, Australia, and the United States. What happens in one growing region can influence price and availability in the rest of the world.

We encountered our first hop shortage in 1980, the year we started the brewery. We didn't have a lot of experience buying hops other than for The Homebrew Shop, when I had mainly bought just small lots or samples. While planning the beers we were going to produce for the year, we projected that we would need to purchase about ten 200-pound bales of whole-cone hops to cover our needs. Our beers contained a little over a pound of hops per barrel, and we hoped to produce about 1,500 barrels. With our decision to feature Cascades in our Pale Ale, we needed more of them than anything else, but our other recipes called for other varieties that would provide higher levels of the primary bittering component, Alpha acid, and some other aromatic qualities to give our range of beers distinctive flavors.

When it came time to place the order for our first year's production, we were told there was a scarcity, and on top of the lack of availability of varieties, we were also informed that prices had shot up dramatically from historical levels. After many years of the market having surplus hops and seeing spot prices lower than contracted prices, some brewers chose to play the odds and began purchasing nearly everything on the spot market. That strategy came back to bite them in 1980–1981, when there was a shortage, and growers couldn't deliver completely on their contracts and were left with few spot hops to sell. Prices went from averaging $2 to $3 per pound on the spot market to more than $14 per pound for some varieties.

Luckily we found the hops we needed but at a price almost three times more than I had budgeted. Because there is no realistic substitute for hops, you either change your recipe or you pay up. Our needs were so small compared with those of other brewers that we got what we needed as spot buyers. When there is a hop surplus, spot buyers often pay less than the brewers who have contracted for hops because the excess is generally viewed as a surplus without a guaranteed home.

If there's a big crop, hops' value can drop dramatically, sometimes to the point that they're nearly worthless if they don't get sold that year. As we learned that first year, buying on the spot market can be risky in the event of a major crop failure, but back then I really didn't know any better; because we were so small, I'm not sure anyone would have bothered writing a contract for the few bales I needed anyway. We learned our lesson and started contracting the following year for the majority of our needs, and we haven't been exposed to the wide market swings since then.

We had our ingredients. Now it was time to start brewing.

5

A BAG FULL OF DREAMS BUT EMPTY POCKETS

Wine is but single broth, ale is meat, drink, and cloth.

—English Proverb

Paul and I spent October of 1980 putting the finishing touches on the brewery in preparation for brewing our very first batch of beer. Katie's and my birthdays were coming up on November 11; we were born on the same day, but she is one year my senior and many years wiser. It had become a tradition for us to hike in the Sierra Nevada on our birthday, so I took the day off. I had a few more welding classes later that week, and I planned to weld the last few pieces of stainless steel fittings and put the final touches of the brewery together. This schedule dictated our first brew date as Saturday, November 15, 1980.

I still needed to find a small tank that would serve as a hop strainer—a key component in brewing—and had been looking for several months during my scrap pilgrimages for a suitable tank but hadn't found what I was looking for. I had some small pieces of stainless sheet left over and found a section of screen I thought would work to get us started. The small rectangular tank that I welded to fit under the kettle outlet with the first brew was meant to be temporary. We used this simple, homemade hop strainer for the next seven years.

THE FIRST BIG BREW

Our first test batch of beer was five barrels (150 gallons) of Stout. We had been test brewing 5-gallon batches of Pale Ale for months, but we both loved dark beer and thought a heavy, dark beer would hide the sins of our first attempt. We also planned to brew Porter, and with this third selection, we hoped to round out our portfolio. We had brewed enough homebrew to know that we could make decent beer. Sure, it might take a few batches to scale up our homebrew recipe from 5 gallons to the 310-gallon batch our equipment would accommodate, but we felt reasonably comfortable that it would take only a handful of brews to nail the recipe.

I started before 5:00 AM that Saturday morning. It was pitch black and cold out when I began grinding the nearly 400 pounds of pale and dark malt we would be using to brew our first batch of beer. My homemade malt mill was loud and dusty and shook badly. This was the second mill I had constructed for the brewery, and although it did a decent job of grinding malted barley, it broke down regularly. My limited budget and initial lack of design skills resulted in both mills being under engineered and lacking the robustness required for daily brewing. I ended up replacing the second mill after a couple of years. The milling of the malted barley is a crucial step in brewing beer—if it is ground too coarse, the starchy interior of the barley doesn't yield itself very efficiently to the enzymes, and not enough sugar is produced. If it's too fine, the husk of the grain can be pulverized, creating a porridge that prevents the easy separation of the sweet malt sugars.

The start of the brewing process after milling the grain is called mashing and involves mixing the crushed grains with hot water in order to activate the natural enzymes in the malted barley. These enzymes turn the starchy interior of the grain into the sweet extract, or wort, that will provide the sugar for the yeast to convert into alcohol and CO_2. We modeled our mashing process after the simpler single-temperature infusion method that had been practiced for hundreds of years before steam heating, motorized raking and stirring machines, and accurate temperature controls were available.[1] In many breweries, complex calculations are used to arrive at the ideal water temperature to mash, using factors such as the moisture content of the grain, its ambient temperature, and the type of beer being brewed. Instead of following this method, I used my homebrewing technique and mashed with water at 176 degrees Fahrenheit, which I hoped, when mixed with

---

[1]With the availability of inexpensive microprocessor-controlled heating and stirring systems, many homebrewers today have more sophisticated gear than we had in our original brewery. As simplistic as the single-temperature infusion method is, it's still practiced in many present-day breweries, and with fully germinated, well-modified, low-protein barley, it still can produce world-class beer. Before thermometers existed, it was said that brewers would heat water just to the point of steam (presumably around 180 degrees Fahrenheit) and would then turn off the heat and stir in the dry-ground malt. The room temperature malt would drop the overall mash to 150 to 160 degrees, which would activate the natural malt enzymes to convert the starches into sugars. I have to assume the resulting beer had some variation in how it tasted because this complex natural chemical and biological process is very temperature dependent and produces a range of sugars whose makeup dictates the sweetness, body, and final alcohol content of the beer. The Germans discovered another way to optimize their brewing process before the advent of thermometers. They would boil about a third of the mash and then add it back to the balance of the mash; this decoction served to both degrade the starch of less-than-ideal barley malt and allow a controlled method to bring the mash up to temperature. They would do this several times to achieve the correct overall temperature. Maintaining the correct sugar profile from batch to batch is critical for consistency. Higher temperatures produce more complex sugars that the yeast can't easily ferment, whereas the lower range produces very simple sugars that are easily converted into alcohol, leaving the finished beer drier because it then lacks the balance of malt sweetness. The simple infusion process, conducted with modern methods utilizing accurate thermometers, can produce very consistent results.

the cold grain, would hit the desired 152 degrees that we felt would give the Stout the correct balance of malt body, sweetness, and alcohol. I had found a very large water heater in a scrap yard that had come out of a commercial laundry and had repaired the leaky coil. I had plumbed the heater into an old insulated dairy tank so that we could stockpile enough water at the exact temperature in it to provide the nearly 200 gallons of hot water we would need to mash and sparge the sugars out of the grain.

I dragged the crushed malt from the mill room through the front roll-up door of the brewery one 40-pound tub at a time and dumped them into the mash tun, stirring each tub in as quickly as I could with a canoe paddle that we had carefully sanded down to remove any traces of lacquer. It was important that all the malt was adequately stirred in and evenly mixed so that there were no dry, hot, or cold spots in the mash tun. If the starch in the grain wasn't completely converted to sugars, it could create off flavors or haze in the beer.

Paul arrived later that morning to start readying the fermentation room for the first brew. He started by scrubbing and sanitizing the open cooler and fermentation tank. We had done some water brews, essentially pumping and heating water as if it were a batch of beer, so I had some comfort that the pumps and kettle would work. The actual brew day was a lot more challenging because we now needed to hit all the temperatures correctly. Our mill had done a good enough job that we didn't have a stuck mash, but it had taken a lot longer than we had planned to run off the approximately 175 gallons of wort into the brewing kettle. The kettle boil accomplishes many desired changes in the wort. Over the course of several hours, it evaporates approximately 15 percent of the volume to concentrate the sugars, unwanted proteins are coagulated, the wort is sterilized, and hops are added to extract their flavor and bitterness. The length of the boil also has an influence on the flavor and color of the resulting beer.

The day passed in a blur. It took more than 13 hours to finish the brew—quite a bit longer than it typically took us to do a homebrew. For the first brew, though, everything mattered, so we did lots of troubleshooting along the way. We still had to refine some equipment and processes, but at least we knew we could produce wort, the first step in the brewing process.

We had divided up the responsibilities according to our skills. I would do all the brewing, packaging, maintenance, and so on, and Paul would handle the office work, fermentation, and laboratory. As it turned out, my responsibilities were never-ending and required countless hours of problem solving and plain grunt labor. Paul mostly worked an 8-to-5 shift from the start. I was happy doing what I was doing, so the labor disparity didn't bother me at first, but it would eventually become a major friction point in our partnership.

It took a long time to get there, but having brewed this first batch of beer was a major milestone. Because it was such a momentous occasion, several close friends dropped by to congratulate us and check in on our progress.

The next morning, Sunday, November 16, I went in to check on the fermentation. There was a nice head of foam as I had hoped for—the yeast was starting to digest the malt sugars, performing the alchemy of converting the wort into beer. Even though we weren't confident that the rest of the equipment would work as smoothly as we wanted, my spirits were good because we were finally on our way. We planned to brew the first batch of Pale Ale two days later, hoping that we'd be able to sell it. We didn't have any intention to sell the Stout but certainly expected that it would be drinkable and figured it would allow us to work out any issues we might have with the bottling line. Our first batch of Stout fermented beautifully, allowing us to test the rest of the process.

Bottling is one of the trickiest aspects of running a brewery, and the bottle filler and entire bottling line were the biggest unknowns we still had to face. On top of the many potential pitfalls, we still weren't sure the bottle filler—previously used to bottle carbonated soft drinks—could handle partially carbonated, foamy beer. As far as anyone knew, bottling beer using a soda filler had never before been attempted. Even with great beer and flawless processes before filling, the beer is at risk from picking up oxygen during packaging, which will cause off flavors. If beer is bottled with high oxygen levels present, the beer degrades in days rather than months. We had a good safeguard against oxygen with our bottle conditioning process. Adding yeast and fermentable sugar just before bottling means that any oxygen picked up in the process would be quickly assimilated by the yeast and would do minimal, if any, harm to the beer.

Sanitation is another challenge because beer touches numerous fittings, valves, and gaskets on the way to the filler; without proper cleaning, each one has the potential to harbor beer-spoiling bacteria. Because the necessary level of diligence is just too difficult for many operations to maintain, many breweries pasteurize their product after bottling, which eliminates possible problems but can sacrifice the flavor of the beer. Our filler was at least as difficult to clean, if not more so, as a proper beer bottling machine. Paul and I erred on the side of caution when it came to cleanliness and beer quality. Our protocol for preparing the bottle filler before filling was a rigorous 60-minute flushing and sterilizing step with 180-degree water before every start and then a hot-detergent cleaning and dismantling of every filler valve with a manual scrubbing before reassembling them for the next day's run. We ran the filler until we had packaged all the beer that was ready. When we divided the tasks of brewing between us, this task became my responsibility and contributed to some absurdly long days, initially taking about 12 hours for the run of 125 cases that we produced per batch.

On the first day of packaging, bottles were breaking and exploding as they went through the filler. Because we had a mix of used bottles, we needed extra space to allow the different sized bottles we were feeding into it. We had to stop and modify the bottle handling parts repeatedly, grinding the parts down to allow additional clearance out of the star wheels that transferred the bottles in and out of the machine.

The bottle washer was still a major challenge with our need to wash every bottle twice, adding many hours to an already long day. Our labeler was another issue that I fought every day until I finally replaced it. It was built in the 1940s and didn't have the gentlest design to move the bottles smoothly in and out. Instead, it just knocked them into place with a steel arm and regularly blew them up, but we had to use it until we bought a 1960s vintage World Tandem a few years later. It was significantly better but a far cry from being modern.

Brewing the First Pale Ale

With the kinks worked out of the brewing process, we were ready to tackle a production batch of our flagship Pale Ale. On November 21, I made a few adjustments on the malt mill and prepared for the first batch. We had settled on our strain of yeast after doing many test brews with a wide range of different brewing yeast cultures. The one we chose wasn't necessarily the most robust or fastest at fermenting the wort into beer, but we liked its flavor; it had all the characteristics we were looking for, particularly the ability to form a compact sediment in the bottle that wouldn't be disturbed easily during pouring. This feature would be important for bottle conditioning because most beer drinkers weren't used to sediment in the bottom of bottles or too cloudy beer. We didn't have much experience using yeast in a production environment, which required the harvesting and reusing of yeast from one batch to the next. We had been brewing test batches once a week, and we would either start a new culture for every brew or harvest and repitch only one or two generations.

Long before Pasteur isolated bacteria and brewer's yeast, brewers realized that the foam and sediment from one batch of beer were vital to fermenting the next batch. They didn't understand that the foam and sediment contained the vital yeast but knew that if the next batch of beer went back into the same vessel that still contained the sediment, or if some of the foam was saved and mixed into the next batch, it would result in a better beer. The amazing ability of yeast (of course, at that point they didn't know that it was the yeast doing the work) to be used over and over was referred to as Godisgoode. Another brewing tradition was the passing down of a special prized mixing stick. Brewers didn't realize it at the time, but using the same stirrer served to inoculate their brews with yeast.

If all went well, we would be able to harvest the yeast from the first fermentation and use it later that day for fermentation of the next brew. This is common practice for breweries that rely on a particular strain of yeast to ensure consistent flavor between batches. In some cases ale brewers reuse, or repitch, the same yeast for dozens or, in rare cases, even thousands of brews in succession. Lager yeast typically does not offer the same degree of vigor or stability, and its fermentation characteristics drift after just a few brews. Typically, it is used for only a few brews in a row before the yeast strain changes enough in performance that it needs to be repropagated from the mother culture. This would have added about a week's time to our schedule for each propagation and complexity to our operation.

Having only two fermenters limited our ability to brewing just 12 batches per month and meant we needed to be on a tightly controlled schedule. Each batch would require about five days for fermentation and for the yeast to flocculate, or settle out. Once all the fermentable sugar in the beer was consumed by the yeast, it would flocculate from the beer. In the case of top-fermenting yeast, the majority would rise to the surface. We would then crop the yeast using a large bowl and stainless steel pot, skimming it off and whisking some of the CO_2 gas out with a large restaurant whisk. We stored the harvested yeast in a refrigerator before adding about 1 pound per barrel to the next batch. This was basic brewing with a lot of hands-on steps, and everything had to be meticulously cleaned and sanitized to ensure success.

Our first batch of Pale Ale fermented well and tasted good, so we thought we were on track as far as the recipe and overall flavor. We let it ferment for a few days and then planned the next brew. After tweaking the recipe a little more, we brewed Pale Ale number two on November 28 of that year. We were starting to notice that the fermentation wasn't going quite as fast as we had planned, but production brewing was all new to us; we weren't that concerned. We decided to keep at it and hoped things would get better. Pale Ale number three was brewed on December 15 and tasted even better. By the third batch, I had figured out how to run the bottling line. We packaged this batch to share it with our friends and solicit feedback. We wanted to make sure we had the recipe right to meet the expectations of a discerning audience and command the $0.85 a bottle price we planned for the retail shelf because we couldn't afford six-packs. Paul and I were so cost conscious that we even went as far as assembling the case dividers rather than buying them assembled. In hindsight, it was a stupid thing to do; I assume the box supplier had a machine to do it, probably costing only a few cents more to get assembled dividers, but we spent hours fitting the cardboard pieces together and putting them into cases.

Brewed on December 23, Pale Ale number four wasn't as good as number three. It wasn't that it was bad, but the fermentation had dragged on a few extra days; it was just a bit different than the last one. Now we were starting to get concerned by the lack of consistency because we had made the decision that we couldn't sell beer until we could replicate the batches every time. We reviewed all of our brewing texts and thought we had ruled out most of the obvious fermentation pitfalls—yeast pitching quantity, temperature, and nutrients. Because we were brewing with no adjuncts and using pure malt, we should have had adequate amino acids available to nurture the yeast.

Brewers who supplement malt with corn, rice, or simple sugar additions sometimes lack the amino acids needed by the yeast, but all the literature indicated that this wouldn't be a concern for us because we were brewing traditional all-barley-malt beers and weren't supplementing our malt. With those issues ruled out, we looked at our equipment next. We were using an open Baudelot cooler that looked like an 8-foot-tall stainless washboard. Wort trickled over the outside, and chilled water flowed through pipes on the inside. With that type of cooler, along with open fermenters, we didn't suspect we lacked the oxygen needed by the yeast for the early steps of growth and metabolism, so I started looking at a wide range of possible problems that could have caused our slow fermentations. Because I still had friends and knew faculty who worked in the lab, I was able to gain access to the Chemistry Department at Butte College. I decided to perform some advanced analytical testing, and I ran samples at the lab to look at calcium, magnesium, and zinc levels in the wort. We knew these minerals were required by the yeast, but most literature stated that other than the possibility of zinc levels being insufficient because of soil depletion of the barley fields, the malt and water should sufficiently provide the other compounds.

Our trial brewing slowed down because we didn't want to throw away another batch of beer. By then we had already dumped nearly

10 brews and didn't have the financial resources to continue on without a plan to solve our problems. We tried making changes in the water mineral content, but as we brewed several other batches, it became apparent that we still hadn't solved the problem. We were just about ready to scrap our chosen yeast and start test brewing all over again with a new strain when we decided to talk to the laboratory that had supplied our yeast to see if they could find someone who had brewed with our strain or one like it with repeated success and consistent results. They put us in touch with a retired brewmaster who had brewed ales, possibly with our culture. We explained our sluggish fermentation issues, and he said it sounded like the yeast was starved for oxygen. In his experience this yeast had a very high requirement and, at least at the start of fermentation, the more the better. For the next brew I modified the pipe leading into the fermenter and made a small stainless steel nozzle out of a flattened piece of pipe, mounting it so that it sprayed into the top of the tank in a fan pattern. This simple change did the trick; the next batch fermented very quickly and tasted great. Months of trials and troubleshooting had tested our patience, but our drive and unwavering desire allowed us to stay the course and not compromise our ideals. But we were still determined not go to market until we were confident that each batch would taste the same every time.

6

TO MARKET, TO MARKET

Prohibition makes you want to cry into your beer and denies you the beer to cry into.

—Don Marquis

While we worked on perfecting our beer production, we started looking at the next step of the process: getting our beer to consumers. We met with Pat Lawing, one of several local beer distributors in Chico, to discuss the possibility of enlisting him to sell our beer. We had little knowledge of the world of beer distribution, and he was willing to guide us. Pat was an independent thinker and had previously worked as a representative for a regional brewery. When the opportunity to buy a distributorship came along, he jumped at it and named the company Stash, which was a fitting name for the local community and culture at the time. The distributorship handled a range of brands, including Budweiser. (I doubt if the senior management at Anheuser-Busch understood the meaning of the name Stash, but locals saw the humor.) Pat wanted to sell our beer and was very supportive of our venture and excited about the notion of a small brewery opening in town.

Fortunately, some states such as California allow brewers to deliver their beer directly to the retail tier. (This is called self-distribution.) By the time we finally had beer ready to go to market in early 1981, we realized that we couldn't afford to turn our beer over to a distributor. Giving up 25 percent of the sales price wouldn't have provided enough cash flow to pay our bills and we wouldn't have survived. We were planning on selling only in Chico at first and figured that with Steve Harrison working part-time, we could easily pay off the $600 cost of the delivery van (a slightly beat-up, used, white Ford Econoline passenger van I had purchased from a friend), and his wages by distributing the beer ourselves. Our plan was to save every penny we could to generate enough cash flow to survive our first year. Then, after we got some critical mass, we could consider turning our beer over to outside distributors. Pat was disappointed that we weren't going to use Stash to distribute our beer, but he understood our reasons and was pleased that we agreed to give him all the territory he covered outside of Chico's city limits.

THE THREE-TIER SYSTEM

At the time, Chico was like most communities across the country, with several beer wholesalers, generally independent small businesses that sold a wide range of brands from national brewers to the then-almost-extinct regional brewers. Before the three-tiered system was enacted, most breweries distributed their beer in and around their home markets on their own trucks. Eventually the challenging economies of scale of running a small brewery dictated the need to increase volume and expand distribution to support continued growth to survive. The national landscape of beer distribution had been forged in part by breweries seeking markets outside their local footprints. Wider distribution was greatly facilitated by an expanded national rail and truck route system as well as national advertising made possible by syndicated radio and later TV, but there were still challenges. Delivering beer farther away from the brewery increased costs and necessitated making fewer, more distant stops to deliver fewer cases per account. Trucks that dropped off a load of assorted brands from consolidated warehouses provided a solution for most brewers because only the biggest brands had enough volume to justify their own dedicated distribution warehouses.

Everything changed when Prohibition was enacted in 1920 and drove alcohol distribution underground, which fostered the involvement of organized crime in every aspect of brewing from production to the distribution and sale of illicit beer and booze.[1] One of the supporting platforms of its repeal with the Twenty-first Amendment 13 years later was a system of states' rights for regulating the sale and distribution of alcohol. Although there were some broad federal requirements, the majority of alcohol regulation fell to each state, which had to develop its own set of criteria and market systems to define where and how alcohol could be sold. A wide range of state- and county-based systems supposedly reflecting the wishes of the constituency emerged across the country. After Prohibition's repeal, some counties, and even states, remained dry, whereas others established state owned and controlled liquor stores. Sentiment about when and where alcohol should be available ran the gamut.

One of the overarching restrictions outlawed tied houses, preventing the manufacturer of alcohol from owning the retailer, in essence breaking any financial connection between the manufacture and sale of alcoholic beverages. Before the advent of Prohibition, the United States didn't prevent breweries, or any alcohol producer for that matter, from owning as many bars, restaurants, or stores as they pleased. These tied-house arrangements curbed competition and had the tendency to promote unfair or unethical sales practices and inducements. The situation worsened during Prohibition because organized crime had

---

[1]The bottle filler that I purchased from Anchor in the early 1980s had originally been used at Chicago's Siebens Brewery, which was reportedly controlled by two underworld gangs and continued providing beer during Prohibition. The story I heard said that the gangs had been paying off the local police, but the unrest that ensued between them is supposedly linked to the St. Valentine's Day Massacre.

largely taken over control of the nation's alcohol industry, and a large effort went into creating a way to break the stronghold that could have resulted if the Mafia had been allowed to legitimize their operations after the repeal of Prohibition. Today, this separation of manufacturer, distributor, and retailer is known as *the three-tier system*. It requires brewers to sell their beer to distributors (also called wholesalers) who in turn sell it to accounts (bars, restaurants, and stores), who sell it to consumers. Thankfully, some states allow breweries to self-distribute, which helped us get our start. The goal of the system is to regulate commerce in a consistent and transparent manner. Although certainly not perfect, it serves to help level the playing field and prevents large manufacturers from owning retail outlets, which would limit consumers' choices and small manufacturers' options to get to market. One of the tenets that advocates of the current three-tier system cling to is the idea that having an independent middle tier serves to regulate and create a more orderly, controlled, responsible means for enforcing the rules.

Federal limitations were also enacted to prohibit practices, such as slotting fees that many retailers receive for shelf or cooler placements for nearly every other consumer product. Because new brands regularly appear on store shelves, highly competitive products, such as soda and potato chips, fight with a significant amount of money for every inch of the prime, eye-level shelf space to sell their products. Thankfully it's illegal for retailers to extract slotting fees for beer, which would present a major barrier to entry for small brewers. Most states have also enacted strict limitations on alcohol producers that prohibit or limit providing anything of value that may be considered an inducement or incentive for a retailer to feature one brand over another.

Collectively, this complex web of seemingly arcane state and federal laws has done a lot to allow the craft movement to flourish. Many other countries don't have a prohibition against the vertical integration of manufacturer and retailer, which has generally stymied the growth of small and independent breweries. For example, in England breweries had a long history of owning pubs, and through consolidation a handful of brewers controlled tens of thousands of pubs that sold only their own brands, making it nearly impossible for start-up breweries to get their beer in front of consumers. Under Margaret Thatcher's government the system was overhauled, and a 2,000-pub limit (per brewery) was set. The resulting divesture by brewers of tens of thousands of pubs created its own challenges in the marketplace and opened the way to huge operating groups that now monopolize the retail sector. Also, even though pubs could sell other brands of beer, their sheer purchasing clout drove down brewers' margins, driving many to leave their less profitable breweries in favor of operating pub chains, thereby creating new challenges for small brewers to navigate. In other parts of Europe and the world, it's common practice for brewers or distributors to cut exclusive deals with bars and restaurants and provide tables, chairs, furnishings, and other equipment in exchange for exclusivity in the brands the retailer sells. These market-driven systems may be aligned with some people's notion of free enterprise, but they limit choice and independence, favoring a consolidated industry in which a large supplier that can provide beer, spirits, wine, soda, and so on, has a significant upper hand that eliminates a level playing field for competition.

That said, dealing with a myriad of state regulations can prove challenging for a small company, and often rules are bent or broken by both large and small brewers trying to gain an advantage in the marketplace. Some small brewers have told me they don't understand the value of many of these laws. Why shouldn't they be able to supply a new draught system to an account they want to get into or provide a few free kegs in exchange for getting a tap handle in the bar? After all, isn't this is a free country? Yes, the craft beer segment is growing and our beers are much in demand, but all of America's more than 2,000 craft brewers still represent only approximately 6 percent of total beer sales. Our major competitors have huge market share and are very powerful. What some small brewers often fail to grasp is the power and leverage that the global brewers, vintners, and distillers hold in the highly consolidated alcohol beverage industry. If you include the wine and spirits segments when you look at the industry as a whole, craft brewers are truly minuscule. The wine and spirits companies are some of our biggest competitors and often operate with their own set of seemingly crazy laws, some of which give them the upper hand in the marketplace. (They must have better lobbyists.) Even if our brands are highly desirable, we can't compete when we aren't at the table. Removing the restrictive laws wouldn't help, though—whatever craft brewers could do, bigger brewers could do more. Most of the laws work for our benefit, and we need to fight as an industry to uphold them. (Okay, most of them are good for us; some of them, such as laws pertaining to limiting brewers or wholesalers from cleaning draft lines, are truly silly, and we should work collectively to change them.) Still, to be fair, we should all play by the same rules.

As these state regulations were being developed, they were often crafted to give small, independent, local distributors some additional legislated power to deal with larger national breweries and their growing domination of the beer scene, with significant leverage over small distributors. Understandably, it was seen as a matter of fairness for small companies that needed some degree of protection. In many cases, the tables have now turned, with very small brewers being disadvantaged in their dealings with large, multistate distributors. Again, it's a matter of fairness, and hopefully better common ground can be established to allow more fairness for small brewers.

Complicating the landscape, as regional breweries faltered and the major brewers consolidated, the distribution tier did the same.[2] Although some distributors have kept focused on single-supplier portfolios, others went a different direction as a consequence of the craft boom and took on many new brands creating huge portfolios, both because of the higher profit margin and the fact that craft has been the only growth segment in the brewing industry for the past several years. At the same time, major brewers have been pushing and facilitating the consolidation of their distributors to improve operational efficiencies, profitability, and market dominance. Larger-scale operations can more easily justify the investment costs demanded by the big breweries in a whole range of operational

---

[2]A town the size of Chico may have had four or five distributors in the 1960s or 1970s. Today, no distributors are based here other than Sierra Nevada distributing the beer we sell in Chico.

infrastructure investments, from information technology to new trucks and paint jobs.

Most people in the distribution business are honest, are a pleasure to work with, and treat us fairly, but some hide behind protective laws that hinder our companies' growth. Brewers of any significant size need the middle tier to get to market—we can't succeed without them—so we truly share a common vision and goal. Over the years we've tried to understand and acknowledge distributor concerns, and I hope they'll continue to try to understand our concerns and support our efforts to make fair and equitable improvements to the beer distribution system.

The US system has allowed small, independent brewing companies more opportunities to get their beer to market, which ultimately provides the consumer with a much wider choice of beer than in almost any other marketplace in the world. For the past 30 years, the US brewing industry has been the global leader in brewing innovation and has seen the establishment of thousands of new brands. I strongly believe that this evolution could not have succeeded anywhere else in the world. The American brewing revolution serves as a model that is being emulated around the world and has affected the global beer marketplace in amazing ways. Similar to our brewery's meager beginnings, the volume of specialty beer sold around the globe by these upstart brewers is minuscule, but just like in this country, it is rapidly expanding, creating tremendous excitement about beer and a new beer culture in countries that never had a historical tie to this tradition. China, Brazil, Italy, and Japan all have fledgling craft cultures, even with significantly more challenging market barriers. Consumer drive and savvy entrepreneurs have created new opportunities and methods of carving out a niche in a competitive marketplace marked by consolidation.

Retail channels have also been affected by the wave of consolidation that swept across the brewer and distributor landscape in the past 10 years. Although some states limit the number of liquor and beer licenses a retailer can hold, consumer preferences have also done a lot to change where and how beer is sold. More people now shop and buy their beer at large chain markets and discount warehouses. Early on, several of the more progressive chains, particularly those on the coasts, saw the value of the high-end beverage sector and devoted significant shelf space to the expanding varietal wine and fledgling craft beer industry. Sierra Nevada benefitted from the early focus, which went a long way to expose our beer to a wide audience. Still, many of these large chains have broad regional or national footprints and until fairly recently were difficult for most craft brewers to engage. Buying decisions are usually made at a central office headquarters, and making a compelling presentation to a sophisticated buyer was generally beyond the skill set of all but larger breweries. Due to the incredible success and excitement that craft beer has garnered in the past few years, almost every chain now puts significant focus on supporting our segment both for the more sophisticated shopper it attracts, as well as for the greater profit margins. Selling a premium 6- or 12-pack generates a much better return than a 30-pack of budget beer in addition to the other items premium craft consumers put in their shopping carts.

OUR FIRST SALES PITCH

By the spring of 1981, we were finally brewing a beer whose flavor we loved and could consistently repeat, so we proudly set out to sell our first cases in downtown Chico. During the struggle to perfect our beer, my wife was pregnant with our second daughter, Carrie, who was born February 8, right as we had finally figured out our fermentation issues. My long hours didn't end, and Katie was now home with two young children. I felt even more pressure to get the new brewery up and running, but I also felt torn about not being able to spend more time with my family. Still, I had obligations to fulfill and had to make ends meet, so we kept working. Paul, Steve Harrison, and I made the first sales calls together on March 16. We removed the seats from the delivery van I had bought, giving us seating for our tasting and hospitality area in the brewery. We packed an ice chest with a few samples of beer into the van and walked around downtown Chico, hoping to land our first few accounts.

We sold our beer in a 24-bottle loose case. We had only a one-case minimum, but at $15.00 plus a $1.20 deposit on the bottles, it was still about twice as expensive as almost every other American beer. Even so, we were able to convince a couple of bars and a couple of restaurants, as well as several stores, to buy a case. By that point, there was no money to buy printed six-pack carriers, so our plan was to sell cases to retailers, and they would sell individual bottles to the customers. We hoped consumers would come back for more until we could sell enough beer to cover the cost of the printing plates and the minimum order of six-packs, which was about $12,000, well beyond our means at the time.

The initial feedback on our beer was mixed; many people enjoyed it, but some felt the flavor was intense and bitter. Still, we had enough sales our first few weeks that we were convinced that our brewery was an instant success. People were buying it, the volume was growing, and we were getting new placements in bars and stores every week. We were now professional brewers!

Sierra Nevada was actually profitable from day one if we left our salaries out of the equation, but that wasn't possible much longer. We were still broke and cash flow remained incredibly tight. We had used every penny we had to open the brewery; we weren't comfortable asking our families for more money, so we had to manage what limited money we had. Paul's family was helping him out, but I was still working a few shifts at the bike shop every month to make some money we could live on. I also picked up a little extra work rebuilding tractors and farm equipment at the farm we lived on in exchange for rent because we couldn't pay ourselves any salary yet. It was months before we were finally able to draw any income from the brewery. Our first salary was $200 per month each. It would be some time before we got up to the comfortable level of $500 per month. We soon realized that our business plan's projected profitability at the proposed production goal of 1,500 barrels a year was not realistic, and we needed to think about how we could ramp up production faster and increase capacity ahead of our original plan.

The brewing was going well, but I was still working through several production issues. The malt mill I originally built regularly broke down, with shafts and chains breaking generally at the most inopportune time, such as at 5:00 AM in the middle of grinding malt for a brew. I had purchased lightweight well casing for the crushing rollers because it was the cheapest large diameter pipe I could find. I had cut out some steel discs, welded them in the sections of pipe, and welded some apparently undersized 1-inch shafts in the center, but when I put them in a lathe to turn them smooth, I realized that the thin walls were not ideal. They chattered and rang loudly in the lathe and did the same when milling grain. I also didn't have enough experience with engineering, and in an attempt to keep costs down, I used an undersized shaft and bearings to mount the rolls. Although the shaft didn't immediately fail, it didn't take too many batches before the flexing of the shaft took its toll and the shafts and chain drive started breaking. I also realized that I needed to improve the dust enclosure I had built around the mill and come up with some sort of room ventilation. I had read that high amounts of mill dust could cause explosions, and my design needed some tweaking to avoid that danger.

A BOTTLENECK IN PACKAGING

Brewing was hard and laborious, taking three long days every week just to produce 30 barrels. Packaging took two even longer days. Our piecemeal soda bottling line worked sporadically at best and required constant cleaning and tweaking that was extremely time consuming, but we certainly didn't have the resources to upgrade it. All of the used refrigeration equipment I salvaged needed regular maintenance and repair, in part due to my rudimentary refrigeration engineering skills and all the old salvaged equipment I tried to bring back to life. I had taken two quarters of basic refrigeration repair courses and had been a little bit out of my league when I adapted the dairy tanks with their old compressors and the other equipment I had picked up from the boneyard of a sympathetic refrigeration repair shop. All these things kept me busy welding and fabricating as we continued brewing and tried to figure out how to improve the operation.

Soon I couldn't keep up with the daily production demands as well as try to increase capacity. I didn't know it at the time, but balancing the two competing needs would be a decade-long struggle. We initially hired a few part-time employees. Paul and Harrison chipped in to help me on bottling days, but I was still working long hours seven days a week. I soon hired a few full-time employees and started delegating more and more of my brewing duties to them. Harrison was one of my first full-time hires. He had voiced an interest early on that he wanted to be part of the new brewery and had been helping out wherever he could. He had experience selling beer because he had worked in a liquor store, which certainly gave him more industry knowledge than we had, so we hired him to be in charge of sales. Most of the early employees were just short-timers, but one of my first brewers, Steve Dresler, is still at the brewery, heading up the Brewing Department. I kept running the packaging line for a while longer because it was a challenging area to master, but I finally delegated it as well. Because we were distributing only to stores, bars, and restaurants in Chico, we were acting as our own distributor and selling the beer directly to retailers. With the roughly 25 percent markup that stores charged, our beer had a retail price of about $0.85 per bottle. We had set our price about as high as we felt we could while still being competitive with the typical imported beer price on the liquor store shelf. Our market competition was almost exclusively imports because there were so few American breweries making the style of beer we were. We hoped we would be competitive enough to generate enough sales and profit to cover the high operating costs associated with our meager and inefficient production volumes.

CASTING A WIDER NET

After a few months of limiting our distribution to Chico, we had mastered most of our production challenges. The bottling line was running better; we decreased our brew time by several hours through the use of larger, faster pumps and improvements to the malt mill; and we made improvements to the troublesome labeler. We were able to start brewing at our goal capacity of three brews a week or 1,500 barrels a year, which allowed us to expand our distribution. We started to explore markets in the Bay Area but had difficulty finding a distributor who would work with us because we had no brand reputation and because we had nothing to offer them as far as a marketing plan or a sales organization to help generate sales. Harrison took it upon himself to approach bars, restaurants, and liquor stores all over the Bay Area, trying to find a few retailers that would be willing to carry Sierra Nevada, a beer no one had ever heard of—it was a very hard sell. Once we were able to show that there were at least a few places that were willing to give it a try, we finally convinced a distributor in San Francisco to handle our beer. They didn't carry any major brands, just 100 or so small, eclectic imports and weak regional brands, but that didn't bother us. We sent one pallet (70 cases) of each of our three brands and hoped for the best. The distributor had no real sales force, and with all the other beers they carried, they certainly weren't pushing an unknown, expensive American beer sold in single 12-ounce bottles.

Things didn't really take off as we had planned, and we struggled to get more accounts to take our beer. Harrison would come back from a few days in the Bay Area after trying to get people to listen to our story and place an order for a case or two; he was generally depressed and demoralized by the experience. He would visit 15 or 20 stores and bars to present the beers. If he was lucky, he would get to meet with the decision maker and a few of them would agree to try the beer. On a good day, he would get a positive response and a commitment from one or two establishments to buy a case, but many days he had no success although not from lack of trying.

Regardless, getting a prospect to place an order was only the first step in getting beer to our consumers. From there, our distributor had to set up the account, enter the order into their system, and deliver the beer. If the bar or store that placed an order with Harrison wasn't one of the distributor's existing accounts, they would sometimes decide it wasn't worth their time to deliver the small one-case orders we were getting; sometimes the beer wasn't delivered. We would stop back in at the account a few weeks later only to find out the order had never been fulfilled.

The first time I visited our distributor's warehouse, they couldn't find our beer. The warehouse employees assumed it must have all been sold, but I happened to spot a full pallet and another partial pallet behind stacks of other beer. It turned out that they had been unable to locate our beer in the warehouse, so they hadn't sold a case in weeks. We were pissed by their lackadaisical attitude, but there wasn't much we could do about it because at that time we had no other options in San Francisco. Nonetheless, it wasn't a great way to start the relationship with our first distributor.

Sales slowly improved as we set up a few more accounts and established a bit of brand awareness in the area, but it would take time before we achieved some nice distribution in the Bay Area. We found a second distributor down the peninsula that was also willing to take our beer. Luckily, they had some experience with the fledgling craft brewing industry, having represented a few other small start-up breweries. We hoped they would be a little more focused on our beer than our first distributor had been.

To save on shipping costs for the single pallet of beer the new distributor had committed to carry, I decided to deliver the beer myself. The warehouse manager roared with laughter, and probably some dismay, when I pulled up in my 1957 Chevy flatbed with a pallet of beer on the back. I was a little taken aback by his reaction, but at the time I didn't understand what a spectacle I was. They were used to receiving deliveries of beer in shiny, 48-foot trucks with larger-than-life logos on the sides driven by professional drivers, and here I was, the owner and master brewer, dressed in jeans, driving a rickety old truck with a bed made of scrap two-by-fours, delivering one pallet of beer. I think it was the only time I delivered beer that way. Instead, we scraped by, by having other companies ship our beer in their trucks.

For several years we worked with Oy Vey Bagel, a Chico company, because they had a contract with Lucky Supermarkets and a light-weight product. It helped them out, and they charged us less than it would have cost to ship it on our own. They'd drop bagels at Lucky's distribution center and then take our beer to our beer distributor down the road. We finally bought our own truck in the late 1980s and started our own trucking company.

With a second distributor in the Bay Area, we were selling all the beer we were capable of producing every week, which helped improve cash flow, but selling through a distributor cut into our profitability because we had to decrease our price to $13 a case to try to achieve a reasonably competitive shelf price.

The American craft brewing industry started to gain recognition in the mid-1980s as the new wave of small American craft beers began to be compared to many of the imported beers, and often our beers were in the top of the ratings. Many of these blind tastings were published in newspapers and magazines, and we started to get a lot of great free press. Oftentimes we had no idea our beer was in the competition until we received a phone call or happened to run across an article. Just as some American wineries were gaining recognition for producing wines comparable to the finest French Bordeaux wines, American beers were beginning to beat out many of their imported counterparts in blind taste tests against centuries-old European and domestic beers. Moreover, the craft beer scene was starting to gain a small foothold in some of the more progressive cities that either had or were developing a food and wine culture. Restaurants wanting to feature unique and interesting beers were turning to craft brews because they were often fresher and more complex than the increasingly uniform American and imported beers.

We entered our beer in the first Great American Beer Festival, hosted by the fledgling American Homebrewers Association, in 1982 in Boulder, Colorado. Twenty American breweries attended, although only four were true small craft brewers.[3] Although there was no formal voting the first year, we received a lot of accolades. During next year's popular vote we received first and second place for our Pale Ale and Porter, helping establish our reputation as great brewers in both the craft and regional brewing circles.

---

[3]Although terminology is currently an area of friction and debate in the brewing industry, the Brewers Association (BA) defines a craft brewery as small (produces less than six million barrels of beer annually), independent (less than 25 percent of the craft brewery is owned or controlled by a non-craft brewery alcohol industry company) and traditional (having an all-malt flagship beer or at least 50 percent of the volume in all-malt beers or in beers that use adjuncts to enhance flavor rather than lighten it). As a sign of the tremendous growth of the craft industry, the BA recently raised the maximum production from two million barrels to six million barrels.

Given our extremely tight cash flow, our market plan was to add capacity as our distribution grew. Early on we didn't have a grand distribution plan; we operated in a mode that was essentially opportunistic. We would typically wait until we were unable to meet demand and then scrape together what cash we could to add a piece of equipment or tank that would add just enough additional production capacity. I returned to spending whatever free time I had scouring central and northern California for more dairy tanks that we could use to expand our fermentation cellar. By our second year of production, we were already knocking down walls and adding capacity—continual expansion and construction would be the norm for the next 30 years. In the long term this would create challenges.

LEARNING THE ROPES

The American brewing industry was reshaped by Prohibition. With federal Prohibition laws repealed, a state-based system of regulation and control was implemented. Each state established its own set of laws to regulate every aspect of alcohol beverage control, from taxation and alcohol strength limits to supplier-distributor contract enforcement within its borders. In many states strong franchise laws were established, giving in-state distributors an upper hand and superior rights in dealing with out-of-state brewers; in many cases these state regulations supersede any contractual language established between a brewer and distributor.

Having no experience and even less knowledge about how distributor relations worked, we enthusiastically, although somewhat blindly, entered into contracts with new distributors. We didn't understand the significance of those contracts' complex language and that in some cases we would not be able to alter them if future conditions warranted a move to another distributor. We had developed a rudimentary contract, but in some of these early situations, it was just a handshake agreement. Our first distribution contracts were simply horrible. The first version was only three pages and didn't contain any performance criteria. Unfortunately, some of them are still in effect today.

Sierra Nevada also started to gain notoriety in the Bay Area food and beer scene with both critics and consumers. As word about Sierra Nevada spread, we started getting approached by distributors and retailers that wanted our beer in far-flung markets. In many cases the distributors willing to carry our beers were not mainstream beer distributors, but rather, smaller operations that had less-than-stellar portfolios, often with no major brands or with a combination of beer, wine, and spirits, which generally means less focus in the marketplace. Had we known enough about the distribution game, we would have recognized that some of these distributors weren't the top players. Many of the better distributors had a full portfolio already or were exclusive distributors for a major brewery. Even if they weren't exclusive, often their major suppliers dissuaded them from expanding their brand portfolio for fear that they would lose focus. Besides, why would a major distributor want to mess with our little brand? We had no real sales support staff other than Harrison, and he had limited time to work in the marketplace. We had no advertising budget, had little to no marketing materials, and were a completely unknown brand in most markets. If we had been lucky enough to talk our way into a major powerhouse distributor, our sales results may not have differed much because back in those days, most markets had only a handful of appropriate accounts that were both receptive to craft beer and had a clientele willing to purchase it.

The early distributors that we did have successful relationships with were boutique, specialty houses that ended up being the ideal partners because they understood our brands and could do the necessary work of hand selling our eclectic style of beer. These boutique distributors had been on the leading edge of the better beer movement and foresaw the shift in consumer taste and desire for something other than light lager beer. They started to import a varied portfolio of European specialty beers, and as the craft movement was born, they added these newly minted labels to their stable of brands. We are still with one of these small niche distributors that we started with 30 years ago in one of the most competitive markets in the country. Our businesses have grown together, and the distributor still provides a great route to market for our brands.

THE GROWING REVOLUTION

While we were figuring out how to meet increasing demand for Sierra Nevada, new craft breweries began opening at a staggering rate. We had become part of the vanguard of what became the craft beer revolution. The craft brewing industry was still very much in its infancy but was quickly gaining momentum. By 1981, six craft breweries were in operation in the United States, and by 1982, 10 more had opened. The change in the brewing landscape caught the attention of the media; Sierra Nevada's focus on quality served us well, and we emerged as the top craft beer in many tastings. Our beers began showing up in tastings in various publications and events on the West Coast. The *Daily News* in Southern California held a taste test of the top European and American ales in 1982, and Sierra Nevada came out on top. In 1983, we were voted favorite beer in the *San Francisco Magazine* blind beer tasting. As publicity grew, so did demand as well as recognition that allowed us to expand our distribution into prestigious accounts. Chico's proximity to the Bay Area also allowed Sierra Nevada to take advantage of the growing foodie revolution. Our first very progressive and cutting-edge restaurant placement was in Chez Panisse in Berkeley. Owner Alice Waters was a true trendsetter in local and fresh cuisine. The principles behind the craft beer movement aligned with her ideas and vision about food.

Another indication that craft brewing was gaining legitimacy was a well-televised and well-publicized beer event at Hall Street Grill, one of the early craft-centric upscale bars and restaurants in beer-loving Portland. The famous critic and British beer writer, Michael Jackson, attended to conduct a beer tasting of primarily American craft beer. It was a pivotal point in American beer culture. Besides myself, beer celebrities of the time turned up—Bert Grant from Yakima Brewing and Malting Company; Charlie McEveley, the brewmaster from the newly opened Redhook; and Don Younger, knowledgeable publican of the well-known Horse Brass Pub in Portland. The mayor of Portland even made an appearance, giving credence to the role, both social and economic, that craft beer played in the city. Although this event was monumental, these kinds of gatherings quickly became more common as craft breweries continued to pop up around the country. The craft industry has always been a tight-knit community, and the genuine camaraderie that exists between brewers helped define our unique trade. We were at the forefront of the fledgling craft brewing industry, but we worked hard to contribute to the sense of community because we all faced the same challenges.

7

GROWING PAINS

Give me a woman who loves beer and I will conquer the world.
—Kaiser Wilhelm

In December of 1982, through the network of craft brewers we knew, we received a lead on a used 100-barrel German brewhouse. It came available after an aspiring brewer in the California Central Valley realized that the cost of entering the business with such a large brewery was well out of his budget. His wife had grown up in Würzburg, Germany, the town next to Kitzingen, where Huppmann, one of Europe's oldest and most respected manufacturers of brewing equipment, was headquartered. He had contacted Huppmann during a visit to his wife's family and tasked them to find a used, smaller, traditional copper brewhouse. Huppmann located one, so he asked them to prepare a quote for it that included some modifications to the equipment. Because he didn't have a boiler, he wanted to be able to directly fire the kettle with gas. He also asked them to supply some additional equipment, bringing the total for the equipment to hundreds of thousands of dollars—much more than he could afford. He knew we were in the market for a larger brewhouse, so he contacted us and passed on the details. He couldn't afford to proceed with the project, but he thought we might be interested.

By this time stainless steel had replaced copper as the material of choice for brewing equipment because of its greater ease of fabrication, resistance to corrosion, and unsurpassed durability. Copper had been used for brewing equipment for hundreds of years, having replaced the iron and wood that had been used in very early breweries. Its malleability and rapid heat transfer made it the perfect choice for many industries that required vessels for cooking and boiling. When used in brewing, however, copper reacts with the slightly acidic mash and slowly wears down giving it a finite lifespan, although some brewers felt the slight erosion of copper and its contribution to the brewers wort was vital as a micronutrient for the yeast. A few brewers who replaced their aging copper vessels with more durable stainless steel have achieved the same outcome. The brewers added plates or sections of copper pipe to allow their degradation to contribute those sacrificial copper ions.[1] During the 1900s coppersmiths perfected their art and produced beautiful polished copper brewhouses that were both elegant and functional. Once techniques were developed to produce, weld, and fabricate the much tougher and more resistant stainless steel, its use in brewing became widespread. After, the copper vessels were rarely produced and the art of coppersmithing was rapidly lost.

The same plight that had decimated the US brewing industry after Prohibition hit Europe. The German brewing industry boasted more than 1,000 breweries during the 1980s, but shortly after, they started closing at a rate of about one per week, leaving many defunct breweries offering used equipment for sale. The brewhouse Huppmann found was a used, traditional, 100-barrel copper brewhouse with two vessels in the not-too-distant town of Aschaffenburg. The brewery was called Bavaria Brau. Although located on the edge of Bavaria, the town's

---

[1]Brewing trials have proved that using sacrificial copper is probably not necessary and may be actually detrimental. The addition of copper later in the production process is risky because if even small amounts of copper make it through to the finished beer, it can contribute to increased flavor degradation caused by unavoidable oxidation.

inhabitants claim to be Lower Franconians, not Bavarians. Huppmann had manufactured and installed the beautiful copper brewing equipment in the original brewery in 1961. From the limited records the manufacturer could supply and the research I conducted, it looked like the brewery had struggled through most of its history, never achieving much market share from the start but floundering even more after World War II. The brewery struggled for years, but by 1968, it was producing only about 25,000 barrels a year. The brewhouse had been producing less than one brew a day—little use by normal production standards—and was still in great condition. The aging owner of Bavaria Brau had no offspring willing to run the brewery and closed it in November of 1981, one year after we had started.

Paul and I decided to take a trip to Germany in December of 1982 to inspect the equipment. I hadn't been to Europe before, and even though we had to go on the cheap, we were pretty excited. The flight left Oakland, California, for Los Angeles, connected through Baltimore and London, and terminated in Frankfurt. It was 23 hours total. We arrived without sleep and met an English-speaking salesman, Mr. Berthold, from Huppmann. We had a delicious German meal and plenty of beer. Although it was all lagers, drinking fresh all-malt beer was a real treat, and Paul and I imbibed heavily.

The morning came early. We met the engineer from Huppmann who was delegated to drive us out to the brewery to inspect the used Bavaria Brau machinery at 8:00 AM. Paul had had a bit too much to drink and had a rough night, but we met the engineer and had an interesting drive to Aschaffenburg. Once we arrived, we met with the owner of the brewery and began making arrangements to buy the brewhouse. We were essentially buying the copper brewhouse and all its associated parts for its scrap value—about $15,000 at the time. Much to their chagrin, because we really didn't have any money, we had decided not to have Huppmann do any of the modifications or upgrades that had been proposed; we decided to take it as it was and deal with any issues later. We negotiated for removal, crating (which cost about as much as the equipment), and ocean transportation (which cost another $30,000, bringing the total up to almost $60,000). Paul and I were pleased with the deal we struck, but it was far from being closed when we left Germany.

Back in Chico we had to figure out how to pay for the brewhouse we had just agreed to buy. We scraped together the $18,000 deposit but didn't have the balance. Once again, my father and Paul's mother agreed to cosign a loan, but the loan covered only what we needed for the equipment; we were still just making ends meet at the brewery. Shortly after we had committed to purchase the German brewhouse, we were dealt a severe financial blow when one of our largest and seemingly best distributors decided to close his operation. He had recently entered the distribution business after successfully running one of the early specialty beer- and wine-focused restaurants. The closing of the distributorship was our first major crisis and caught us completely off guard. We had extended a significant amount of credit to him, in part due to state label requirement issues that prevented some of our beer from being sold until stickers were applied to correct them. Even worse, we had just shipped an additional truck days before he notified us of his intention to close. I tried to get the shipment of beer back but was told he needed to sell it to cover other obligations. I was furious. He owed us around $13,000—a significant percentage of our overall operating budget. Paul, Harrison, and I believed we had a good working relationship with the distributor. We attempted to resolve the matter without involving attorneys, but because I couldn't get anything tangible in writing that gave me any assurance that I would ever get paid, we hired a lawyer. After months of wrangling we received a settlement of $0.10 on the dollar, all of which went toward legal fees.

I was afraid our business couldn't weather this financial blow and considered trying to pull out of our deal to purchase the brewhouse. In the end we went forward because we knew we needed a larger brewhouse, and the deal was too good to pass up. We learned an important lesson in the process—contracts may have felt overly formal, but they were a necessary part of our business, as was making sure we dealt with companies with integrity. Still, our naiveté had put us in a financial bind at the worst possible time, and no amount of hindsight could fix it. Instead, we faced our mistake, tightened our belts, and made the best of a bad situation. I'm happy to say this is still the single largest loss we have absorbed to date.

OVER THE OCEAN AND THROUGH THE WOODS

I arranged to travel to Germany with my old friend Dave Sheetz to assist in the removal of the brewhouse. Huppmann assigned two experienced employees to dismantle the brewhouse. Eric was the senior man with many years in the field, but he spoke virtually no English. Fritz was a young shop mechanic who had learned English in school but hadn't had the occasion to use it much and like many was not that comfortable with it.[2] Dave and I spoke no German other than the basics required to order beer. The language barrier provided many challenging and often humorous moments. For example, the Germans would shout "auf," which of course we thought meant "off," but it means "on or up" in German.

The removal was supposed to take around a week. Huppman's directive was to cut the vessels free with saws and torches, leaving all the plumbing and wiring behind. Being the frugal scrounger that I am, I wanted to take it all. Who knew? Maybe I could use some of it when I reinstalled the brewhouse. The owner was just going to have to pay someone to remove it and have it hauled off for scrap, so he didn't care if I took everything. In my naiveté I hoped that some of it would be worth taking. In reality, vintage 1961 German wiring was essentially useless; besides being designed for 50-hertz, 380-volt power, it didn't meet any current US standards. Unhooking and disassembling the piping and wiring added a lot of time to the removal, so Dave and I were compelled to do as much work as we could to assist the technicians. Although I couldn't understand much of the dialogue, I knew Eric was getting grief from the Huppmann office to get the project done. They had a firm bid, and the project was taking much longer than planned.

---

[2]Fritz still works at Huppmann, and I've had the opportunity and pleasure to work with him again many times over the past 30 years as we continue to expand and upgrade our brewery.

I took photographs of all of the equipment as it was being dismantled with the idea of using the photos as a guide when we would have to reassemble and install the brewhouse in Chico. Usually delivered and assembled by the manufacturer, these types of machinery don't come with assembly manuals with illustrations showing where the thousands of parts and pieces go. I would have to figure out how to put it back together myself.

Up to that point, my experience with rigging and removing large equipment was limited, but I got a crash course on that project, at least in the German way. The building the brewhouse was in was going to be demolished, so there was no concern about damaging it, which was a good thing given how we proceeded. The brewhouse extended across three levels of the building, and some parts weighed more than 5,000 pounds. The removal was accomplished without the luxury of a crane, but we were provided some timbers, slings, large hand winches, jackhammers, and cutting torches. To lift a piece from below, we would jackhammer a hole in the floor, attach a sling to a large timber laid across the hole, drop a cable through and attach it to the equipment, and then crank away with the hand winch. Working as part of their crew and trying to understand the German commands they were shouting made for plenty of scary moments as we removed all the equipment in this fashion. The most excitement came when we had to stand the 13-foot, 5,000-pound lauter tun on its edge and roll it between two columns through the brewhouse. Even back then, I knew that most of these rigging methods and techniques wouldn't pass muster with the Occupational Safety and Health Administration (OSHA). Thankfully no one was hurt, and the equipment suffered only minor bruising. The brewery owner came by almost daily to check on our progress. I got the impression that no one other than Dave and I thought that this brewhouse would ever be brought back to life.

Once we freed the equipment from the old brewery, it went to Huppmann's plant in Kitzingen, where it was carefully inspected and crated for shipment to Oakland, California. When the equipment finally arrived several months later, I received another good education in importation and dealing with dockworkers. The crates were larger than anything I had dealt with up to that point—the lauter tun was 13 feet in diameter, and in the crate it had an overall width of 14 feet, which required special trucks, permits, and flag cars, all of which charged by the hour. I went to the docks to meet the trucks and showed up right as the forklift driver was taking his break, so we had to wait until after he finished before we could get the load. When he returned, he said he wanted $50 cash or he wouldn't start the lift. I didn't have $50 or a quick way of getting it. This was before ATMs, and I didn't have a credit card. Although I had applied for one, I had been denied; I ended up borrowing money from one of the truck drivers. Once we got the $50, it was lunchtime, so we had to wait again. The whole time I was watching the clock and the dollars go by—two trucks and two flag cars were costing us a few hundred dollars an hour, and I didn't like spending my hard-earned money waiting around. After lunch they finally got the crates loaded, and it seemed like we were on our way.

The trucks pulled away from the docks and toward the gate. The drivers stopped to get their customs paperwork checked. Just then, a US Department of Agriculture (USDA) inspector strolled by to look at our load. He was waiting around for a load of duck eggs from China to arrive and was killing time. He saw a hole in one of the crates, started poking around with his pocketknife, and discovered a small dead beetle. He immediately impounded all the trucks; the load couldn't move until the beetle was identified. He said the bug would have to be mailed to San Francisco and analyzed at the USDA lab, taking several days or more to get the results. I was in shock. I couldn't believe what he was telling me. The truck drivers said they had other jobs and would have to unload the trucks and head home, but I convinced them to let me try to work out another solution. At this point the dockworkers were also close to getting off work and didn't think they could get the trucks unloaded, so I had at least another day of truck costs and more forklift fees. I started to try to negotiate with the inspector. I could see San Francisco clear as a bell just a few miles away and offered to drive the bug to the lab. He said I couldn't do that but did offer to drive it over himself since the duck eggs hadn't arrived yet. Several tense hours passed and finally the customs office got a call saying that they had identified the beetle, and it was native to California. By that time it was rush hour in the Bay Area. Our wide load permit prevented us from moving until after hours, and we couldn't be on the road after dark. We had one bit of luck on our side—because it was summer, we had more than an hour to get out of the Bay Area before we had to stop along the road for the night. We urged all the truck drivers to head out of the impound yard and park outside the gate to get out of the dock in case another inspector with a different agenda happened by. That evening, we made it only as far as Dingville (a place too small to be called a town along Highway 99) before we had to park the trucks and wait for the next morning to finish the drive to Chico.

Upon arrival we used borrowed forklifts to unload the German brewhouse into the trucking company's yard, where it stayed until we were able to reassemble it. We knew we had a lot of work to do before we could get the financing together to install it, so in the meantime, we continued to expand our homemade 10-barrel brewhouse.

FROM RELICS TO RELIABILITY

In February 1983, we were cranking out six brews a week and trying to add additional capacity. By that time we had signed with distributors in Southern California, Oregon, and Washington but were struggling to meet demand. I desperately needed to improve efficiency and decrease the labor required to brew. The constant inability to keep up was wearing on me and anyone I hired to help out. I was able to use a few parts and pieces I had scrounged while dismantling the ancillary equipment in Germany. Once again, my scavenging paid off. I had collected all the old grain handling and cleaning equipment in Germany. The owner had no use for it, so he had given it to me. Until then we had been grinding malt into pails and toting them up to the brewhouse before lifting the 50-pound tubs up a few feet and dumping them into the mash tun. Needless to say, it was a very arduous task.

I also purchased a small, very old malt mill sight unseen from the shuttered Ortlieb Brewing Company in Philadelphia to replace the rickety, maintenance-plagued one I had built. What I bought was not their main mill but a true relic that had been in the brewery for years. Joe Ortlieb had just closed the brewery after struggling financially for many years. It was a sad time for the company and the family, which had run the brewery since 1869. Joe sold me the mill for a few hundred dollars and threw in a large industrial vacuum designed for cleaning up potentially explosive malt dust that I thought I could use in my dusty mill room. The old mill was built around 1910 and would have been better off in a museum, but I thought I could still make it work. The bearings were cast out of Babbitt (a lead and tin material that was easy to cast) just like a Ford Model T and needed replacing. Fortunately, my friend had a business restoring old vintage cars, and he cast some new bearings. The mill's motor was vintage 1906 and needed to be replaced altogether because it came from the era when manufacturers produced their own direct current power, and it couldn't run on modern electrical power. It also had a large unguarded drive that relied on a brass and leather gear. I installed a new motor and belts and used the mill for the next five years. I cobbled together the dust vacuum with some parts from the grain handling system from Germany and an old meat scale that I got when I bought the butcher shop refrigeration unit. With bits and pieces from here and there, we were able to weigh and transfer grain to the mash tun automatically. These upgrades helped us crank out a few more brews per day and lessened some of the physical demands of the job.

As it turned out, it would end up being many years before we were able to make use of the beautiful copper kettles from the Huppmann brewhouse. Not only did we need money for the installation, but we also needed funds to expand our already cramped facility on Gilman Way.

Even though our business was growing, banks were still turning us down for a loan. Our meager volume and profit didn't justify the significant investment in their eyes. Paul and I spoke with a few venture fund people, but we were so unsophisticated and wet behind the ears that I don't think they took us seriously, and we weren't so desperate that we wanted to give up ownership or control anyway. Our new brewhouse sat crated in a storage yard for almost five years until we were able to increase our sales and profitability enough to justify its overhaul and resurrection.

GETTING BIGGER AND BETTER

Over the next few years, I found myself focusing on our ability to increase and maximize production. The pressure to grow continuously was compounded by the addition of our third child, Brian. With my energies split between work and home, I still had to figure out how to get close to 10,000 barrels of beer per year out of the original 2,500-barrel brewery to have enough sales to justify the million-dollar investment we thought it would take to grow Sierra Nevada to the next level, which would involve essentially starting over from scratch and building a new brewery from the ground up. The original Gilman Way building was only 3,000 square feet when we leased it, and we had added on another 495 square feet just to barely cram in the bottling line. Our office was a 10-by-10-foot space, and at times Paul, Harrison, and I all worked in it. The office also served as the main entrance to the brewery, so there were always people passing through. We had framed clean rooms inside the metal shell for our lab that gave us a crude second floor for storage over much of it, but the access was up a wooden ladder, so it wasn't very convenient and was crammed full of equipment.

We needed space to expand production, but we hadn't purchased all the new equipment we'd need or have a final equipment layout yet. When the metal buildings on either side of us became available, we moved into them: first one, then the other. They were cheaply constructed, uninsulated structures, so we had to make improvements if we wanted to use the space for more than boxes or empty bottle storage. The extra space allowed us to move our office, refrigerated beer storage, maintenance shop, and general warehouse area out of the brewery and free up production space. The brewery was turning into a shantytown full of jury-rigged equipment and infrastructure. The building didn't have the industrial three-phase power that was required for some of the equipment, so I had hooked up several used transformers. The water line to the building was undersized and kept breaking due to being poorly installed. I solved that problem when I rented a trencher and ran 500 feet of new pipe to the meter early one morning without telling anyone. Still, everything I bought was used and installed with the notion that it wasn't permanent. I stationed as much equipment in the dirt lot out back as I could to allow more room for fermentation indoors. I ran pipes to several dairy tanks that served as my hot water storage system, and I used an old ice builder that I had found at an auction for wort cooling.[3]

Because we had made so many improvements to our facility over the years, I was reluctant to get the city involved with permits or inspections when the larger scale work began. Instead, I justified and approached our projects as temporary structures. I built a new malt room on timbers that allowed me to pick it up and move it with a forklift. I set it in the backyard of the brewery, so I rationalized that didn't require a permit. Another improvement we made was to weld a higher skirt on the brew kettle to hold more wort, so we could almost double the amount of beer we could brew per batch from 10 to nearly 17 barrels. This modification meant that the kettle would be filled to the brim. I had to be careful to keep it from boiling over, but it added a lot of capacity. Being able to brew more helped, but we still had to start brewing around the clock as our markets continued to expand. We also increased the size of our fermenting tanks, first to 17 barrels, then to 35, until finally adding tanks that could hold 70 barrels of beer. With the 70-barrel tanks, we could then blend four brews into one tank, which helped even out minor variation from batch to batch.

Even with our accelerated growth and continuously expanding operation, we were very focused on the quality of our beer. We knew Sierra Nevada would not become a brand people loved if we didn't turn out beer with a consistently rich and full-bodied flavor profile. Paul and I had always had the philosophy that our company could grow only at the rate of our capabilities. We wouldn't overextend ourselves by brewing too much beer, by compromising quality for

---

[3]The ice builder was the first of many energy storage projects that we've installed at the brewery over the years. At night it froze water in a large tank and then used the stored energy during the day to cool the brew.

speed, or by spending money we didn't have, so we were always just behind the curve with demand exceeding production.

Inevitably, any extra beer we had as a result of the improvements to the brewery would sell immediately, requiring us yet again to find a way to increase production. We maintained this frugal and conservative approach to our beer and business for many years. Although it probably initially hampered our potential growth rate, it kept us from making some of the mistakes that plagued many other small brewers of our time. Some of the early craft brewery start-ups were struggling to find success and making what we perceived as obvious mistakes. The most prevalent was a lack of consistency in their beer; several also borrowed heavily from banks or took in many partners or investors to help fuel their growth. Brewing on a small scale is fraught with challenges, but some brewers were able to figure out how to grow their businesses with fewer resources than others. I credit much of our early success to our ability to be resourceful and innovate.

Most early craft brewers starting out were severely undercapitalized. Although Paul and I probably had a little more money than some, we heard of new brewery groups raising much more money than the $100,000 we finally pieced together to get Sierra Nevada going. As we connected with them, we saw that they had less to show for their money and often made equipment and plant design choices that would end up being detrimental to the long-term survival of their companies and brands.

Several of the breweries that had opened were already struggling financially just a couple years into their endeavors. By 1982 the fallout began when Cartwright Brewery—Oregon's first microbrewery—which opened just ahead of us in 1980, closed their operation in large part due to quality issues. DeBakker Brewery in Marin County, California, closed about the same time—just three years after opening—when the rigors of being a full-time firefighter and part-time brewer became too much for the owner and his wife when they decided to start a family. The original River City Brewing Company in Sacramento, California, closed soon after, suffering from both quality and style acceptance issues. The owner, Jim Schlueter, who had brewed at a major brewery prior to opening River City, had tried to produce a lighter lager-

Mountain climbing at North Palisade Peak in the Sierra Nevada Mountains, c. 1976.

DEPARTMENT OF ALCOHOLIC BEVERAGE CONTROL

PUBLIC NOTICE OF APPLICATION
TO SELL ALCOHOLIC BEVERAGES

APPLICANT Paul Camusi, Ken Grossman, et al, Ltd. Ptnrshp.

TYPE OF LICENSE Small Beer Manufacturer

ADDRESS OF PREMISES 2539 Gilman Way, Chico, Butte Co.

APPLICANT HAS FILED FOR: (NEW LICENSE)   PREMISES TO PREMISES TRANSFER
CHANGE IN LICENSE PRIVILEGES

IF A VERIFIED PROTEST IS TO BE MADE AGAINST THIS APPLICATION, IT MUST BE RECEIVED BY ANY OFFICE OF THE DEPARTMENT OR DEPARTMENTAL HEADQUARTERS, 1215 O STREET, SACRAMENTO 95814, WITHIN 30 DAYS OF DATE POSTED. PROTESTS MUST BE VERIFIED. FURTHER INFORMATION REGARDING THIS APPLICATION AND VERIFICATION FORMS MAY BE OBTAINED AT

YUBA CITY A.B.C. DISTRICT OFFICE
577 AINSLEY AVENUE
YUBA CITY, CA 95991
TEL. 916-674-4331

PREMISES ARE (NOT NOW) (ALREADY) LICENSED TO SELL ALCOHOLIC BEVERAGES.

WARNING
Every person who intentionally defaces,
obliterates, tears down or destroys this
notice prior to 30 days from the date it was
posted is subject to fine or imprisonment
in the County Jail. Section 616, Penal Code.

Mandatory posting of our beer license at Gilman Way, April 22, 1980.

Steve Harrison checking bottles of Porter as they leave the filler at the Gilman Way Brewery, c. 1982.

I did most of the building and upkeep at Gilman Way. Working on the kettle, c. 1982.

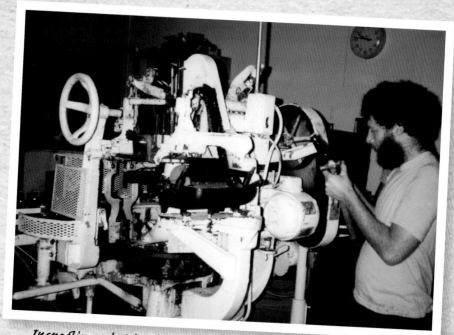

Inspecting a bottle of Porter as it comes off the labeler, c. 1982.

A stack of returnable bottles we used in the early days, before we could afford to buy new glass. Preparing a pallet of beer for shipment, c. 1981.

An early shot, with Paul, of Sierra Nevada's first lineup of three beers, c. 1982.

The arrival of the first German brewhouse at Gilman Way in early 1983; it was put in storage for five years and not installed until we built the 20th St. brewery.

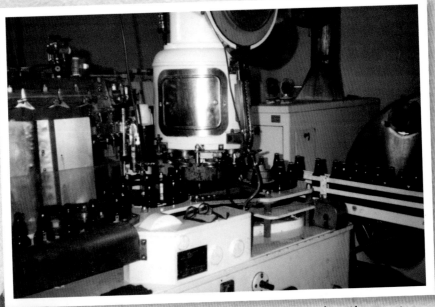

The filler from Anchor Brewery at the Gilman Way brewery, c. 1983.

Loading bottles onto the bottling line from outside; the addition of a canopy made the work a little more pleasant, c. 1983.

The office at the Gilman Way brewery, c. 1984.

Steve Harrison was always an early adopter of new technology; he had the first computer at Sierra Nevada, c. 1985.

BY MICHAEL CASTLEMAN

THE BEER THAT'S MAKING CHICO FAMOUS

The cover of the San Francisco Examiner Image Magazine in May 1986. This article launched us into the spotlight and helped fuel decades of growth.

Working with Dave Sheetz on the filler in 1987, prior to the installation of the German brewhouse in the 20th St. brewery.

Construction of the 20th St. brewery, our current home, c. 1987.

The arrival and placement of 400BBL fermenters in 1994. I've always been hands-on and overseen the installation of all new equipment.

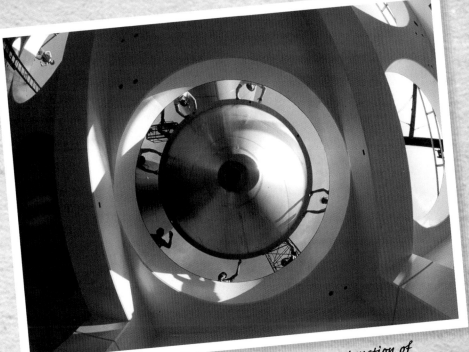

Installation of an 800BBL tank during the construction of the West Side at the 20th St. brewery in 1996.

The West Brewhouse at night with our hand-polished kettles, c. 2004.

One of our 250-kilowatt fuel cells. When they were installed in 2005, we had the largest privately owned fuel cell system.

We have a 9-acre hop yard on site, providing the hops for our Estate Ale. Early summer 2009.

Freshly harvested Centennial estate hops. The lupulin that flavors the beer is a resinous substance, making harvesting a dirty but fun job.

Aerial view of the brewery in early spring 2009.

Harvest of our estate barley in June 2009.

*Brewing Life & Limb®, our first collaboration
brew, with Sam Calagione, owner of
Dogfish Head Brewery, in July 2009.*

The chapter house at the Abbey of New Clairvaux.
Sierra Nevada's Ovila® beers reflect tradition
combined with brewing innovation.

One of our brewers, Scott Jennings, skimming the foam off an open
fermenter full of Kellerweis during fermentation, 2009.

The open top of a hop torpedo before beer is circulated through the bed of hops, 2009.

The first batch of our Sierra 30th Anniversary series, Fritz and Ken's Ale, an imperial stout brewed with Fritz Maytag, previous owner of Anchor Brewery, 2010.

Estate hops grown at the brewery, c. 2010.

Bottles of Pale Ale on the bottling line in 2011. Pale Ale makes up 70 percent of our sales.

At the announcement of our North Carolina brewery with former North Carolina Governor Bev Perdue, and my son, Brian Grossman, on January 25, 2012.

The Sierra Nevada Beer Bike in front of the brewery in 2012. A Beer Camp counselor steers while campers provide the pedal power.

style beer, which was a challenge to pull off with any consistency in his crude facility. He occasionally came to me to buy malt and would comment that nobody would want to drink our hoppy style of ale. Although we were saddened each time a fellow craft brewer closed his doors, what shook our confidence the most was learning that New Albion had brewed its last batch of beer and was closing. The very earliest pioneer, Jack McAuliffe opened the brewery in 1976 and was a role model and inspiration for us. To watch him run out of time and patience trying to raise funds to expand his unsustainable barrel-and-a-half operation was disheartening to watch.

New Business Models for Craft Brewers

Even against this less-than-encouraging landscape, the buzz about new American brewers continued to grow. People who wanted to own their own breweries and be brewmasters started coming out of the wood-work. Running a brewery seemed to promise the fulfillment of many adolescent fantasies, but aspiring brewers soon learned that running a brewery was as difficult as running any other kind of business—hard work, long hours, low funds, and tough decisions. We had dozens of loyal fans and aspirational visitors who regularly trekked out to Gilman Way to take tours and see our little operation. Some were serious about learning how to start and run a brewery, but most were just dreamers. In spite of our crazy schedule, and although we were always tight on time, we made sure to make time for our visitors and share our story because we had benefitted from so much counsel from large and small breweries that freely shared their time and experience with us when we were just starting.

Aspiring brewers began to exploit strategies that dramatically lowered the barriers to enter into the brewing industry. A couple of brewers who had very limited resources cut major corners and set up a commercial brewing operation with the same level of technology and skill that a beginning homebrewer would utilize. They skipped the entire mashing step, and instead purchased canned extracts and packaged yeast. One of the earliest, Thousand Oaks Brewery in Berkeley, operated in this fashion, brewing in the basement of the owner and producing a very palatable beer. Some of the brewers who adopted this alternative model struggled with quality and consistency or by design or circumstance failed to develop consumer acceptance. Their failures dealt a blow to the fledgling craft industry, so we kept a concerned eye on them. We were all competing for a small, knowledgeable consumer base willing to shell out $1 a bottle, which was a lot at the time. We knew that a bad experience with one craft beer could taint us all in the eyes of consumers, so we tended to help each other out to solve problems when we could.

Another business model that arose was contract brewing, in which the brewer didn't have to have a brewery or, for that matter, be involved with the production at all. This model was probably the most threatening to the brick-and-mortar craft breweries that struggled to add capacity and was the source of much discussion and debate amongst those in the industry. Contract brewing played out in many different scenarios—some companies simply asked a brewery to develop a special style of beer for them or purchased an existing recipe from an established brewer, with the only difference being the label. In another permutation contract breweries would work with the company's brewmaster and take a more active role in procurement and product development. This business model allowed entrants to avoid all of the challenges of building a small brewery. With less risk, owners could deploy their financial resources for branding, packaging development, and sales and marketing efforts. Because of the route Paul and I had chosen, we didn't devote any significant budget to branding, marketing, or sales our first years in business. We believed that because of our unwavering commitment to quality, our beer would sell itself. We couldn't afford to advertise at first, but down the road, our low profile and understated reputation became part of our brand identity. Luckily, our humble, no-frills approach resonated with our consumers.

This wave of contract production gave a short-lived shot in the arm to some of the surviving small regional breweries in the early 1980s.

Their ongoing struggles gave them excess capacity, so finding a brewery to produce under contract was relatively easy. All types of people entered the industry through this route. Some thought they had a cute name or were marketing geniuses; others had family members who had once brewed and had sold out or left the industry, and they or their offspring wanted another bite of the apple; and still others thought they were going to get rich. Engaging in contract brewing probably helped some of the struggling legacy breweries to see and better understand the emerging high-end beer market and another means of maximizing capital by producing styles of beer with higher margins that didn't go head to head with the dominant big brewers' brands. Brewing these beers was becoming increasingly necessary for struggling breweries to survive, and some eventually achieved success by developing their own higher-end brands. Unfortunately, the lack of transparency and distinctiveness in some of these contract brands created a situation that was often divisive for the still-emerging craft industry.

As Sierra Nevada struggled to add capacity and I poured my heart and soul and countless hours into my brewery, I often became frustrated with the so-called craft brewers who had the ability to get on the phone and order up a few hundred more barrels to fill an order. Around this time, we were so strapped for brewing capacity that when we had orders in hand that we couldn't fill, we would consider getting involved in contract brewing and having someone else brew our beer. The conversation always ended with us deciding that even if we believed our style of unpasteurized, bottle-conditioned ale could be produced elsewhere (which we didn't think was possible at the time), it wasn't what we wanted to do. Paul and I knew that going down that path meant selling our souls with no hope of redemption; our brand would be forever sullied. This type of business model is fairly common in many other industries, including processed food and wine, and in many cases the consumer is oblivious to a product's origins. The lack of transparency and authenticity usually has little effect on the viability of the brand but at other times has been met with consumer negativity, particularly when imported beers have tried to move their production to US contract producers.[4] Instead we continued to focus on adding capacity. Even then, year over year our growth rate was close to 20 percent annually, but our output still remained small relative to our demand, and it was painful to watch contract brewers easily eclipse our volume. We knew we had more opportunities if only we could make more beer; we just needed to figure out how to raise money for our expansion.

---

[4]Most of the brands launched via contract brewing have run their course, completely disappearing or significantly declining in market share. As many regional breweries finally succumbed to years of declining brands and the inability to reinvest in their ailing plants, most closed, leaving only a few contract brewing options available.

8

MOVING ON UP

Do not cease to drink beer, to eat, to intoxicate thyself, to make love, and to celebrate the good days.

—Ancient Egyptian Credo

By the mid-1980s the craft industry had been established long enough that it was no longer viewed as some sort of fringe movement, but we certainly weren't headline news, either. That changed in May 1986, when the *San Francisco Examiner* featured an article about Sierra Nevada in their Sunday *Image Magazine* titled "The Beer that's Making Chico Famous." The article included a five-page color spread that immediately catapulted us into the mainstream press in our biggest market, the Bay Area. Within a few days of the article being published, we were immediately sold out at most of our distributors, and we had no ability to meet the increasing demand, underlining our desperate need for a bigger facility. We produced a little over 4,000 barrels in 1985, and with some significant plant improvements and larger tanks, we added around 50 percent capacity that year. We were quickly able to fill it, producing almost 7,000 barrels in 1986. Paul and I now believed we had solid track record and enough momentum to justify both to ourselves and to a bank the financial risk of a new, bigger brewery.

It was finally time to install the much bigger brewhouse we had in storage. We had been casually looking at existing buildings in Chico for a few years and now began to look more seriously at locations for our plant expansion. Our biggest hurdle was that under zoning requirements packaging breweries had to be located in a manufacturing zone. At that time, Chico had very few areas with that designation and even fewer that would be suitable for our needs. We knew we wanted to add a small restaurant and pub and had focused on several downtown sites that had the correct zoning. One of the buildings we considered, on the outskirts of downtown Chico, was an old brick building on the corner of 8th and Main; it had a great history. It had housed Pullins Cyclery where I had worked soon after moving to Chico, but even more significantly the building was the original Chico Brewery that had closed around the turn of the century.[1]

We thought it would be exciting to move our brewery into the original Chico Brewery building. It was in poor shape and didn't have enough space for even our first-phase construction plans, but the

---

[1]The Chico Brewery was advertised in a Chico newspaper in December 1865 as recently built, having "all the appliances of the business," and "for sale at a bargain." At the time of its construction, the building was one of the finest commercial brick structures in Chico and remained the only brewery in the area for many years. Charles Croissant, a Bavarian brewmaster, bought the half block the brewery stood on from John Bidwell in 1874 for $1. He apparently tore the original building down and rebuilt the present structure. The Chico Brewery served the area for 25 years. The ground floor front rooms were occupied by a saloon and card room, and the upper floor functioned as a boarding house. The beer was brewed in the rear of the building. A wooden warehouse for grain was constructed in the back of the building. The brewery building has been consistently occupied for more than 100 years with a variety of businesses, including saloons, hotels, restaurants, antique stores, crafts shops, and a bicycle shop. It is one of Chico's oldest buildings and the oldest remaining building in the Junction area, the area where the Chico-Idaho Line, the main supply route between the Sacramento valley and the Idaho Mine, began.

whole block was correctly zoned; we thought it might be possible to get the other businesses to relocate. A construction firm evaluated the old brewery structure and the news wasn't hopeful. Most of the building couldn't be salvaged, and it would be very expensive to bring it up to current code, even if we used the historic building only for the pub that we wanted to locate downtown. The city also voiced concerns about the additional truck traffic that a brewery would bring to the area. Paul and I were discouraged, but we realized it would have been a horrible choice and probably would have resulted in a much different outcome for Sierra Nevada because we would have been landlocked and unable to grow past the original 60,000-barrel size we had designed.

At that point, we had not predicted our growth past 60,000 barrels, which we ended up exceeding in the fourth year after we built the new plant. When we began planning our new brewery, we were modest in our expectations, not thinking we could continue to grow like we had. I had decided that 60,000 barrels was a lofty growth target that would be close to the maximum design capacity of the brewhouse of two brews a day, 300 days a year. To keep things in perspective, we were now producing fewer than 12,000 barrels, and the only small brewery that was close to that size was the grandfather of the movement, Anchor. The craft industry was still in its infancy. Although there were certainly some successes, there were plenty of struggles and challenges for most of us, and examples of growth from a start-up to 60,000 barrels was unheard of. We had less than 10,000 feet of building space, factoring in the other two adjacent metal warehouses we took over, so from a plant and growth perspective, almost anything would be an improvement.

New Neighborhood

With downtown Chico ruled out, we had to look in other parts of town. In the course of building the Gilman Way brewery, I had met Lou Chrysler, a commercial contractor whose office was around the corner from us. He took a liking to me and knew about our plight and need to build a new plant. He had recently started working on a small commercial project on land he owned at the southern end of Chico, situated at the end of a small road destined to have a freeway off-ramp. The land was in an area designated for future manufacturing zoning and development. Next door to the site was a company that processed walnuts. Directly across the street were the Royal Crown Cola bottling company, which had just closed, and the recently constructed and relocated 7UP bottling plant. The city planning commission thought it was the ideal location for another bottling and food processing operation and encouraged us to locate in the area. We started working with Lou on plans to purchase a small section of his parcel. At his suggestion we hired local architect Ed Hoiland to draw up some preliminary designs so that we could come up with a budget. I had been working on an equipment budget and estimated that we could equip the brewery for $1,000,000, besides the building and land, but we had a very limited amount of money and hadn't lined up all of our financing. To help us out, Lou agreed to build the building and lease it to us with an option to purchase it from him at a future date; however, we decided to go a different route. Paul's mom, Sybil, was a shrewd investor in Southern California real estate and had a lot of investment properties; she offered to sell one to pay for the construction of the new brewery building and lease it to us. Although Lou was willing to build and lease the building back to us, this seemed like a better alternative because we believed Paul's mother would be a more sympathetic owner for the lease period and offer a more favorable price when it came time to exercise our purchase option. We had been working with Lou and our attorney to define a buyout protocol, but when Paul's mom stepped into the picture, we didn't finalize the terms, assuming that because it was family we could sort it out later.

Because the lease price would be determined by the overall cost to build the building, we scrimped as much as we could on the design and parcel size. We ended up settling on a 25,000-square-foot brewery with a 2,700-square-foot pub attached. Sandwiched on 1.7 acres on 20th St., the building and required parking came within 10 feet of the property line, leaving no room to expand in the future, but it was all we could afford.

I worked with a project estimator, Dave Heric, at Modern Building to refine the building budget. I had been so used to doing my own construction, as well as plumbing and electrical, that I was shocked by how expensive the bids for the job were. I kept eliminating nonessential items and tasks that I thought I could do myself. The resulting structure was a metal building with wood-framed offices and an attached pub shell. Since it wasn't an essential part of the brewery, we decided to finish the pub later when we could afford it. Once we decided on the final building design and budget, I was again in full salvage and fabrication mode. In true Sierra Nevada fashion, Paul and I first set about determining which of our current equipment we'd be able to reuse in the new brewery. Some of the newer 70-barrel aging tanks that we had purchased the past couple of years were the only candidates to make the move. It would take two 100-barrel brews to fill three of the 70-barrel tanks, which would be a bit of a hassle, but they were in good shape; reusing them would save us money. We planned on adding only a few more 200-barrel tanks to get us up to a production level of 20,000 barrels per year—the first phase of our expansion. I decided that I would do the design and installation of all the refrigeration equipment for the brewing operations because we couldn't afford to hire it out. I found some slightly used cold box panels that would work for our hop freezer, which I assembled myself. I had several friends in the air conditioning and refrigeration business and scrounged through their back rooms for compressors and cooling coils.

The building across the street from us was an old Royal Crown Cola bottling plant. The large warehouse there provided a perfect staging and fabrication shop. The short walk between the two areas would allow me to keep tabs on the construction and oversee the rebuilding and fabrication of the new brewery, so we rented the space and moved my office into the uninsulated building.

OLD WORLD COPPER, NEW WORLD BREWHOUSE

The Huppmann brewhouse had remained in the crates we shipped them in from Germany for years while we struggled to get our volume up to a point at which we could justify the investment and look for a home for our new brewery. Now that the construction of the new brewery was under way, we began inspecting the equipment to see just how much work would be required to ready the German brewhouse to brew our American-style ale. We had more work ahead of us than we expected.

What shape the components were in; how much of the piping, steam valves, and electrical equipment I had salvaged could be reused; and what we would need to do to get up and running had been, until now, a mystery. One big issue facing us was that industrial power in Germany was 50 hertz, 380 volts, instead of 60 hertz, 480 volts, which is the standard in the United States. Additionally, the equipment had been built in 1960, and several of the motors for the specialized gear drives didn't have any American replacement parts. After much searching, I found a local motor shop that was able to rewind and convert the motors to run on US power.[2] As if those challenges weren't enough, all the measurements on the pipes and threads were of course in metric sizes, so I had to convert and adapt all the fittings to US sizes for dozens of connections. I developed a set of swaging tools to expand the German copper pipe enough to mate with the American sizes. I became adept at brazing and switching back and forth between the two different systems. I purchased a small sandblaster and spent the next few months dismantling equipment, rebuilding valves, and painting. I also purchased a lathe and used it to salvage many of the valves and flanges, refacing them and turning them down to couple with domestic pipe. Unfortunately, the other electrical equipment I had salvaged that controlled the operation of all the motors and pumps was worthless because it didn't meet US standards.

We designed the new room to house the copper brewhouse using the original German building prints, so that part of the building was the exact same size, which I thought would help facilitate reusing some of the shafts, beams, and other parts I had scavenged in Germany. The original 1961 installation of the brewhouse in Germany happened at the tail end of the mechanized industrial period before the advent of

---

[2]This would have been a much simpler proposition today with the development of inexpensive frequency and voltage converters.

electronics to automate valves and temperatures for process control. All
the control valves were actuated with shafts and couplings connected
through universal joints to knobs and wheels on a spectacular polished
copper control panel. Although elegant and functional, it wasn't the
easiest thing to maintain because the valves were so tightly grouped
that servicing the unit was complicated. Parts for the control panel also
weren't available in the United States, so I had to order parts from
Germany or modify the panel and replace the parts with domestic parts
adapted to fit.

On the upside, this brewhouse had better control over the temperature of the brewing process than our old simple infusion brewing
method did. In our original brewhouse we had no means of heating or
stirring the mash, which was a more simplistic way to brew but had
some inefficiencies and was not as flexible in dealing with different
malt types.[3] Our new brewhouse was able to do both infusion and
decoction methods. The lack of automation would require a lot of skill
and experience because to control the temperature of the mash, the
brewer had to watch a temperature gauge to predict how fast it was
increasing and throttle the steam back. This completely manual control
scheme would take a little getting used to but offered increased flexibility in our brewing options.

I found an older, used, American-made bottle filler at an equipment
dealer that had originally been in the Latrobe Brewing Company
plant. Ironically, my current plant manager, Al Spinelli, operated
this same piece of equipment in the 1970s at Latrobe when he

---

[3]This brewing method was still common in England but had been largely abandoned
in the rest of the world in favor of either decoction mashing or upward infusion. The
Germans favored decoction mashing, which had been developed to deal with lower-
quality barley more efficiently, increasing its yield. The process involved boiling a
portion of the grain first before the mashing process, allowing for a greater solubi-
lization and breakdown of the starch. This boiling and pumping of portions of the
mash took a lot more time and energy. During World War II many breweries
switched to upward infusion because they were forced to cut back on energy usage,
and with improvements in malting barley, they were able to adopt a system utilizing
heating and stirring in one vessel, allowing for greater temperature control with less
energy.

first began his brewing career. This type of long tube filler had been the workhorse of the US brewing industry since the 1960s, and although filling technology had been dramatically improved, it was a big improvement over our current equipment. Better and more efficient technologies out of Germany were slowly replacing them, but at the time it was a step up for us from the original soda filler whose maintenance had taken up so much of my time. We had to do a complete overhaul of the filler from the base up, but the effort was worth it because it was much faster than our old filler and would easily handle our production for years to come.

It was too much work for one person, so I located and hired a few great fabricators, welders, and mechanics to work on the project. Dave Sheetz, my childhood friend, rounded out the team and helped rebuild the old bottling line. I also ran across a very handy fabricator, John Visel, who had assembled bottling lines for several small wineries and was out of work and up for the challenge. John was a very meticulous and talented worker but a bit of a rogue. He ended up pitching a tent and living in the warehouse to save money. He worked long days and consumed a significant quantity of beer as he worked. He favored Schaeffer as his work beer and typically drank a dozen a day, saving Sierra Nevada for evening consumption.

I went to equipment auctions to look for pieces of equipment that would make up the balance of our bottling line; with our rapidly dwindling budget, we couldn't afford any more new equipment, so, yet again, I had to scrounge together old machinery to create the packaging line from several equipment dealers and soft drink bottlers. We made the decision to build all of our own conveyors from scratch because we wanted them made out of stainless steel and couldn't afford to have them made. I had enough room in the warehouse to set up the entire bottling line and tediously rebuilt every part as John welded and fabricated the conveyor sections with Sheetz helping where he could. It turned out to be a large project and a painfully slow part of our construction process, but we were all proud of the bottling line when it was done.

As the building plans wound their way through the city's permit process, we began readying the equipment for its future home across the street. While I focused on the new brewery, we were stressing the equipment and our 15 employees at the old brewery to the maximum limit. We had been at full capacity and were forced to ration beer sales and limit shipping to new markets. The new brewery had been a long time coming, and with delays of several years, the staff was starting to think it might never come to fruition.

On top of those frustrations, Paul had been going through a nasty legal dispute with his father's estate. Paul's father had died, and his will had been changed to leave all his assets, including the brewery stock, to his new wife. Paul and his sister spent months trying to get the will overturned, but in the end all they received was the brewery stock. Our corporation documents contained a provision for a buyout agreement that would have addressed this situation, but it required the participation of all shareholders. Because Paul's father died unexpectedly, there was no time to execute it. Unfortunately all of this came at a critical time for Sierra Nevada and, of course, divided Paul's attention.

HELLO 20TH STREET

We finally broke ground on 20th Street in the fall of 1987, and threw a big party across the street in the Royal Crown Cola warehouse. Not only was it a momentous occasion for us, but it was also a big deal in a small town like Chico, bringing out a local television station and the mayor for the obligatory groundbreaking ceremony.

The polished copper kettles from the German brewhouse looked magnificent on display at the party, but I had a lot of rebuilding and fabricating to do. We still had a lot to do to coordinate the installation of the rest of equipment in the new building.[4] The kettles needed to be installed in pieces and assembled in place exactly as they had been removed. I had taken a lot of pictures when we took it apart in Germany, but so many years had passed; I hadn't had the opportunity

---

[4]Because we eventually added on to the 20th Street brewery, it became necessary to differentiate between the original brewhouse and the portion that came later. We call the original part of the plant the East Side, and the newer portion is the West Side.

or reason to think much about the process of reassembling the kettle until I had to reinstall it. I had a few conversations with the mechanics at Huppmann in Germany but couldn't afford to bring them over to help. By now I had years of experience in fabricating, and I wasn't too fazed by the project. Maybe I should have been, but like the challenges of the past few years, if I looked at the obstacles we faced all at once, I would have thrown in the towel. So, instead, I took things one step at a time, solving each problem as it came up and then moving on. I had to do it that way—if I had looked at the project in its entirety, I never would have had the courage to start.

Fortunately, we had become very handy at rebuilding equipment, and for the most part, the brewhouse went back together as planned, although resoldering the dome back to the kettle base was very difficult. I also went to a few closed breweries and industry auctions and bought a few specialized items that I couldn't make myself. The Hudepohl Brewing Company, which was founded in 1885 by a German settler in Cincinnati, Ohio, had recently closed and had a suitable malt mill that I purchased for a fraction of the price of a new one. It was bigger than we needed and from the 1950s, but it was a huge step up from what we were using and cost just a few thousand dollars. Also for sale was some packaging machinery that would have been great to have, specifically a glass depalletizer, which was one of the last pieces I needed to get the bottling line running. I bid against another brewer for Hudepohl's old one, but I was running out of money and put in a low offer; I didn't win it. I cobbled together my own system, thinking it might be good enough to start with until I could find another used depalletizing system to unload bottles. The temporary unit, nicknamed the glass launcher after a few exciting hiccups, was cobbled together from a scissors lift and some conveyors that I picked up at various scrap yards and auctions. It ended up lasting for five years.

By November 1988, the building wasn't finished and many details, such as tile and paint, were still left to do. But we were close to having all the brewing equipment in place. To mark our eighth anniversary, I had the harebrained idea to make our first test brew in the new kettles at the annual party, which we planned on having in the almost completed building. The pub was still just an empty shell, but it was certainly much more spacious than trying to pull off the party at the now overloaded and deteriorating original brewery on Gilman Way. Because we were so close to making our first batch, it seemed like a fun target to shoot for, even though I hadn't tested any of the grain handling or mashing equipment yet. We started the brew on November 15, our anniversary, several hours before the party started; everyone was in a festive mood, and I had a few beers to celebrate as we tried to figure out the new system. A string of mishaps followed. We had to abort the brew partway through the process. Then, the spent grain handling system didn't work as planned, and we ended up with most of the grain in the basement, blocking the drain and filling the basement with hot, sticky wort. While hundreds of people walked around admiring the almost completed building, I was in the basement trying to clear the drain, the wort nearly over the top of my boots. It was the first of many memorable parties at the 20th Street brewery.

GOODBYE GILMAN WAY

This first brewing trial pointed out some serious, but not insurmountable, issues that I had to rethink before we would be able to brew beer in the new facility. I tackled the spent grain system first because I had no desire to flood the basement again. It took a few more months to finish the building and solve some of the other problems that popped up as we did brewing and packaging trials.

When we thought we had resolved all the major problems, we made plans to officially pull the plug on the old brewery and move everyone over to the new plant. We didn't have the labor to run both breweries and had to make the call to sink or swim. We also needed to move some of the tanks that we intended to use at the new plant until we could afford more of the larger tanks. We brewed the last batch of Sierra Nevada beer on Gilman Way in April of 1989, and started up full production on 20th Street. The larger fermentation tanks were the only pieces of equipment we took from the old brewery. We found buyers for the rest of our equipment; some went to established craft brewers who were also expanding, but the majority was going to one of my old homebrew shop customers, Bob Smith, and my old friend, Jean Harvey, who were starting up their own brewery—Mad River Brewing Company—on the north coast of California.

The old brewery was in rough shape when we moved out. I was a bit embarrassed by the dilapidated condition we had let the plant fall into during the construction of the new brewery, but we were in full production mode in our new facility with no time or inclination to paint or fix anything in the old building. The owner of the building had insisted we pay an additional security deposit when he saw how much we had done to modify the building. In addition to cutting up the slab to install sloped floors and drains, we had cut through the roof and tin walls for vents. The increased deposit allowed us to walk away from the Gilman Way building when we were done, and that's pretty much what we did. On one hand, it was fun knocking holes in the walls to facilitate the removal of tanks, equipment, pipes and wiring, knowing it was the last time we would have to put up with the cramped facility. On the other hand, it was also the end of a long, hard era that had required a lot of sacrifice and held many memories. Still, I was so tired of some of the makeshift systems that I had built and had to maintain constantly that I felt little remorse leaving them behind.

STEPPING UP PRODUCTION

With the new, much larger brewery, we planned to brew one batch per day, three days each week, compared to the three brews per day, seven days a week way we had been operating for the past year. The German brewhouse was designed to produce up to two brews a day, nicely matching the 60,000-barrel-per-year plant capacity that we planned on ultimately growing into in the new facility.

Even with this adequate capacity and more efficient machinery, the first few months were a little rocky. On our early brews, we had our first-ever problem with some minor but definitely unwanted bacteria in a few batches of beer. Our new aging tanks held three times the amount of beer our old tanks held and had a much deeper layer of yeast in the bottom after it settled out. We found out the hard way that the thick sediment would degrade after a few weeks of storage, creating the perfect environment for bacteria to multiply. We ended up dumping several batches and modifying our storage protocol to eliminate the deep yeast sediment, and the nuisance bacteria went away.

To meet pent-up demand, we rapidly increased our production from brewing a few days a week to almost every day. I soon realized that the smaller tanks we had moved from Gilman Way were creating additional labor and complexity, limiting our capacity, so we quickly decided to order additional larger aging tanks. We had designed the new plant to be a scaled-up version of our old brewery with four 100-barrel open fermenters and a small complement of conical tanks.

That year, 1989, we saw an almost 80 percent increase in sales from a little over 12,000 barrels to over 20,000 barrels. Because we had also started to make a little extra money, we decided to go ahead and purchase the building from Paul's mother. When we approached her with the idea, she wasn't all that anxious to sell, and if she did sell, she wanted to maximize her return. She proposed getting the building appraised to set the value rather than receiving a fixed return as would have been our arrangement with Lou. This unexpected twist caused a bit of stress my relationship with Paul. It wasn't that he supported his mother's position, but he didn't argue with her, either. I was shocked and upset that she would put us in this unreasonable situation, and I'm sure it was awkward for Paul because having a family member own the building was supposed to be financially better, not worse, for the company. I knew Sybil was a very shrewd businessperson; perhaps this was her way of ensuring a good return after taking a big risk with her initial investment in the brewery. I didn't feel like any of our other investors viewed the business that way, nor did I think they'd try to take advantage of the situation like I felt she was. It was true that she had stepped up when we needed money, but we didn't need her money anymore. I'm not sure what finally convinced her, maybe behind-the-scenes pressure from Paul, but Sybil finally relented; we purchased the building under terms similar to what Lou had proposed.

Unfortunately the stress of buying the building cemented my growing sense of resentment of Paul over the balance in the business. In the early days Paul put in a fair amount of time. While I had been working in the bike shop and Homebrew Shop, in addition to working on the brewery seven days a week, Paul had been getting support from home to live on, so he had devoted all of his time to brewery activity. When I sold the brew supply shop, I still had to work seven days a week to build the brewery, take shifts at the bike shop to support my family, and attend classes to weld and fabricate equipment. When we opened Sierra Nevada, I was responsible for all the brewing, bottling, and maintenance, so my days started much earlier than Paul's and most often went late into the evening. I was aware from the beginning that Paul's capacity for work was not as great as mine. I was driven (I still am) and a workaholic. Paul generally worked close to 40 hours per week, at least in the early years, so there wasn't a problem at first. As we grew and added more people and complexity to the company, Paul became less and less engaged and started to put in fewer hours. He also avoided our infrequent employee meetings and took a backseat in charting the overall direction of the company. He began to work even shorter days, and during the planning and design of the 20th Street brewery, he was only peripherally involved in the project. On one hand, it gave me a free hand to do what I thought was right without much pushback, but if I made a mistake I owned it.

We were growing fairly quickly without putting a lot of effort into sales, unlike many of our peers who were much more aggressive and seemingly better marketers. Several of my friends at other craft breweries used to give me grief that we had only one salesperson even when we reached 30,000 barrels. It made no sense to me to spend resources on sales when we couldn't make enough beer to fill orders anyway. Early in the growth of our company, we were not a very sales-focused organization, and we didn't have a lot of layers of management or, for that matter, any formal management or financial systems. I controlled every major project and practiced slow, controlled growth, only adding capacity for the sales we had at the time rather than what we might need in the future. It was nice being able to invest in the business without having to worry about a large marketing budget. We were very much a production-focused business, and for years my almost singular focus was continually working on projects to supply the ever-increasing demand for our products. Once our sales volume passed 10,000 barrels, we had decent, although not huge, cash flow that provided enough revenue to fund our consumer-driven growth. Growth, though, meant more work, and Paul no longer seemed willing to do his fair share.

By 1990, Paul was working less than 35 hours a week and starting to distance himself from Sierra Nevada. Nonetheless, we were getting paid the same monthly salary, and aside from what I viewed as a serious inequality in effort and immediate remuneration, I felt that my hard work was building his equity. It really started to bother me, and one day when I was very frustrated, I wrote up a proposal that would give me a significant boost in salary over Paul. He didn't balk because the inequality was obvious. The salary increase addressed the current compensation differential, but the equity I was building in the business we shared equally still made me felt like I was being unfairly compensated for the long term, and my animosity grew.

BACK TO THE MOUNTAINS

When we first started the brewery, I lived about 10 miles outside of Chico and later moved down the road a little closer to Chico, but when the kids got older, we moved into town for school and to be near other kids because we were totally isolated on the ranch. From very early on at the first location, I had been so involved in the design, construction, and operations of the plant that I was also the on-call person for problems. It wasn't uncommon for me to have to go to the brewery in the middle of the night to deal with boilers that had tripped off, leaking pumps, or a plugged grain handling system because Paul didn't have a clue about those types of things. I had the same role when we moved to 20th Street, but by that time I lived 18 miles out of town, making the midnight calls even more stressful. Being in Chico just added to my angst and workload, though, because I was just a few minutes away and would get called in to deal with almost any issue that came up. I was particularly bothered by fire engines, a paranoia that started at the old brewery, given its piecemeal construction. Hearing sirens put me on edge and made me think that the brewery was on fire, a tank exploded, or someone got hurt or burned. I envisioned all sorts of disasters and would breathe a sigh of relief when the fire engine or police car passed by. When I heard a siren, I frequently drove to the brewery to make sure everything was okay, often multiple times in one day. We had finally decided to move out of town and into the mountains we loved.[5] Right around that time, I hired another mechanic who had a broad skill set that at least allowed me some time away without being on call every night. If I got called now, it was probably a real emergency. Even with mechanical help, I was still at the brewery all the time, and Paul remained oblivious to the fact that I may have spent all night at the brewery fixing something. He would stroll in at 9:30 and leave at 3:30, adding to my feeling of inequality and frustration.

GROWING BOUNDARIES

The first few years after we opened the 20th Street brewery, I focused on keeping up with demand as we grew from 12,000 to 20,000 to 30,000 to 45,000 to 60,000 barrels. Thankfully a lot of vacant property surrounded us, and as our cash flow allowed we bought what land we could afford. Lou still owned some empty parcels behind the

---

[5]Katie wanted to get out of the valley, and when she was pregnant with Brian we finally scraped together enough money for a down payment on an $85,000 house on 5 acres. The salt frame box house had one loft bedroom, one bathroom, and a big walk-in closet where we set the girls up. We thought we could add on another bedroom later when our modest income allowed. Even though we could afford the down payment, the owner carried the note because the house probably wouldn't have qualified for a conventional loan. It had only a wood stove for heat, and I still hadn't established much personal credit.

brewery and sold them to us, one or two acres at a time. Acquiring the adjacent vacant properties allowed us to expand our operation with a buffer zone. Still, we had several neighborhood conflicts over the years. At one point a church wanted to establish a facility with an elementary school on the property directly adjacent to us, creating an awkward public situation. Churches are a bit in limbo as far as zoning is concerned, and the property was zoned for manufacturing. The church had been trying to relocate for some time, but we really didn't think it would be a good fit with our trucks, pub, and 24-hour operation. It was maddening that our business was established, but they still wanted to move next door, presenting the possibility for future conflict. It's happened before that businesses in that situation have been forced out, so we had to address it. The Chico Chamber of Commerce joined in our fight, and we all publicly and privately received flak for dissuading the church from locating next to us. I received hate mail and nasty phone calls, and the battle appeared on the front page of the local newspaper. It wasn't the kind of publicity we wanted, but in the end the church opted for another location; I still think fighting it was the right decision.

Later, we had to challenge the rezoning of the property directly to our west when the owner wanted to rezone it from manufacturing to high-density residential. He thought he could get government funding for a low-income housing project to be built adjacent to an existing project. The property butted directly up against our property line, and we felt that we needed to create a buffer strip, at a minimum. We convinced the city to create a larger setback, but for whatever reason, the project didn't get funded, allowing us to purchase the parcel eventually. Because the zoning had already been changed, we had to petition to change it back to manufacturing, which then added additional restrictions for us that had not been in place before the housing project was proposed. We've tried to create a large enough buffer around our operation to mitigate our impact on the neighboring community. Over the years we have weighed in on most of the rezoning that has converted the limited amount of designated manufacturing space into retail or commercial space. All the other manufacturing businesses that had been in this part of town when we moved in are now gone, and the neighborhood has changed tremendously.

ADDING INFRASTRUCTURE

By 1992 we were producing 60,000 barrels, the maximum I had originally designed the brewery to produce. Once again, we were running out of fermentation capacity and didn't have space to add any more inside the existing structure. On one of the additional acres we purchased from Lou, we built a larger beer conditioning warehouse and a much larger fabrication shop. Freeing up the old warehouse space allowed us to install an automatic palletizer, one of the first pieces of bottling equipment I purchased new. It saved the time, cost, and labor of having two people manually stacking and wrapping hundreds of cases of beer a day, a mundane and backbreaking task. I figured it paid for itself in less than two years, not including the value of the opportunity to eliminate the possibility of a workers' compensation claim. With the extra space, we could add additional malt storage to help with our increasingly busy brewing schedule. I also started to build the first of many outside fermentation tank structures based on my design for a freestanding concrete building similar to what I had seen on my travels throughout Europe, only much smaller in scale. We built a heavily reinforced concrete deck adjacent to the building to support the tanks, and just their cones protruded inside the room. With the majority of the tanks outside the building, the fermentation cellar could remain clean and open. It added to the project cost considerably compared to tanks just sitting on legs, but having a wide open, clean working space below made for much easier maintenance.

Our growth rate since we had moved had been nothing short of phenomenal, but we were still cautious and tried not to leverage ourselves, so we expanded a little at a time rather than doing one major expansion. At a 50 percent growth rate year over year, we were constantly adding capacity because the infrastructure was really only laid out for the initial 60,000-barrel projection. I had to tear out undersized systems or, more commonly, add a second parallel system because we were so taxed to keep brewing that we rarely had time available to shut down the plant to reconfigure systems properly, leading to a complex and sometimes ill-thought-out web of pipes and wires. I acted as engineer, designer, and fabricator for many of these early projects and, to make matters worse, was never very good at documenting what I had done or why my design made sense at the time.[6]

FINEST QUALITY

As I tackled one area at a time with increasing revenue and cash flow that allowed for better equipment, laboratory instruments, and more people to share the increasing complexity and demands of the brewery, I never allowed anyone to lose sight of quality. Many people believe that smaller is better, but in reality as we grew, we continually improved our quality in almost every aspect of our operation, and in fact, being small has its challenges for a complex and involved process such as brewing. Trying to produce a consistent product, batch after batch, utilizing agricultural products that change from year to year and from field to field is not easy. Brewers have to rely on good hygiene, quality control, and plant design, especially to go down our path of shunning pasteurization. The majority of beer produced in this country and, for that matter, in the world is pasteurized, not because beer will make you sick, but to destroy bacteria that may cause off or unpleasant flavors. Some purists (I fall into that category) do not generally believe in pasteurization for beer, viewing it as a crutch for technically deficient or lazy brewers and as unnecessary if you pay attention to your yeast and the cleanliness of your plant. This is a bold statement and one that requires you put your money and focus where your mouth is. Quality failures can be disastrous, which is why many brewers have opted to go the safe route of pasteurization.

---

[6]Almost 20 years later some of these puzzles remain in operation, and my staff occasionally struggles to unravel, often without drawings.

Do I think less of them as brewers? No, not necessarily, but a number of small brewers utilized pasteurization because they could not keep on top of cleanliness or had plants that were not capable of producing clean beer. For brewers operating in old plants that don't have the luxury of modern hygienic equipment or buildings, where the task of producing clean, unpasteurized beer would present a costly, if not impossible, challenge, it is understandable that they require pasteurization to get a quality product to market. They may be great passionate brewers but just can't overcome the obstacles. I have wondered if the decision to install a pasteurizer is an indicator that a good company is turning the corner from being a true small craft brewer, connected and in touch with their beer and their consumer, to running their operation more as a factory, turning out a mass-produced product. I am sure that many of my peers will take offense to my stance on pasteurization and disagree with me, but Sierra Nevada proves that it's possible to brew consistently great beer without relying on sterile filtration or pasteurization. It's incredibly tough to do, but it can be done. I once had a brewer from a large brewery ask me how I slept at night because Sierra Nevada didn't use a pasteurizer. In truth, I haven't slept that well for the past 30 years, although not owning a pasteurizer is pretty far down the list of things that keeps me awake at night.[7]

Growth and cash flow allow you to choose where you want to invest. In some cases owners may prefer not to keep investing and take resources out of the company; after all, isn't that why you're in business, to make money? What drove me and many others into the business was the desire to make great beer. Sure, I was a businessperson, too, and realized making a profit was essential to my ability to brew beer for a living, but I was not enticed into the industry based on profit motive. Don't get me wrong; breweries can be very profitable,

---

[7]The current wave of aging beer in wood poses another challenge to beer quality. The reuse of wine, brandy, and scotch barrels lends beer interesting flavors, but invariably these porous surfaces harbor a multitude of unwanted microfilaria. In sour beer styles these organisms might be desired, but either way they may require flash pasteurization to render the beer stable. We've recently added barrel-aged beers to our portfolio and with our emphasis on quality, we've found it necessary to utilize flash pasteurization on these limited runs.

especially when you get some critical mass, but whatever size you are, breweries require a staggering amount of money to run and maintain. How ownership and management address the many demands for financial resources is key to long-term survival for the company and brands. It's a little like the nest of hatchlings that need to all be fed— even if one screams louder, Mom has to try to keep them all nourished before the worms run out. For me, continuing to invest in our beer and its quality whether it be through equipment for our labs, improving infrastructure or, more recently, in marketing and brand support, was never a question. Running a brewery requires balancing competing demands and understanding their short- and long-term consequences and how they impact the values of the company. Many of these seemingly small decisions were critical and set the stage for failure or success.

9

THE TIME OF TROUBLES

Many battles have been fought and won by soldiers nourished on beer.

—Frederick the Great

In 1988, Sierra Nevada was finally making enough profit that Paul and I began drawing a little bit more salary, at least enough to live on, but for all our time and investment, we were still not taking home much money. Anything extra went back into the brewery. In 1989 and 1990, with continual construction at the brewery taxing all our finances, we both drew a bare-bones salary. Early on, we had established a profit-sharing and 401(k) plan for all employees. When money was tight, Paul and I opted out of the plan so that we could afford to fund it for our employees. Even with better cash flow and the ability to borrow, the constant need to expand strained our resources.

In 1992, we decided to buy back company shares to rectify the fragmented ownership that limited finances had forced us into when we established Sierra Nevada. I approached my grandfather and asked him if he would be willing to sell his shares back to me. We worked out a note with a modest down payment and monthly payments thereafter. A little while later I arranged to purchase my father's shares as well.

Paul tried to buy out his family's shares, but they didn't want to sell. My frustration with Paul's lack of efforts was mounting, and his family's unwillingness to sell their shares only made the situation worse. By that time, Steve Harrison was much more involved in charting the direction of the company and was more invested in Sierra Nevada's success than Paul, who seemed to be just along for the ride. Paul voiced his disapproval or at least unease with the growing size and complexity of the business, and although he was never very outgoing, he was becoming more withdrawn and reserved. I couldn't ignore the situation anymore because we needed to build additional warehouse space, which required buying additional land and borrowing significantly more money. I wasn't keen on having more debt *and* the majority of the workload until I knew what Paul was going to do. I had repeatedly asked him about his retirement and exit plans. He acknowledged that he wasn't as involved as Harrison or I were, but at the time he said he was comfortable with his role and was too young to retire and didn't know what else he'd do. I was receiving almost twice the compensation he was, which in the scheme of things wasn't a lot of money, and continuing to compensate him despite his diminishing involvement didn't feel right to me. We didn't have an adversarial relationship at that time, but he was certainly aware of my feelings and frustration about the state of affairs.

Eventually, I got more serious about pushing Paul for his exit plan, and we started discussing a sale of his shares. We had kicked around some ballpark values and arrived at general terms that we both believed would be fair and would hopefully allow me to borrow what I would need from a bank. At the beginning, Paul's plans to separate from the company weren't malicious—he had helped build the company and wanted to see it succeed—but he also wanted enough compensation to be financially secure, which was understandable. Unfortunately the situation was complicated by his sister's and mother's retention of their shares, forcing their involvement in our negotiations. They didn't have the same emotional connection to the company or its employees and saw it more as an investment to maximize for their benefit than a labor of love.

In October 1993, Paul told me he had hired an advisor, someone he had met in the Bay Area, to help us negotiate the sale of his shares. Before the meeting, Paul and I had established a target price range, and I had been making plans with that in mind. We all met in our corporate attorney's office in downtown Chico. The meeting didn't go well. Paul's advisor was not there as a neutral party to facilitate an amicable deal, even though he introduced himself as a mediator for Paul and I to finalize our split. Within a few minutes, it was evident that the level of open discussion and cooperation we had previously enjoyed was gone. In our attorney's office, Paul said he was willing to sell but thought he needed more money and announced a proposed value higher than we had agreed upon. The amount was more than I was able to come up with, but it wasn't outrageous; I was willing to consider it to finalize the deal. Paul and his advisor stepped out of the room to talk. When they returned, Paul's advisor told me that he was now in charge of the process and whatever Paul had agreed to was off the table. After the meeting our corporate attorney said he couldn't advise me because he represented the company. He recommended that I find my own attorney. It was obvious that we were in for a battle.

LEGAL JOUSTING

I retained the services of another Chico attorney, and we—the corporate counsel, Paul, his advisor, his personal lawyer, my lawyer, and I—arranged to meet again. This set the stage for what would be nearly four years of bitter deliberations and legal jousting. It was one of the most difficult and stressful periods in Sierra Nevada's history and tested every bit of our patience, drive, and will.

Being 50 percent equal owners certainly had its challenges, but what's more, it prevented one party from being able to take the company in a direction the other half didn't want to go. When we couldn't agree on a direction, the result was an impasse. During our protracted separation, Sierra Nevada continued to grow, and our partnership terms required that the value be split evenly. Because Paul was rarely coming to work and not contributing meaningfully when he did show up, I requested another increase in salary to compensate me for running the brewery almost singlehandedly, but my requests were rebuffed or ignored. After waiting months for approval or at least his willingness to discuss it, I told him I was going to take a salary increase anyway. Of course, that prompted the next round of legal escalation, with Paul's team threatening to take me to court. My local attorney was not a litigator; it seemed like we might end up in front of a judge or even possibly a jury, so with his input I decided to beef up my legal team and hired a large, high-profile law firm that had an office in Sacramento. Paul's team finally agreed to meet to discuss my compensation, and we decided that I would receive almost four times Paul's salary. It was a significant difference but a small consolation because by working tirelessly to grow the business, I was also adding greater value to his stock than to my salary increase.

After Paul's father's death we worked on a valuation methodology and a new buy-sell agreement, but unfortunately it was not completely vetted or in effect when the negotiations for the buyout of Paul's and his family's shares began. Paul and his family weren't in a hurry to make decisions about the brewery because as long as it was growing steadily, its value continued to increase significantly. We now spent months debating hiring an appraisal firm while the attorneys postured over how the valuation of the brewery should be tied to a possible sales price because neither side wanted to be bound to accepting a value they didn't like.

Not until 1995 did we finally receive the valuation, and both sides tried to make their case as to why it was flawed: in Paul's case, why it should be raised, and in mine, why it was inflated. Either way, it was significantly more than we had been discussing internally and factored in continued growth at least up to the plant's capacity, which with some additional investment was projected to be close to 250,000 barrels per year. Because the business was still growing and craft brewing across the country was on the rise, we got the sense that they were in no hurry to settle. Why would they want to sell now that the company's value continued to increase with little or no effort from Paul?

More than a year went by with little forward movement. The situation grew increasingly contentious as I continued to build value for the other owners. With litigation one of the few options left, my attorneys and I discussed going to court and asking for the dissolution of the corporation to split up the assets—essentially, the nuclear option. Going down that path would be a big gamble and would certainly hurt our value and momentum. Because of the nature of the negotiations, I had to limit what information I could share with my staff, and I tried my best to keep the ongoing deliberations out of the press. Public battles are never good for morale or supplier, distributor, and consumer confidence, but we also thought having this on the table might help Paul's team focus more seriously on finding a mutual path forward and completing a transaction. Besides being costly, the legal jousting was slow and contentious. Still, I remained reluctant to go to court because the outcome was so uncertain, and I wasn't prepared to possibly lose the brewery.

CONTINUED GROWTH

Despite all the friction and distractions, the business continued to grow at a double-digit rate. At that point, we could have sold the business for a nice sum, but I loved what I was doing and was committed to Sierra Nevada. I continued to work diligently on building the business and adding incremental capacity. I was deep in the planning stages of a new brewhouse, essentially adding on an entire new brewery because the current infrastructure was rapidly approaching maximum capacity.

By September 1995, the output from the 100-barrel German brewhouse was reaching its limit. I had added an additional mash tank and was working on adding another wort-holding vessel to get us up to eight brews per day, up from the original two-brew limit the brewhouse was designed for. But even with that increase, at our current growth rate, we would run out of capacity within a year.

Designing and installing a new brewhouse would cost close to $30 million and take 18 to 24 months to complete. It would be by far the largest capital project to date for Sierra Nevada. Paul and I had spent a few million dollars when we opened the 20th Street brewery in 1987, but this new project would be 10 times the scale. The new brewhouse would be added onto the west side of the existing brewery and would ultimately get Sierra Nevada up to 600,000 barrels from the original 60,000 barrels. The alternative was rationing or limiting growth. With many of our peers fighting hard for growth, it just didn't seem prudent to put the brakes on now, especially because we were experiencing an increase in demand with little effort.

The addition of a strained partnership that came with a group of attorneys who looked over my shoulder and questioned my decisions complicated the process. I prepared documents that explained the project and provided a financial analysis to build a pretty compelling case for the expansion.

The plan essentially called for building an entire new brewery with a new brewhouse, boilers, refrigeration, and packaging hall. We needed a more state-of-the-art and labor- and energy-efficient operation rather than continuing to cobble used equipment and parts together. In the past, I was able to do most of the projects without any shareholder input, but now I had to get the approval from Paul's group when making any substantial decisions or investments. For such a large undertaking, I needed all the stockholders to agree to the significant debt the expansion plan would entail. They understood that a capacity-constrained company was worth a lot less than one that was poised for growth. It was obviously in everyone's best interest to approve the plans because it didn't look like we were going to resolve the partnership situation any time soon.

My projections were accurate and by 1996, we were starting to stress the entire plant. I started implementing the major plant expansion plan. If we didn't start construction soon, we would be unable to meet demand in under a year, so they approved the plan. I set about juggling the challenges of designing the major expansion.

The negotiations for Paul's exit strategy also continued to drag on. Since Paul's team hadn't accepted the appraisal price offering the highest value for Paul's family's shares they were pushing for other options, including taking the company public or selling to a large domestic brewer. They were trying to get me to take the company public or sell out because they were aware of the high valuations of some recent transactions. Pyramid Brewery had gone public, and Redhook Brewing and Widmer Brothers Brewing had sold a portion of their companies to Anheuser-Busch for a significant amount. One of the benefits they thought they would get, selling equity to a larger national brewer, would have allowed them to plug into a national distribution network almost immediately. But sales either hadn't panned out or eventually faltered without the synergies necessary to make the acquisitions work for these small breweries. In addition to these possible pitfalls, I worried that selling any portion of Sierra Nevada to a big corporation would be viewed negatively by our customers and fans. Also, being in the fold of a major brewing company would take a lot away from the independent nature of who I was and what I had accomplished. The few people I knew who had taken their small companies public counseled me that it was the worst decision they'd ever made. But even more than that: As far as I was concerned, going public was off the table—I didn't want to work for or run a public company and refused even to consider it.

Running a public company often drives you to think about short-term returns rather than long-term vision. It is much more difficult to be a leader in a business that out of necessity is almost totally driven by the bottom line and much tougher to follow your heart because you'd have to satisfy analysts and shareholders on a quarterly report card. If you run a public company, it's your fiduciary responsibility to maximize value for your shareholders, so you can face opposition to initiatives outside that focus. Investing in solar energy, CO_2 recovery, vegetable gardens, or other marginally cost-effective technologies wouldn't be seen as prudent.

After almost three years of legal wrangling, we enlisted a financial group to market the deal for a buyout of Paul's family's shares. I didn't want to sell my shares, so 50% of the company was for sale. Using the group represented movement, so I thought it was the best option. The potential acquirers were limited to a select group of international brewers and the financial markets. Many hours were spent preparing growth scenarios, plant expansion, and operational models. I screened the list of possible international brewers and singled out the ones that I felt had good brewing cachet and wouldn't hurt the brand too much, at least from an image standpoint. I had limited knowledge of how they operated but hoped they would still allow me some autonomy in running the company.

Finding the resources to buy Paul out myself was the final option, but as the negotiations slowly progressed, that became less likely because the brewery's volume had been rapidly increasing; the company's market value had risen from where we had started several years earlier. It was frustrating to know while I was focusing on growing the business, these efforts only served to increase Paul's share value—which would be the funds I'd need to come up with to buy him out. Paul's advisors thought it was improbable that I could ever match the amount they thought a strategic sale would bring. They insisted I take on a financial or strategic partner to give them the profit they were seeking and made a point of forcing me and my attorney to acknowledge that fact in an effort to disabuse me of the notion that I could do the deal myself without an investor or financial partner.

FORWARD MOTION

The mergers and acquisitions group we ultimately hired was affiliated with our bank, so I was comfortable with a few of the principals on the team. They had a base fee but were also working for a percentage of the sale, with bigger returns if they hit a certain price, so they were also motivated to maximize the value to Paul's family. We worked with them on putting out an offering book, a marketing piece that contained industry background and company and brand history with several years of operating performance and five years of future growth scenarios. As expected, agreeing on the contents of the book was another onerous process. From my standpoint, future growth scenarios were highly uncertain. Our current business model was unsustainable and unrealistic in the marketplace with the rapidly growing competitive landscape of craft brewers. Even though we had grown faster than most of our peers, with the least spent on marketing and brand support, it was just a matter of time before we would need to alter our approach. It would be my responsibility to deliver on the projections or potentially lose equity or even my job at the helm of the company I had built, so we had a lot of debate about ongoing costs and future growth scenarios. Our operating margin at the time was close to double that of the few public small breweries we could measure ourselves against, but there were no perfect comparable companies; we each had to make our arguments for growth and cost scenarios.

We finally agreed on an operating model. Paul's side started circulating the book, even though it was supposed to be kept confidential. Word soon leaked out to the industry press and rumors started flying. Interest from foreign brewers was minimal, and fairly quickly it became apparent that the highest offer would come from the financial sector. At the time this avenue seemed preferable to me; at least from a public brand affiliation and association, there was much less baggage with a financial investor. In reality there are probably more operational issues with partners that are strictly in it for the money rather than the beer, but the world of investment banking was all new to me; the only exposure we had had was when we purchased the German brewhouse and needed money for its installation. The craft industry was in the midst of its first surge in popularity, and there had been quite a bit of public financial activity with some acquisitions and initial public offerings (IPOs). The fledgling industry was now viewed as a hot segment; maybe microbrewers would follow the microcomputer industry in providing the next investment windfall.

CONSIDERING PROPOSALS

After several months we had a list of nearly 60 interested companies. By June 1997, we had 21 proposals and from that selected 10 for the next round of due diligence. As part of the deal, some groups had proposed an increased ownership stake for me, which at first blush appeared attractive. It was obviously intended as a means to entice me to favor their offer, but upon further analysis of their proposals, the degree of deliverables and financial leverage required on the company was worrisome, and failure could have resulted in my loss of control and equity. Other proposals diminished my ownership or management role, and even though some were at the top of the estimated value range, I insisted that they be tossed out. What wasn't apparent when we started the process was the amount of leverage each group had planned on saddling the company with. I was aware that most of the deals proposed by the venture groups would involve the brewery assuming some limited debt, but I had wrongly assumed that much of the funding would be provided by the venture group. None of the strategic buyers (brewers or other beverage industry players) indicated they would add debt to the deal, but their offers were well below the average offered by the majority of financial suitors. Paul's group rejected them out of hand because their stated goal was to walk away from the deal with the maximum amount of cash. The beverage industry players didn't like the fact that they wouldn't have a con-trolling position in the brewery because one of the stipulations was that I would remain chief executive officer (CEO); they therefore didn't put forth the highest bids. A few of the strategic offers contained provisions for putting a mechanism in place to buy the balance of my shares, something I wasn't ready to commit to.

The highest offers were heavily leveraged proposals. I was upfront and made my resistance to such a speculative approach well known to everyone. I had always been very conservative when it came to assuming debt; if the market changed for the worse or there was an unforeseen change in our business, I didn't want to have a bank over my shoulder threatening to pull the plug. Their ability to raise capital for the riskier deals they were proposing came with a steep expectation of a high return and disastrous consequences if I didn't perform. At that point, I realized that the direction the deal seemed to be heading in just didn't feel right to me, but we kept going because we had exhausted the other exit scenarios for Paul.

The investment groups chosen reviewed financial and business details and spent time with Harrison and me discussing the industry and getting a better understanding about the company. Because, presumably, I was going to be the successor, it was my responsibility and in my best interest to meet with the interested investors to give them my vision for the future and projected growth strategies. We spent much of June meeting with them, all of whom were engaging and excited about the prospects for our future together. We usually met over dinner in Chico with several key principals from the firms; they were typically from big-city offices in New York, Boston, or Chicago. It was a challenging role for me to play because I had to balance my level of enthusiasm for the future with concerns about delivering the long-term sustained growth and profitability that the proposals were based on.

The changing marketplace was also becoming a concern. The momentum of the craft beer movement was beginning to slow and may have played a part in prompting Paul's group to move more quickly to conclude a transaction before projected growth and valuation of the brewery would be affected. For the past four years, they had been the beneficiary of rapid growth and increasing value, but signs were indicating that growth was now starting to slow. Moreover, much of the company's future value was predicated on continued strong growth, so with softness starting to affect a few small brewers, the future growth scenarios were not looking as promising. So far Sierra Nevada hadn't seen a slowdown in sales, but because we were becoming capacity constrained and had started to ration beer to some markets, it was hard to know exactly how the shift might affect us. We were brewing all out—seven days a week, 24 hours a day with no scheduled downtime or holidays other than Thanksgiving and Christmas. In 1997, we brewed a total of 363 days. Production was still lagging sales, so we continued rationing markets and distribution of some styles of beers in a way that we felt would do the least long-term damage to the brands and company's future. We tried to protect the draft business because we knew we'd lose our placement in pubs and restaurants if we couldn't supply them; once a brewery loses a tap handle, it is generally difficult to get it back. We limited Celebration®️ Ale to certain markets and had an outcry from consumers. A newspaper article told the story of one devoted fan who used his frequent flyer miles to fly from the East Coast to San Francisco and back the same day just to pick up a few cases.

The next round of due diligence took up most of July, with lots of questions and clarifications back and forth. Because we were supposed to conclude the process in a couple of months, I needed to pay close attention to these firms' intentions; soon one of them would be my partner. We had agreed that if the proposals all offered the same value to Paul, it would be my decision who purchased the shares. In almost every case the amount of money being put in by the venture fund was one small component of the total deal, with the majority of funds being borrowed by the brewery; I would have been personally liable for a significant portion. Essentially, I would be putting everything I had on the line and at best would own only roughly 50 to 80 percent of the company. My objection to the degree of leverage sent many groups back to recast a deal with a little more upfront cash, but invariably this approach reduced the return for Paul's group, so it wasn't met with much enthusiasm.

Contrary to my expectations about venture funds, most of the firms assured me that they were in it for the long haul and would be a great partner. Most of these funds had a 6- to 10-year investment horizon and expected large returns on the order of 35 percent annually, achieved in large part by highly leveraging the transaction. They acknowledged that with such a large expected return, many of these types of deals fail. As we evaluated and refined the proposals, the lawyers worked through the tentative sales agreement for whichever company we accepted to acquire Paul's family's shares.

Although I was no longer in direct communication with the other shareholders, I was aware of increasing strife between them. Paul's second marriage had recently fallen apart, and other family members were still hoping for a higher valuation. By this time, most if not all of the family members had retained their own counsel to vie for their fair share. The stock that had been purchased for several thousand dollars was now potentially worth millions.

By August we had a final offer from one of the venture funds that met Paul and his family's financial objectives and seemed to be the best to me. The leverage was slightly lower than many of the other proposals, and I would increase my ownership percentage to 80 percent if I met all the return objectives. I had long been unhappy with Paul's efforts and contributions, but at least I knew what to expect. Accepting the proposed deals meant trading a known partner for an unknown entity. My new partner would potentially be more onerous and demanding than my current one, with greater expectations on the company's performance.

THE CHANGING INDUSTRY CHANGES THE DEAL

By late 1997 the craft industry was struggling, and the lofty valuations of the few public small breweries had plummeted 75 percent from the highs they had hit the previous year. I had mounting concerns about the strength of the industry moving forward, the level of debt, and the almost certainty of being back in the same situation in five to seven years when my new partners wanted out. In September my lawyer notified Paul's advisors that the current proposed deals had too much risk and we could not go through with any of them. With a faltering industry, a heavily leveraged buyout made even less sense to me than when they had originally proposed it. Paul's side had ridden a huge wave that had swept across the brewing industry and that I had helped increase. Now that it was starting to crest and looked like it could come crashing down, they wanted to get out quick. I had the sense that several people involved had already been counting their money, so my stopping the deal at what was essentially the eleventh hour wasn't well received. We had been close to concluding a deal that had been in the works for almost four years. My halting the sale was certainly a blow to their plans. In hindsight, it was probably one of the wisest business decisions I have ever made. Of course, this started another round of accusations and legal posturing. Luckily, I had a very wise attorney who convinced all parties that finding an acceptable resolution to these new developments was preferable to the nuclear option of dissolution or court sale that could have ended in what was left of the company being sold at a fraction of the current value after a drawn-out legal process. Given the level of frustration on the part of all parties at this point, this outcome was a distinct possibility.

Throughout the lengthy legal battle, I came to realize that all of the venture funds had proposed deal structures that included significant leverage with fairly minimal cash infusion. If the projections were conservative enough, they validated that the company could handle the required leverage necessary to retire the debt.

But if they could make it work, why couldn't I? All I had to do was to raise the same amount of capital that the venture groups were going to invest. This would also mean not having to fund another buyout in seven years. My attorney introduced me to a colleague who was experienced in negotiating with banks and who ran a firm that readied companies for sale or to go public. He was well versed in handling all types of financial deals, and besides having contacts, he knew the ins and outs of structuring leveraged deals such as I was proposing to undertake. I was now in a race to come up with a financing package that could match the offer on the table. One option was for Paul's family to carry a note for one-third of the debt. I would raise the majority of the money from the bank, which would loan me only about two-thirds of what was needed. The proposal was received with a lukewarm response, but it was better than further impasse.

The proposed bank's interest rate was high, and there were a lot of conditions that Paul's group would want to impose; my team and I looked for other ways to fund the buyout. We wanted to look for options that gave me a clean break—I didn't want to be scrutinized by Paul's family and to have to justify my actions to them. As with many things in our lives, timing was everything. Unlike the late 1970s, when I tried to raise capital for the original brewery, in 1997, the financial markets were prospering and credit was relatively easy to get.

My advisors had contacted a range of large banks and we had several workable options, but Wells Fargo put a great deal on the table. They would underwrite the entire deal with two different levels of debt—the main loan and a second loan with a slightly higher interest rate, which would be based on the perceived risk. Wells Fargo would be the lead bank, but they would syndicate a portion of the loan to other banks, a practice common on highly leveraged deals in order to lessen the risk. It also meant a higher rate to attract other financial institutions. I had to go through another round of sales presentations to other banks to try to convince them to fund the second tier loan.

I had gotten fairly proficient at pitching investors, but now I had even more at stake. First I had to convince them to loan me the money, and then I had to make sure I performed up to projections and met all the covenants and ratios to avoid defaulting or triggering a higher interest rate. I also had to give a personal guarantee, so everything I owned was now collateral. We finally hammered out a deal with Wells Fargo in March of 1998, concurrent with the new brewhouse getting up to speed. When we got the new brewery up and running, the pent-up demand from the limited production helped us greatly exceed our projections and boosted cash flow, making paying back the loan less daunting. The final month leading up to the purchase was spent poring over hundreds of pages of documentation both for the bank and for Paul's and my buy-sell agreement.

We picked March 12, 1998, as the closing date and started the final countdown. Everyone involved went to my attorney's office in San Francisco to sign the papers. It was a bittersweet moment. I was finally on my own, but the weight of the financial commitment I had just agreed to was all I could think about. When Paul and I started out, I never expected it to end this way. Although my purchase of the company wasn't how anyone had envisioned it ending, the day we finally signed the papers was long overdue and welcomed by all. I was still doing what I loved, but it had come at a high cost in every sense.

10

THE WINCHESTER MYSTERY BREWERY[1]

[I recommend] . . . bread, meat, vegetables and beer.
—Sophocles (on his philosophy of a moderate diet)

The end of the partnership represented an important new chapter not only for me but also for the entire company. After the deal was final, I called all the employees together to announce my purchase of the outstanding shares of the company. For years there had been speculation and rumors, among employees as well as the general public, about the future of Sierra Nevada. Even though the negotiations were supposed to be kept confidential, it was impossible to keep information from leaking out; there was chatter around the brewery and in the trade press. With numerous closed-door meetings and

---

[1]Located in San Jose, California, the Winchester Mystery House is known for being under continuous construction for 38 years without an overall building plan.

visitors parading through the brewery for many months, employees were certainly aware that the situation was finally coming to a head. Confidentiality clauses prevented me from talking freely about what was going on or commenting on speculation, even if I had wanted to.

The past four years had been such a struggle, and now the uncertainty, legal battles, gamesmanship, and acrimony were finally behind us. Telling employees about what had transpired was a catharsis for me. The staff was relieved when I told them that I hadn't sold out or brought in a partner, which almost certainly would have prompted drastic or unwelcome changes. I didn't sense any concern about my sole ownership of Sierra Nevada. Because Paul hadn't been around the brewery for months and hadn't been involved in any significant role for years, there wouldn't be any shift in daily life at the brewery.

Despite all the drama and turmoil finally culminating in the buyout, most of the time I had also been busy planning and building our major plant expansion—the biggest project Sierra Nevada had ever undertaken to date. The start of the project had initially been delayed, in part due to my reluctance to move forward with such a huge endeavor when the future of the company and my role in it was so uncertain, but also because of the objections Paul's family raised to the investment. With the legal battle behind me and a significantly improved and expanded infrastructure we could meet our current, backlogged demand as well as the future growth I hoped for.

We were building essentially an entire new brewery with the required infrastructure except for bottling, which at the time was still adequate to handle some additional volume. We had purchased several acres directly to the west of the brewery, and the project was, and still is, referred to as the West Side. I had already invested more time and money than originally intended on a range of state-of-the-art equipment and technology, as well as splurging on aesthetic details. Because I imagined this would be the last brewery I would ever build, I wanted to make it as spectacular as the finest I had seen anywhere in the world. I had started designing the expansion several years earlier, working closely with engineers, architects, and brewing specialists to make it both a technological and architectural masterpiece. Ideas collected during trips to Europe and around the United States to visit modern and classic plants also fed my vision.

Given the scope of the project and the distraction of the legal battle, I had decided to hire a full-time project manager. Dave Heric was a contractor whom I had worked with on the first phase of the 20th Street brewery; he had a good understanding of the quality and design standards of Sierra Nevada, and I knew he would ensure that they were met. It also helped that we got along well. With almost an entire new plant to build, I would oversee the brewing infrastructure, and Dave would handle the construction of the buildings and facilities. In the early days I had always overseen both sides, first out of necessity and later on because I enjoyed it. I had a solid grasp of brewing and process flows and enough process engineering, refrigeration, and electrical knowledge to know what needed to be done.

Construction on the West Brewhouse started in 1996, but the integration of an entirely new brewhouse into our existing operation wasn't without its challenges. It took more than a year to smooth out the kinks and put the finishing touches on the facility.[2] The West Brewhouse took a lot of stress off the frenetic pace we had been operating at with the single-kettle, 100-barrel East Brewhouse running seven days a week. With the West Brewhouse we had the capacity to produce twelve 200-barrel brews a day, but even with twelve new 800-barrel fermenters, we had fermentation capacity only for about three days' worth of brews and would have to wait until bottling to start a

---

[2]We celebrated our anniversary and the commissioning of the West Brewhouse on November 15, 1998, 18 years after I made my first batch of Sierra Nevada beer. We had a large multiday party for employees, suppliers, and friends of the brewery, including guests from around the country and Europe. Huppmann, the German manufacturer of the brewhouse, arranged for a traditional German chef to travel with them to prepare food for the celebration. I first met the chef on an earlier trip to Germany; he ran a fantastic brewery restaurant that was located in an old castle in the heart of the Hallertau hop-growing region of Germany. With suckling pigs, Leberkäse, and abundant beer, we had a memorable party; it was a fitting celebration for all that we had accomplished.

new brew. Because I had so grossly underestimated the market receptiveness for flavorful beer when I built my original brewery, I designed the West Side to allow growth to reach 1 million barrels per year.

Although overall growth of craft breweries had reached a standstill, which was negatively affecting many of our peers, for us the growth rate was well above my projections. We had seen 50 percent annual growth rates in 1992, 1993, and 1994, but I knew we couldn't expect to continue growing at that rate forever. We dropped to 30 percent in 1995 and 1996 and grew only 14 percent in 1997, in large part because of our capacity constraints. Because we had shorted markets in years prior and hadn't aggressively tried to increase distribution at the sake of compromising quality with the new brewhouse operational, we experienced a period of significant growth. The growth of the craft segment as a whole slowed to nearly zero annual growth at the end of 1997, but with the addition of the West Side, Sierra Nevada saw growth of nearly 30 percent in 1998.

Once the brewhouse was up and running, we had to look at the downstream infrastructure to match our larger output. I started working on a plan to install another fermentation cellar with 10 more 800-barrel tanks, a big project that would typically take around a year-and-a-half barring any major snags with permitting or equipment suppliers. We had a lot to do as far as adding additional equipment and buildings to handle the almost 200,000 additional barrels that the West Side cellars afforded us, but thanks to my optimistic thinking, we acquired enough adjoining real estate for my big plans.

By the first year after we completed the West Side, I started thinking about the next phase of expansion. After coming off a year of rationing in 1997, the following years saw sales growth of 28 percent, or almost 100,000 barrels. We were growing fast enough that we needed to start planning our next steps, but I had to temper my vision with the reality that I was heavily leveraged; if our trends followed the industry trends our growth would also slow down. I had plenty of sleepless nights those first few years after the buyout, wondering if our growth trends were going to slow down and how I'd keep the company afloat if they did.

NEW BREWERY, OLD HABITS

Even though we had built a new brewery, we were still operating much the same way as we had at Gilman Way—build just enough to meet demand, and then stretch it to the limit before adding more. Over the past 18 years, Sierra Nevada had managed to grow steadily without taking the conventional approach of sales and promotions to sell our beer. Sierra Nevada was a production-focused brewery from the very beginning, not a market-driven one. We brewed what we loved to drink and it sold; obviously our model had worked well for many years.

Our growth was truly organic and fueled by word of mouth. Free publicity was the only media coverage we received, and we had no outside public relations company. Other than placing a few ads in our local free newspaper, we had no media budget at all.

The fact that we had a minimal sales force and lacked any sales or marketing plans hadn't hindered us so far, so it wasn't an area we focused on improving. I wasn't so naïve that I didn't recognize that our business model had flaws, though, and I knew we couldn't expect it to last much longer. For many years I left overseeing the sales operations up to Steve Harrison and focused on making beer and expanding production. I often struggled to keep production ahead of sales, so ramping up or changing our sales strategy didn't really seem warranted or even prudent when we had steadily seen double-digit sales growth for 10 years.

Harrison, who had started out at Sierra Nevada driving the delivery van, was managing our small sales force, and he wholeheartedly embraced our bootstrapping ways. As Sierra Nevada's first employee, he experienced our many years of struggle and learned to keep tight reins on any unnecessary spending in his jurisdiction of marketing and sales. He stood by that mentality his entire career. Harrison was often referred to as Mr. No by members of the sales force because any promotion or hiring request was usually met with the singular word "no" or sometimes "hell no" if it involved spending much money.

In 1992, almost 12 years after we had started the brewery, when we were producing 68,000 barrels annually, we hired our first outside salesperson, Steve Oliver. Steve had worked at one of our distributorships and had been selling our beer for years. He traveled the country, meeting and signing up new distributors that were interested in carrying our brand. We really didn't have a comprehensive or methodical rollout or distribution plan. Because we had no field support, no one from the brewery visited the market or distributors other than an occasional visit from Harrison or Steve and occasionally me when I happened to be traveling on business. We were growing so rapidly without a sales force calling on stores that it didn't make sense to hire any more salespeople, so we didn't add anyone additional until we hit a production level of over 150,000 barrels. Some of our competitors hired something like one salesperson for every 5,000 barrels they produced. We had one person covering the entire United States, and we were selling 150,000 barrels! We unrealistically told ourselves that our beer was so great we didn't need a big sales department. Although certainly not ideal for our brand or distribution partners, somehow it worked and was part of the reason we could fund our plant expansion internally.

We had added a few people over the years only as necessary, and by 2004, we were selling more than 500,000 barrels a year with a sales force of fewer than 15 people, with no formal training systems in place to support that staff. Steve knew we would have to address this. As we grew he often came to me and discussed the need to increase our sales staff and training, but we were both reluctant to make a significant change to how we operated; it was easy to put off the additional investment it would take. We had come a long way on a shoestring, and building a big, sales-focused department would have been a significant departure for us. Most of our salespeople came to us from our beer distributors. They typically had a street-level background doing sales or deliveries, which was great for calling on bars and restaurants, but we also needed people with a higher level of experience to present and develop business plans and formulate sales metrics, something we had never done. Given the importance of a strong and well-supported sales force in the competitive world of beer sales, we had a lot of catching up to do.

During the years of rapid growth, we started discussing our national distribution and both the financial and environmental realities of operating out of a single California brewery. Initially, when the West Coast was responsible for the vast majority of our sales, it wasn't a significant concern, but as our growth rate started picking up in faraway markets and during periods when fuel prices were in flux, transportation costs started to have a meaningful impact on our profitability.

In the late 1990s, the wholesale and distribution channels were generally receptive to our beers, so we managed to expand into new markets with little to no sales support. It was risky in terms of long-term success, but Harrison believed that the window of easy growth would close soon. He believed we'd be better off seeding these new markets to establish a beachhead to build off of. Plus, every additional barrel sold generated a little more profit to help retire the debt.

With growth from just a few hundred barrels to almost 500,000 in 20 years, we had accomplished, to our knowledge, something no one else in the United States, and possibly the world, had done—building a brewery and a brand from scratch with that kind of success and growth rate.

Even with the proliferation of the craft industry, craft breweries made up less than a few percent of the US beer market, and there were plenty of instances when we were painfully aware that we truly were a very small fish in a tank full of predators. In 1999, we joined the ranks of other craft brewers experiencing a decline in growth rates and fell back to 14 percent growth. The following year would be our last double-digit growth year for many years. In 2001, we grew only 8.5 percent, and although less than double-digit growth rates were foreign to us, it wasn't so much alarming as it was a bit of a relief. After the many years of stressful negotiations and then pushing hard to grow enough to reduce the smothering debt, a little slowdown was welcomed, and I could take a breather. We had spent years with our heads down, cranking away with a singular focus—how to meet next week's, next month's, and next year's growth demands. We had long anticipated that someday the market for hoppy, bottle-conditioned beer would hit a ceiling; we thought that as we started to catch up with demand, our growth would naturally slow.

AN INDUSTRY EVOLVED

In 2002, we had only 5 percent growth. The craft industry landscape was evolving rapidly; no longer were we one of a small handful of craft brewers putting out unique and memorable beers. Now there were hundreds of great little breweries popping onto the scene, offering consumers a variety of beer styles. A few had significant financial backing and oftentimes a much more aggressive approach to marketing, but many were just like us with a great story and passion for beer.

At the same time that craft breweries were experiencing robust growth, imported beers were losing some of their luster as high-end growth, and the spotlight was focused on craft brewers. In response many imports refocused their efforts and sharpened their message. Major American brewers who didn't like all of the press craft beer had received as the darlings of the US brewing industry also started fighting back with copycat branding and aggressive tactics to limit our distribution options and prevent us from garnering shelf space. The landscape was getting more crowded, and breweries resorted to all sorts of tactics, some legal and some not. We heard stories of breweries offering bars televisions or an enticement of elaborate European junkets in exchange for replacing a craft beer tap with another of their brews. Even so, the big brewers welcomed our innovation and the excitement we brought into the marketplace because craft beer opened the eyes of many consumers and food writers about the interesting and diverse world of beer. Thanks to craft brewers, American beer became known as some of the best in world, helping to disprove the idea that all American beer is a watered-down, bland interpretation of what real beer should be.

The big American brewers didn't like being left out of the conversation, though, so they began copying craft brands. In some cases they came directly at Sierra Nevada, mimicking our bottle, ingredients, and brand attributes with large, well-oiled marketing machines to help them execute their strategies. In 2006, in an episode of National Broadcasting Company (NBC)'s *Dateline*, one of the major brewers exposed the well-obfuscated fact that big brewers produced beer for some of the so-called craft brewers who didn't have their own plants but operated virtual breweries and contracted out the production of 100 percent of their beer. The unmasking only furthered the decline of the craft industry. Contract brewers, particularly Pete's Wicked Ale and Boston Beer Company, were affected the most by the major breweries' tactics. The slowing sales trends also affected them more than the rest of us because they had larger targets on their backs and a hard time defending their authenticity.

As the growth rates of many of the more established craft brewers declined, those who had made big bets or were already marginally profitable took more desperate measures with increased discounting and at times less-than-above-board trade practices to avoid the slump. Sierra Nevada was increasingly disadvantaged in the marketplace and was being attacked on all fronts. I often told Harrison that if our growth rates declined, and we had to make a choice, I would rather have slow profitable growth than squander all of our profit chasing sales and have nothing to show for it like some of the other craft breweries. Big brewers capitalized on our industry's uncertain position and redoubled their efforts. Not only were we facing the challenges of a depressed market, but we also hadn't created the framework to support our meager sales and marketing staff. We were feeling pressure from our distribution partners, who wanted us to develop programs like coupons, discount scans, and promotional tie-ins like large brewers and many increasingly desperate small brewers.

Even with all of the challenges, we were still growing at a decent clip, but our momentum was starting to decline in some of our most established markets. Still, we didn't panic because we were well ahead of our growth projections, had paid down a big chunk of our loans, and now had a good financial buffer, so we didn't need to emulate the desperate strategies some of the other brewers were employing to maintain volume. For years, I had been adamant about not wanting to alter our business model drastically; we stuck with what we knew, though in the back of my mind, I was concerned about our long-term future if we didn't invest in some significant level of sales and marketing.

As we saw the craft market trends slow down, we started discussing its impact on our business more seriously. We knew that a declining beer brand is a difficult, if not impossible trend to reverse and that managing a shrinking brewery takes an enormous financial and emotional toll. I had attended the Brewers Association of America meetings since the early 1980s and witnessed the fairly rapid demise of most of the remaining small and regional legacy breweries. I was starting to see history repeat itself in the craft industry with the same warning signs of declining sales, inability to reinvest, limited brand support, and reduction of employee numbers and compensation. The psychological pallor of the steady death spiral that some brands succumbed to affected the morale of not only everyone in those companies but everyone throughout the whole industry as well.

To prevent Sierra Nevada from joining their ranks, we acknowledged the need to ramp up the sales force. With a patchwork of brokers and spotty sales coverage in the rest of the country, we had a lot of holes to fill and a lot of ground to make up. Our initial, and somewhat feeble, strategy was to add sales reps in a few key markets slowly, but we were still growing fast enough to require me to continue to add production infrastructure to meet demand. Therefore, I didn't have an extreme sense of urgency to make dramatic changes to our sales and marketing structure. Both areas required financial and personal resources, but for the time being, I was more comfortable spending my money on brewing equipment than sales programs.

I knew at some point we would need to focus more on the sales, but I was concerned that transitioning from a strictly production-focused company to one that focused on sales would greatly affect our company culture and operating philosophy. As we moved forward building the company and brand, I felt finding the correct balance between being production focused and building a more robust sales team would be critical. We had garnered legions of loyal followers without ever spending a penny on national ads or commercials. We had evangelists ranging from beer geeks to Grateful Dead followers. These fans were drawn to our beer not only for its uniqueness and flavor but also for our focus on quality over marketing or slick advertising. Because we hadn't succumbed to the trends toward discounting, a large sales force, or aggressive marking, I was able to build up a small buffer of money, enabling us to fund more expansion projects out of cash flow. The handwriting was on the wall, though. The marketplace had changed and our company had changed; if we didn't focus and invest in our brands we would ultimately fail.

11

FORK IN THE ROAD

A meal of bread, cheese and beer constitutes the perfect food.
—Queen Elizabeth I

I had been so accustomed to the company growing easily with a hands-off approach toward marketing that I had difficulty imagining myself as the person who would change that philosophy. We knew we needed to change directions fairly soon, or it could be too late. We debated industry analysts' theories that beer brands have life cycles that mirror generations—who drinks Dad's beer anyway? We didn't know if our original customer base was still relevant as we approached having been around for at least one generation. A younger demographic tends to drink the most beer, including craft beer. If we retained only our loyal following of original drinkers without attracting younger drinkers, we'd be doomed in the long run. Perhaps we weren't in the same league as most beer brands, though. After all, we had accomplished what almost nobody else had, building a national brand with a homebuilt brewery and almost no marketing effort, so maybe we were an anomaly and immune to the traditional market dynamics of the brewing industry.

Being at the helm of a rapidly growing company required me to make hundreds, possibly thousands, of critical decisions every week. The unrelenting pace had taken a toll, and I didn't have many places to turn to for business support. Truthfully, I was starting to get a little burned out; nearly 25 years of more than full-time focus, pressure, and responsibility had taken a lot out of me.

Sierra Nevada had a flat management structure—a result of our production-focused organization. I had a core group of long-term employees, many of whom had been with me for years. When we started out, we had such limited financial resources that we couldn't pay very much. The people who were attracted to working at the brewery stayed because they loved what we were doing and it was a fun place to work; they certainly weren't there for the money. Most of the people who stuck it out eventually rose through the ranks and became department heads. No one was originally hired for his or her management abilities, and some were more adept than others at developing their own skills. After more than 20 years, we started to bring in resources and tools to help our managers deal with evolving job responsibilities and transitioning from production positions to management positions focused on developing people. Not everyone made the transition; we had some longtime, dedicated staff members who had done a lot to help us build the company who didn't make it. I had to make some very difficult and gut-wrenching decisions and part ways with some bright and valuable employees, but I felt I had to do it for the benefit of the team.

For some time Harrison and others on my senior management team had been discussing the need to take a good hard look at the business—our current management structure, long-term goals for ourselves, and the long-term future of the company. For so many years we had all been working *in* the business, but now it was time to start working *on* the business.

As we worked to position ourselves for the next 20 years, Harrison came to me and said he was getting to a point in his life when he thought he was ready to make a change. He suggested we start talking about his succession plan. Harrison had been with me from day one and poured his heart and soul into the brewery. In the beginning, he had been the first and for many years had been the only person driving our sales growth and, like the rest of us, he had accomplished a great deal with no formal training or industry experience. His gut instinct, passion, and work ethic were vital to our early success; without him playing the role he did, we probably wouldn't have achieved what we did. More than 20 years later, he didn't feel he had the drive, desire, or expertise to help take the company to the next level. He didn't want to do anything that would damage what we had built and promised to help in whatever way he could during the transition.

I had invested everything I had to get to this point, placing several all-in bets. I had beaten the odds, but maybe my luck would soon run out. We were at a crossroads. With Harrison's desire to lead a less stressful life, I had to make some big decisions about the next phase for Sierra Nevada. Weighing the options for the future of the company, I agonized over the best direction for the brewery. I now had hundreds of employees and their families depending on me for their livelihood, so I had to think about their futures as well as my own.

Harrison and I discussed the situation, and we agreed that the timing might be right for both of us to leave the company. I contacted Peter, my business attorney who had helped broker the deal with Paul, and confided to him what we were thinking. I still hadn't decided that I was going to part ways with Sierra Nevada, but I thought I would at least explore the idea and its implications. Katie was supportive of whichever direction I chose, but because I didn't want rumors to start, I couldn't discuss my thoughts with anyone else. It wasn't a decision that I could approach lightly. Although we had grown faster than the entire craft industry for years, we had a big wakeup call in 2003 with only 1.4 percent growth when the industry was up 3.4 percent. The next year the craft industry started to improve even more and was up about 7 percent, but we didn't rebound with the rest of the pack and started losing share in the market for the first time. The business was truly at a crossroads.

PROJECT OCEAN

I had regularly been approached by investors over the years, so I knew there was interest out there. I got in touch with two financial advisors (one of whom I had known from my dealings with Paul) with the strict agreement that they wouldn't disclose anything until I decided what direction I would take. Several meetings with two different financial groups followed. One was a larger group that had managed a wide range of transactions, marketing mainly family-owned companies to primarily strategic buyers as opposed to financial buyers like I had sought out before. I also met with a small boutique firm that was started by one of the bankers I had dealt with during my buyout of Paul and his family. He had followed the craft brewing industry out of curiosity and with the hope of getting involved in another deal. We had stayed in touch, and although he lacked the experience of the more established firm, he was fairly well connected in the brewing community.

After some discussion with both teams, I decided to have them join forces to represent me if I decided to move forward and sell the company because they each brought something different to the table. The project was dubbed Project Ocean because of my desire to buy a house on the coast when I retired.[1] I also spent time with my advisors and attorney discussing how to compensate my key employees and managers during any potential sale. They had been integral to our success, and I wanted to put a plan in place that would guarantee an employment contract or a soft landing for anyone who didn't make the cut or wanted out.

---

[1]For years I have loved scuba and free diving, and I thought that leaving Sierra Nevada would give me more time to spend under water. One nice benefit of diving is that it's hard for your mind to wander back to thoughts of work because of the focus the activity requires and the foreign environment that occupies most of your consciousness. It also helps that no one has yet figured out how to make a cell phone that works under water.

As opposed to when I bought Paul out, I didn't think a financial investor was what I was looking for this time. Besides the fact that I was planning on retiring the day I signed the papers, I didn't think I could face the notion of working for anyone else. Plus, facing all our loyal employees after selling out, so to speak, would have been unbearable. Convincing a financial buyer to pay a competitive price when the founder and chief executive officer (CEO) would be leaving the next day wasn't going to be easy sell, though. The advisors weren't so keen on my intention to walk away the day the deal was done, not that it was a nonstarter, but they felt that it might be an issue with certain buyers and limit our opportunities. At this point, I didn't care if I had to take a discounted price for the possible lack of continuity in management because I didn't think I could bring myself to stick around if I wasn't in control.

While contemplating my retirement, I happened to pick up a book written by Gary Erickson, the founder of Clif Bar & Company, that chronicled his struggle with the direction of his company at a similar point in his life. His story was similar to mine, with a troubled partnership and the near sale of his company to a major industry player. He changed his mind at the absolute last minute and walked away from signing over his company and had since rededicated himself to it. I had met him a few years earlier when we sponsored a bike team together, but I hadn't been in touch since. As I was struggling with my decision, his story hit close to home.

The more I thought about it, the tougher it was for me to move forward with the plan. I had been entirely invested for so long; how could I just walk away? When I told my kids what I was thinking, they were aghast. At the time, Sierra was 27, Carrie was 23, and Brian was 19. I hadn't pressed any of them to work at the brewery as they were growing up, and although they all did stints in various departments as summer employment, none of them pursued studies for brewing or business. They all gravitated toward public services instead. I knew all too well how tough my business was to run, and unless they were as passionate about it as I was, it would not have been a fun or successful livelihood. They were shocked that I would consider selling the brewery; it had always been a part of their lives. The general feeling was that they wanted to be a part of the decision process and have the chance to be involved in the future of Sierra Nevada. After my revelation, they made it clear that they saw the brewery as part of their futures and started making plans for how they'd fit into the company.

Their vehemence and my reluctance sealed the deal—I couldn't sell Sierra Nevada. I never got into the brewery business to make a lot of money. I got into it because I love brewing. I love solving problems. I love being my own boss. My personal future may have been different from what I had imagined a few months before, but with renewed energy, I set about preparing for our future. I called up the financial groups and told them I was canceling Project Ocean.

Sierra Nevada didn't need a complete makeover but did need some added focus on areas we had been neglecting. We built one of the best breweries in the world; we just needed to do a better job of telling our story. We also needed to add employees, develop systems, and build skills. I knew it would take time and money, not to mention having the right people on board, but we were profitable enough to afford the investment. I didn't want to make any radical changes to who we were or what we stood for; we were brewers first and foremost, and we would always be true to our roots and how we brewed our beer.

REFOCUSING

We started a search for an experienced sales and marketing manager. I wasn't entirely comfortable with the notion of bringing in an outside marketing person and wanted to make sure when we did it they would be the right person for the job, so Harrison agreed to stay on as long as it took. His sense of urgency about retiring had waned a little, so we took our time posting the position and then interviewing candidates. It was a big move for the brewery. We hadn't brought in many outside people to be managers, and our company culture was almost entirely homegrown; most of us had worked side by side for years. This was also going to be one of the most critical hires we had made up to this point. The sales and marketing manager would control a large and rapidly increasing department and budget, as well as set the direction for the future development and evolution of our brands. Like Harrison, this person would help chart Sierra Nevada's course.

The job posting garnered a fairly wide range of applicants, most of whom had worked for larger domestic breweries, distributors, or importers. The pool also included a few Sierra Nevada employees and others from the craft segment, but they lacked the kind of depth and experience we were looking for. We were concerned about how someone from one of the major breweries would fit in our organization, though. Because we're truly a family-run business, our culture has grown organically from those roots. We wanted someone who would appreciate our history and our culture and understand who we were, and I knew I didn't want anyone who would dramatically alter Sierra Nevada.

At just about the same time, we were approached by Joe Whitney, who had worked in the craft industry in sales and marketing roles for close to 20 years at both Boston Beer Company and New Belgium Brewing Company. Having directly competed against us for years, he knew our brands well and understood the craft segment intimately. Most importantly, the fit felt right and we quickly decided we had found the right person.

Joe quickly realized he had a lot of work ahead of him. Aside from our small number of sales people and rudimentary training, we also had only basic systems to track sales data, limiting our ability to analyze trends and performance by market. For almost 30 years, Harrison had done a great job with his instincts and gut feelings, but we had known for some time that it wasn't sustainable. Joe dove in and started to develop additional structure and training, allowing Harrison to step back and spend more time doing what he wanted away from work.

LOSS OF A FRIEND

As Harrison backed away from his brewery responsibilities over the next several months, he became increasingly stressed. He continued to be involved in production planning, a role he had taken on because it dovetailed so well with sales and forecasting. As we tried to transition this role to another person, he became convinced that he hadn't done enough to establish any systems and had failed Sierra Nevada and me. Over the years Harrison had kept paper records on dozens of yellow pads covered with notes to himself, but mostly he kept everything in his head and did an amazing job balancing our production capacity to sales. He started to second-guess his every decision and, engulfed in a sense of guilt, felt he had let us down because he had nothing to pass on to his successor. We met often and I had nothing but praise for what we had accomplished under his watchful and cautious eye, but he still felt that he hadn't done enough for the brewery.

Harrison started to appear more upbeat and seemed to be working through his issues, but then one day in August 2007, he didn't show up for work. His car was later discovered along an isolated stretch of the Sacramento River, west of town. For days dozens of friends, Search and Rescue personnel, and brewery employees searched for him with specially trained dogs, watercraft, and divers. After nearly a week, Harrison's body was discovered a short distance downstream from his car, trapped under a fallen tree snag. We still don't know exactly what happened. A sense of disbelief and crushing grief engulfed everyone at the brewery. He had been my friend well before I started the brewery and my first employee—it was a devastating loss. Our old neighborhood friend, Tom Hungerford, conducted the funeral service. Both men had known me since my closet brewing days, and even though I had lost other friends, this death hit me the hardest. Not only was he a dear friend, but he was also an integral part of Sierra Nevada, and I thought he'd help guide the next generation of brewery leaders. Harrison's death was the worst thing the brewery has ever been through. At the same time, the entire experience emphasized how much of an extension of our family Sierra Nevada employees are.

12

GERMINATING A WORKFORCE

I am a firm believer in the people. If given the truth, they can be depended upon to meet any national crisis. The great point is to bring them the real facts, and beer.

—Abraham Lincoln

Although it wasn't necessarily practical in our early days, I felt strongly about wanting to build a company with a culture where people would enjoy working. I had worked for a variety of bosses with various approaches to management; most were the kind of boss I never wanted to be. I knew how important it was to work toward creating a place that people could look forward to going to every day.

Like the plant, Sierra Nevada's employee roster has always been on the lean side. I was afraid our meteoric rise could end suddenly, and I didn't want to build or add people before I was assured that we could support them. I watched as a few of my peers in the craft industry overextended themselves, causing irreparable damage to their companies or resulting in the loss of ownership or control; some were forced to lay off part of their workforce, something I hoped never to do. I would rather operate conservatively with a lean workforce than operate with the mentality that if we build it, they will come. In 30 years Sierra Nevada has never laid off an employee because of lack of work.

When we started construction on the new brewery in 1987, I had almost fully transitioned out of the daily demands of running the Gilman Way brewery to focus on construction of the new brewery. In previous years we had developed a loose management structure and had assigned areas of responsibility to several key staff members: Steve Harrison was in charge of sales and warehousing, Steve Dresler took over brewing, and Bob August handled filtration and packaging. Paul's girlfriend and later wife worked part-time, running the office and helping with the books; after they divorced we brought in a part-time receptionist. To say we were lean was an understatement.

With a total head count of 15 people, we knew we had to make plans for a bigger workforce at the new brewery. Going from a 17-barrel brewhouse (expanded from the original 10 barrels) to a 100-barrel brewhouse meant we would need to brew only a few days a week, and we assumed that when we opened the new brewery we would have surplus brewing staff. One of our brewers volunteered to run the pub at the new location, so we sent him to some classes at Butte College to help prepare him. We also found a person with restaurant and bookkeeping skills to head up the office and act as our first part-time human resources director. Even though she wore many hats, it was a momentous hire because she was the first full-time employee not involved in production in any way. We soon became accustomed to hiring nonproduction employees with the opening of our restaurant and pub, a business venture unlike anything we'd done before.

When I was first designing the Pub, which opened in 1989,[1] I envisioned having a tasting room that showcased our beer and served food. It was a big upgrade from Gilman Way, where we used a small

---

[1] It's officially named The Sierra Nevada Taproom and Restaurant; however, employees and locals simply call it the Pub. The shortened term stuck, and if anyone in Chico refers to "the Pub," it's assumed to mean our restaurant.

space in one of the metal warehouses as our tasting and hospitality center. It was embarrassingly crude, with removed van seats providing seating and décor comprising a few posters on the plywood and metal walls. In the dingy space, we gathered for an afternoon beer or to share samples with the handful of people who sought us out or stumbled upon our cluster of tin sheds—hardly a great brand-building image or experience. As with many things as we developed our business, we had no clue about running a pub or restaurant, but as was my style we just jumped in with both feet. Hell, we had been running a successful brewery; how hard could it be?

Salary and compensation were only part of the equation, but from the very beginning, we knew that without enough money to live on, it was going to be tough to meet people's basic needs, and we would continue to lose the talent we needed to survive. Early on, no one made much money because every penny we made needed to be reinvested to cover the basic financial needs of running the business. Paul and I were barely pulling in any income, and during lean months we had to skip or delay paying ourselves to cover payroll. Even when we sacrificed our salaries, we always managed to pay our employees on time. It was a matter of principle for us.

The only way we were going to be able to provide a decent living for our employees and for ourselves was to increase the volume of beer we produced so that we could fulfill market demand and improve our cash flow. As we started to gain some market traction and add capacity, the cash flow steadily increased, and we were able to increase pay and start adding a few benefits. In 1982, we were able to first offer our employees health insurance and a retirement plan that over the years morphed into a 401(k) plan. It wasn't common for a company of our size to offer those benefits, but we wanted to attract people who would make brewing their career by providing long-term security for our employees. By then, we made the decision to make our salaries more competitive. We still lagged behind the salaries and benefits offered by major breweries, but at least we were no longer paying people a little above minimum wage. Even with our limited budget and frugal tendencies, we wouldn't scrimp on our employees because we couldn't stay in business without them. Improving compensation ensured we wouldn't lose some of our key employees to other breweries or industries and helped attract a wider range of applicants when we had new positions to fill.

Artisan trades, such as brewing, winemaking, cheese making, and baking, conjure up romantic images of sampling delicious products all day long, and sometimes onlookers don't realize the tedious work that goes into creating those products. For me and many others, the lure of working in a brewery, and all that it seemed to imply, was part of the attraction, even if such romantic myths were quickly dispelled. Being a brewer has its rewards, but most of the time it's hard, repetitive work in often hot or cold and wet conditions.

In our early days, brewing beer was very physically demanding. We started the process at 5:00 AM by hoisting 50-pound buckets of grain into the mash tun and stirring the malt in by hand with a canoe paddle. When the mash was done, we shoveled out the 150-degree grain by hand with buckets and scoops. Cleaning fermenting tanks after every batch was also laborious—you had to climb in and manually scrub the tank with strong detergents, scouring pads, and brushes. Our days were often very long and could be unpredictable when a pump or one of our cobbled together, antiquated machines broke down. We had very little automated equipment at first, so every bottle was unloaded and loaded by hand. We didn't have a forklift and relied on a pallet jack or hand trucks to move things around. Who in their right mind would want a job like that?

Out of necessity, the first people I hired did everything. One day the few employees we had would help brew; the next day it was all hands on deck to run the bottling line. I didn't ask anyone to do anything I wouldn't do. We all pitched in. Any time there was a break in the action during the day, the brewer would run up from the brewhouse and pack cases to give the person doing it a break for a few minutes.

We got our share of colorful people stopping by and applying for jobs, so we had little need to advertise when we needed additional staff. Sometimes I hired people on the spot to help out on the bottling line if they happened to come by to ask for a job on a busy day. Several of those early hires stuck with us, and what was probably just a short-term position at the time turned into a career. Some of them are still with us today. Steve Dresler came to us as a homebrewer and had a degree in chemistry and biology; he started working part-time on the bottling line and later became our head brewer, a position he still holds. We hired Steve Johnson as our first warehouseman around the same time. Like all early employees, he worked in various positions at the Gilman Way brewery; he still works in our warehouse today. Although they may not have envisioned that their jobs at Sierra Nevada would lead into careers, they started with us 30 years ago and have been integral in Sierra Nevada's success. None of us could have predicted that this struggling little company would prosper the way it has.

EVERYBODY PITCHES IN

Early on we also attracted a few University of California, Davis, brewing students who came to work for us after graduation. We were competing with the major breweries for recent graduates, and compared with what larger, more established companies were offering, we had little chance or ability to offer a competitive package. Still, a few made the decision to work for our small, fledgling company instead of a major corporation and joined our ranks to be a part of something special. Most of them didn't stick around long; the idea of working for a small brewery sounded better than the reality, and the hard physical labor and makeshift equipment of our primitive plant weren't necessarily what they expected after graduating from Davis with a brewing degree.

Our "everybody pitches in" mentality led to a very flat organizational structure. We've also never put a high value on titles. We don't have vice presidents or layers of management. The employees who were promoted to managers in our early days all worked their way up from production positions and for many years after they were promoted they still spent most of their day with their boots on.

Our flat structure worked well for years, although it certainly had some downsides. In the very beginning, our bench strength remained limited because although we had been able to attract talented applicants, we weren't getting many top-notch brewing graduates or highly skilled candidates. Instead, we got people who wanted to work for Sierra Nevada and were willing to work hard. We were so focused on production that we had little time for training or actively developing employees' skills. Everyone was working *in* the business, including me, and we didn't have time to spend working *on* the business. As a team we were very effective and accomplished a great deal. We weren't necessarily aware of our weaknesses in management and employee development. We were just focused on figuring out how to make enough beer to meet next week's or next month's demand, so nobody gave it too much thought.

Under the constant pressure to increase production, every department faced challenges. Every area was stressed. We battled equipment limitations, staffing shortages, and warehouse and storage constraints. We didn't have the vision, resources, or confidence to do a major expansion of every area at once, so we would put our money and energy into whichever area needed the most attention and was faltering the worst. Of course, our piecemeal method of improvement led to some dissatisfaction and strained resources.

Still, I was most comfortable during those years of solving the problems of growth. It wasn't always easy, but tackling engineering problems was easier for me than addressing people problems. Over the years our turnover rate had been fairly low, but employees were starting to get a bit burned out, particularly those working in brewing and packaging.

Not a Creature was Stirring except for the Brewer

Once you start the brew, it is a living thing. The yeast doesn't know or care about the time of day, and it doesn't sleep until its job is done.

I had made the decision to operate around the clock in the brew-house because we had few other options available to meet our increasing demand. Operating that way makes sense for a variety of reasons, but it takes a heavy toll on the people who work those shifts. The brewing process is a series of roughly 2-hour steps and once started, they can't be stopped until the final batch of beer is in the fermenter. From the start of mashing in the grain to boiling and then cooling, brewing takes approximately 8 hours. Around-the-clock production allows a new batch to be started every 2 hours as the previous brew moves to the next vessel. Once the equipment gets hot, and the process is flowing, it remains in a sterile state. Running continuously also allows the myriad of vessels, pumps, and valves to stay in continuous production, with no lag from starting and stopping the process. Heating the copper kettles from a cold start causes additional stress on the metals, so there are many reasons to start the process and run until enough beer for the week is made, at which point the cleaning takes place.

The production demands of a continuous operation at a busy brewery are not ideal for everyone's lifestyle and can be very hard on employees and their families. Because around-the-clock brewing is the current reality at Sierra Nevada, other departments also operate with night-shift employees. For the brewers, it's a demanding job to stay focused and manage multiple batches as they move through the brewhouse. The night shift can be difficult for people because it can create a sense of isolation from other employees; it's hard for them to feel like part of the group. Some people can thrive in that kind of a work environment, but it isn't for everyone and it's hard to screen and interview for. We found that alternating the night shift worked best for us—very few employees liked it when it was their turn, but spreading it out meant that everyone shared the burden. We also try to acknowledge and mitigate the impacts as best we can. Employees earn a pay differential for night shift, and we make an effort to include night-shift employees in company events and celebrations.

Trying to strike that balance between production demands and people's lives is one of the greatest challenges Sierra Nevada continues to face in all areas of our operation. Some breweries shut their brewhouse down every night and fire it up in the morning rather than finding someone to work around the clock. Some small German breweries have gone to a greater extreme and have installed automation that allows the brewery to operate part of the day with no employees at the helm, thus avoiding the night-shift conundrum while maximizing productivity. The cost of that level of automation can be prohibitive, particularly with our insistence on using whole hops, which almost requires the human touch. Regardless of the advantages it offers, I've always been leery of an autopilot brewery because of the potential for catastrophic problems to arise. Other breweries just forgo the efficiency and build a brewery large enough to cover the production needs on a less than continuous operation, but the bigger you get the less sense that makes.

FOSTERING TALENT

When we're looking for new people to join Sierra Nevada, we look for a great attitude first and skill set second because it's much easier to build skills than change people's outlook and behaviors. We have always had the tendency to promote from within. When we have a good, talented pool of candidates it makes sense, but we've also realized that there are benefits to bringing in people from the outside to help build our knowledge, broaden our pool, and prevent us from becoming too insular in our thinking.

When I realized that I needed more time to focus on general business demands, I decided to look outside Sierra Nevada for someone to take a lot of the daily production and plant issues off my plate. I tracked down an old acquaintance, Al Spinelli, who is an experienced brewery manager, having run a slightly larger brewery on the East Coast for more than 25 years. In 2006, he became Sierra Nevada's first plant manager. For the arrangement to work, I had to be willing to step back and let someone else handle a lot of what I'd been doing for the past 30 years. It took time for me to learn how to do that, and I'm still learning, but having him here has allowed me to look at the business differently.

For the past five years, Sierra Nevada has put more emphasis on employees' personal development plans and company goals, which tie together and allow us to assess an employee's strengths and weaknesses. Sierra Nevada has a lot of great people, but it's inevitable that problems will arise. We have never been very good or timely at cutting employees loose when they fail to meet expectations. Few people I have met like to deal with conflict, and I'm no different. I have had the tendency to give people passes or more chances than I should, so I have probably allowed suboptimal behavior to persist past when we should have addressed it. I've changed how I think about those situations because it doesn't do anyone any good to hang on to employees who aren't pulling their weight. Over time, I had developed somewhat of a cynical view that it's nearly impossible to change a person's behavior. Having seen some people grow and change, I now acknowledge that it is possible, although highly unlikely, for people to make dramatic and lasting changes in their behavior. Overall, we try to act more quickly now to identify problem behaviors and provide coaching when practical. When that doesn't work, we part ways and give those employees the opportunity to be successful elsewhere. Although it's hard to let people go, we try to look at the bigger picture and make decisions to keep the employee body healthy.

EMPLOYEE WELLNESS

One of the perks of owning your own company is that you get to set the tone of how employees are treated. Over the years we've developed a wide range of benefits and perks to recognize and reward how hard our employees work. Good wages along with health and financial benefits are a good start, but other programs have gone a long way toward building Sierra Nevada's culture and morale. We started offering health insurance and 401(k) plans to employees in the early 1980s. All full-time employees are eligible to participate after three months of employment, and part-time employees are eligible after one year of employment (with a small additional cost). Also, we offer the same benefits to our restaurant employees that we do to our brewery employees. To encourage greater participation in our 401(k) program, we offer a 10 percent match on employees' contributions, as well as annual 5 percent profit sharing. I'm happy to contribute to our employees' future, but I expect them to do the same. I also see the profit sharing as a way to recognize everyone's hard work after we've had a good year.

In recent years we've developed a wide range of benefits and initiatives centered on health and wellness. Being in an industry that produces a product that can bring both joy and hardship if abused has probably helped drive my decision to find ways to support and facilitate healthy lifestyles and behaviors in my employees and their families. Keeping one's life and priorities in balance is a challenge for some in our industry. Promoting employee wellness hopefully encourages a sensible approach to nutrition, exercise, and the enjoyment of a long life.

We offer discounted gym memberships, realizing that healthier employees make better employees. We allow them to choose which gym works best for them and do a payroll deduction to cover the cost. Over the years we've also worked toward creating a tobacco-free workplace, although it hasn't been without challenges. We knew it would take many years to achieve that. We learned a lot from our early efforts, but I feel strongly about sticking with the program to improve employee health. Our first attempt met with resistance, so we created an employee taskforce, including smokers and other tobacco users, to promote the program from within. To reach our goal, we offered a three-pronged approach of education, support, and financial assistance. Sierra Nevada covers the cost of smoking cessation aids and counseling for employees who quit tobacco. We also share employee success stories in our monthly newsletter, *Wort's Happening*.

We decided to formalize our program under the direction of a full-time wellness coordinator, whom we hired in 2008. I also thought it would be nice to have an on-site massage therapist, so we hired someone qualified in both massage and wellness promotion. Full-time employees can take advantage of a half-hour, on-the-clock massage or foot reflexology session once a quarter. They also have access to a monthly 15-minute chair massage. Additionally, our wellness coordinator performs Active Release Techniques (ART) for employees as needed.

A HOLISTIC APPROACH

In 2006 Sierra Nevada opened The Oasis, an on-site medical clinic for employees and their families. The idea of a clinic was something I'd been talking about for years, and with the assistance of our human resources director, who came to us with a background in health care, it became a reality. Beginning with one physician's assistant (PA), it now boasts a part-time doctor, several PAs, a part-time accupuncturist, as well as a women's health specialist. The clinic is open five days a week with varying hours to accommodate work schedules. Services at The Oasis are free to employees and their family members. We also allow employees to obtain a pass once a year for a nonfamily member to go to the clinic. The Oasis also houses Sierra Nevada's lactation room and is conveniently located next to our on-site day care.

After years of planning, our parent-run, on-site day care, Littlefoot Childcare Center, opened in 2009. Many of our employees are parents, and I had long wanted to provide high-quality, affordable, convenient childcare. Located directly adjacent to the brewery, Littlefoot also lessens the environmental footprint of each family and reduces emissions, cuts transportation cost, and saves time. The center offers care for children aged three months to five years at rates lower than comparable local rates. The Littlefoot executive director reports directly to a board of parents who determine costs, center needs, fundraising events, and general direction. Parents are welcome to join their children for lunch and can check in throughout the day.

With all that we have going on at the brewery and our much increased workforce, we realized that communication with employees was integral to our successful operation and our relationships with our employees. For a long time, we didn't have time for an employee newsletter or have as much information to communicate during our production-focused years. As our workforce and company grew, it became imperative to improve our communication. Knowing that people retain information through repetition, we try to hit all the bases in our communication—written, spoken, and visual. We have quarterly meetings, dubbed Town Hall meetings, to discuss the state of the industry, the state of our business, and challenges and opportunities. All employees are encouraged to attend, either in person or online, and are welcome to ask questions of the speakers. Once a year we bring in speakers from outside the company to offer a wider perspective on issues that affect our business. Around the brewery we have touch screens that serve several purposes. Employees can check each department's monthly KPIs, read company news, check the clinic schedule, and look at job postings. Much of this information is also disseminated in our monthly newsletter.

THE HEALTH OPPORTUNITY PROGRAM (HOP)

As part of our goal to empower employees to take charge of their own health, Sierra Nevada also created the Health Opportunity Program (HOP) run by the wellness coordinator. HOP covers a wide variety of health initiatives. We kick off every year with an annual health screening to collect data to measure the effectiveness of the wellness program, as well as provide employees with benchmarks for personal improvement. In conjunction with our local hospital, employees take part in a blood draw, physical assessment, and lifestyle questionnaire. All of the information is handled by the hospital and remains completely confidential. Employees who take advantage of our insurance and participate in the annual screening receive a discount on the portion of the insurance premium they pay.

Each year HOP offers a selection of classes, lunch and learns, counseling programs, and social events open to all employees. We also invite speakers from the local university to talk about diet, nutrition, and healthy living. Workshops take place during employee meal periods for convenience, and we provide healthful, delicious meals made by our talented kitchen staff. Past topics have included stress reduction, body mechanics, and nutrition. We've also offered courses led by our chefs that allow employees to get into the kitchen to prepare seasonal, local meals. Although not part of the HOP program, in an effort to walk the walk, Sierra Nevada purchased HUMAN vending machines to provide healthy snacks and drinks in our break rooms. Having our own vending machines allows us to select the offerings. The wellness coordinator also instituted Fresh Fruit Fridays, providing baskets of fresh, usually local, fruit around the facility. We also created a walking path through our hop fields for employees to use during breaks and meal periods.

HOP also dovetails with our volunteer program, allowing employees to count their volunteer time to earn HOP points for incentives at the end of each year. Employees can donate their time to organizations of their choice, and most choose programs that reflect the brewery's values. Some work with the local elder community, and others volunteer at the animal shelter. Sierra Nevada also adopted a stretch of highway that employees clean regularly. We've also worked with a local community group whose goal is to reclaim an abandoned creek side property and create a passive park. Every December, Sierra Nevada works with a local foster agency to provide gifts to children in the county's foster program. Volunteerism is a part of Sierra Nevada's value system, and we focus our efforts on our local community. We also see volunteerism as part of our holistic approach to health that includes physical, mental, and social well-being.

IT'S THE LITTLE THINGS

Over time, as our employee roster grew, the little perks that we offered in the early years solidified into programs based on our desire to foster a sense of pride in what we do and as a way to encourage employees' investment in the brewery. Of course, one of the first perks we offered was free beer. In the beginning, it wasn't an organized program; when we had 10 or 20 employees, it was practical to allow them to take what they wanted. That practice evolved into Beer Bucks, a much-loved institution at Sierra Nevada. For employees who don't drink beer (yes, there are a few), we've established a trade with a local juice manufacturer, so they can still enjoy the benefit. We also give employees T-Shirt Bucks to use for clothing in our gift shop for two reasons. First, some of our jobs can be dirty and hard on clothing; providing shirts takes away some of the burden of clothing cost. Second, and probably more important, people are proud to work here and happily wear the Sierra Nevada logo.

We reimburse employees for classes and training that improve their knowledge base in all things related to the brewing business. This program started small and somewhat informally, but not only has its use grown, its scope has also gotten even broader. What started as reimbursement for employees who took outside courses is now a line item on our budget, allotting funds to each department. In 2007, we also established Sierra Nevada University, an on-site computer lab and training facility. We have courses ranging from basic computer skills to more in-depth coverage of common computer programs. Additionally, we have an employee dedicated to creating Brewing 101 courses that cover every step of the process—history, brewing, fermentation, sanitation, utilities, quality, and so on. Our goal is to have every employee complete 24 hours of training in a two-year period. Many of our employees may never work in production, but I want them to know our business from the inside out. I respect knowledge and don't think there's such a thing as too much. It can only benefit Sierra Nevada to have educated employees.

For as hard as we work, we also like to have fun and celebrate our success. Sierra Nevada has a long tradition of celebrating our anniversary on November 15. In an effort to offer something for families, we alternate between a summer Hop Festival that coincides with the peak of our hop crop and an Oktoberfest, as well as a holiday party in the winter. Several times every year managers and supervisors cook an employee appreciation meal, which is a way for different departments to mix and socialize. Once a year we also celebrate our employees' longevity with an employee anniversary dinner. Employees with at least five years of service are invited to a dinner in their honor. The evening includes a slideshow of old photos and speeches that highlight the fun we've had over the years. It also allows us to reflect on how far we've come.

Striking this balance of perks and programs is a real challenge and, unfortunately, not everyone has the same sensibilities, wants, or needs. The employee who doesn't need day care or value the convenience of a free on-site health clinic may think they're a waste of money and would rather have a few more dollars a month in their paycheck. Just like the premise of socialist programs ranging from health care to social security, not everyone values the benefit or wants to share in the costs, and often it's not until they need it that they appreciate the benefit. My intention with all of these programs and benefits is to create a company culture that supports employees as much as they support Sierra Nevada.

13

NEW MILLENNIUM,
NEW CHALLENGES

The mouth of perfectly happy man is filled with beer.
—Egyptian proverb

As Sierra Nevada sales continued to grow, our original 20th Street infrastructure was taxed to keep up with demand. We made small strides almost continually to increase output, but our staff was starting to burn out. We were brewing around the clock and getting close to around-the-clock packaging, too. Our increasing inability to have sufficient downtime to perform routine maintenance also took a heavy toll, with more unplanned downtime that exacerbated an already challenging production schedule. Our bottleshop was extremely cramped for our 550-bottle-per-minute line. We figured out how to speed things up a little to squeeze out almost 600 bottles per minute, but running the equipment above its design limits ultimately just added to downtime. Because we were barely able to keep up with our demand anyway, shutting the line down to remove and replace the equipment wasn't practical, and I started to look for other solutions.

Not only had we run out of packaging capacity, but we had also run out of warehouse space again. We started planning a significant expansion of approximately 70,000 square feet that we hoped would allow us to reach 1,000,000 barrels, our estimate of the plant's maximum capacity. The expansion also included a new packaging facility, beer storage warehouse, packaging materials warehouse, and large separate warehouse to store and ship point-of-sale items from. The building that now houses our T-shirts is almost four times the size of the original brewery!

Hop Wars

Over the years I've acquired a good understanding of the economics of hop farming. One of the positive aspects of the growth of the craft beer industry has been the change in relationship among hop growers, dealers, and brewers. In many cases we're able to work together directly with farmers and plant breeders, doing pilot test brews to help foster the development of new hop varieties. Hop farming has become a very hard way to make a living, and growers barely break even in many years. To cope with the uncertain market and mitigate the financial risk, most hop farmers in this country raise a diverse set of crops. In the fertile Yakima Valley in Washington, where the majority of American hops are grown, apples, mint, grapes, and pears are common crops grown along with hops to help diversify the risk. I learned about the difficulty of being a hop farmer firsthand when we planted several acres of hops at our brewery in Chico almost 10 years ago; we now organically farm almost 8 acres of hops. I figure that it costs me close to $30 per pound to farm my own hops, nearly 10 times the cost if purchased commercially; it's been a fun project but not a wise investment, particularly if my motivation had been to reduce costs.

For many years brewers around the world have sourced hops globally, with European and American hops crossing paths as brewers mix different varieties and sources of origin to achieve their desired flavor and consistency. Although a few novel nonbeer uses have been discovered, hops are pretty much a single-market crop, which dramatically increases the market volatility. The market is further complicated by the global nature of the industry—if Europe has a huge crop, American prices will fall, and conversely, if American growers have a stellar year, European prices go down. When hop prices hit high marks, farmers around the world hope for a repeat the following year and plant additional acreage, oftentimes resulting in a boom or bust marketplace. The climate in the Yakima Valley provides an advantage over most other growing regions in the world; a newly planted Yakima Valley field of first-year hops of a robust variety will yield 50 to 70 percent of a mature hop yard compared to fields in other countries that will yield almost no marketable hops their first year, so some farmers hedge their bets, hoping to increase their income. However, if it's a good yielding year, the spot prices fall back again, and none of the farmers win unless their hops are all previously contracted. But the opportunistic brewers may end up getting a good deal by picking up the surplus at a large discount, thereby reinforcing the cycle of relying on spot buying. The brewer that spot buys may win for many years, but the lack of contracting has led to a weakening of the hop industry, with growers and brewers making bets that often upset the balance of supply and demand and eventually drive many growers out of business.

The hop market has also been complicated by other factors. As bitterness levels in beer dropped, so did the demand for hops and the Alpha acids they contain. Coupled with slowing demand, the development of much higher yielding and more potent varieties that contain upwards of three times the bittering values of the typical varieties grown in the recent past caused needed hop acreage to plummet, even though beer sales on a global level have continued to grow. Hop farmers were left with infrastructure they no longer had use for, but because most of the planting cost comes from the poles and cables that support the plants, farmers were reluctant to rip out acreage and sold hops below their production costs, hoping for a turnaround in the marketplace; for a period of time, surplus stock continued to rise. In recent years, the development of technologies that could extract and preserve hops' bittering component as almost pure Alpha acids in concentrated syrup allowed surplus hops to be put in a container with almost no degradation and provided a market for surplus hops. Although it's not an exact replacement for natural hops, many brewers started to take advantage of hop extract because it's a more efficient way to bitter beer and, with the flooded hop market, much cheaper to purchase than natural hops. Enough growers finally decided that selling below production cost in the hope of a turnaround market was senseless. Growers idled a lot of acreage or removed the poles from their fields to replant them with other crops. The pendulum finally swung the other way, and by 2005, brewers were using more hops and hop products than were being grown. The surplus was rapidly depleted. In 2007, the crop came up short. Few in the industry grasped the severity of the situation until it was too late. When not enough hops were available to meet needs, it set off a global panic and price escalation. Prices spiked to nearly $20 per pound, and many of the specialty varieties weren't available at all.

These extreme cycles typically happen about once a generation. This time around it caught hundreds of small craft brewers, as well as some large ones who had been relying on cheap spot hops, off guard. Just as when we started, the majority of small craft brewers were spot buyers and had been able to purchase what they needed from the oversupply of hops at generally reasonable pricing, but now there were almost no surplus hops to go around. Brewers had few options.

Several brewers like us who carried a surplus inventory to cover precisely such a situation made hops available to other brewers. We decided to take only a portion of the hops we had contracted that year and sold back some of our excess inventory, working with our suppliers to make them available to small brewers. Unfortunately, the situation also produced less altruistic outcomes, and many frustrated small brewers were pressured into signing long-term contracts at highly inflated prices in exchange for enough hops to satisfy their current needs. Even big brewers were affected. The hop shortage was so dramatic that rumors swirled that many brewers were forced to reformulate their beers. Others opted to change their brewing process to utilize the more efficient extracts that are added to finished beer in place of the traditional method of adding hops to the brewing kettle, where hop oil losses are higher.

The increase in hop prices triggered the planting of significant new acreage by farmers to fill the demand and benefit from the increase in price. This, of course, resulted in an oversupply of some varieties the following year and prices again plummeted. This also prompted an irrational move toward the planting of hops across the country in areas not known to be suitable for hop production by dozens of brewers and small farmers with no prior experience. Driven by the temptation of earning $20 a pound, they planted their fields without the understanding or infrastructure needed to pick, dry, bale, and process hops.

To compound the fragile market dynamics even further, Anheuser-Busch (AB) was taken over by InBev at the same time. Historically AB maintained a huge inventory of hops as an insurance policy, but the new management had a different philosophy both in the hop varieties they used and toward the security stockpile of hops they maintained. As part of InBev's cost cutting measures, they soon liquidated and canceled contracts, putting millions of pounds of hops into the market. Additionally they purportedly changed hop varities, further decreasing the needed acreage. Many small brewers who had signed very high priced contracts, some in excess of $20 a pound, now found they could buy the same hops on the spot market the next year for $2 to $3 a pound. Few were happy with the ripple effect created by InBev's actions. Frustration, anguish, and distrust mounted as some brewers came to believe that suppliers took advantage of the situation.

The volatile hop market affects the craft industry dramatically because our usage is typically 5 to 10 times greater per barrel than the larger mainstream brewers' use. Since then the hop market has regained some stability, and pricing has been more rational. Some brewers were able to renegotiate the contracts they signed during the tumultuous years, but the hop marketplace still presents a particular challenge for brewers. Hop availability has also started to stabilize as growers and brewers work together to balance supply and demand.

There will always be some fluctuation in the market as new hop varieties are developed and as brewers continue to innovate with new beer styles. New designer hops that have a unique flavor profile are sought after by craft brewers and are still in short supply, so they command a significant premium.

THE BARLEY BUSINESS

The malted-barley market has also been on a roller coaster for the past several years. A number of factors are responsible for a decline in available acreage of barley suitable for brewing. While malted barley is not as specialized of a crop as hops, the need for quality malting barley has changed from what was once a commodity crop into a specialty grain. Changes in global food and energy supplies have affected how farmers plant their fields and which crops they plant worldwide. Land once farmed for barley has been converted to grow higher yielding, and often government-subsidized, genetically modified corn, much of which is converted into ethanol fuel. This fuel-over-food mentality drives up the cost of almost all other competing grains. I support innovation and the development of alternatives to importing oil; however, I think the current energy policy and drive towards highly industrialized and subsidized agribusiness is the wrong way to go about it.

Only certain barley varieties are suitable for brewing. Brewers look for barley that is low in protein, plump, and free from disease, requiring optimal weather conditions during the growing season and at harvest. Beyond that, brewers require grain with the proper levels of enzymes and, of course, good flavor. Farmers are forced to sell barley not selected for malting into the feed market at a lower price, where it competes with higher-yielding crops like corn. Because brewers have exacting specifications to ensure quality malted barley, many farmers have elected to plant crops that promise a greater guaranteed profit. Other pressures have forced many farmers out of growing barley. As the climate has shifted, more persistent disease problems have developed in traditional barley-growing regions. There is currently no commercially grown genetically modified (GMO) barley and brewers have not supported the effort to develop it, but many other high yielding GMO crops have been developed and compete for acreage that was once devoted to barley. The resulting monopolization of the marketplace by seed and chemical companies has occurred in corn, canola, and sugar beets, just to name a few crops that are now almost entirely controlled by a handful of global companies that have developed and patented these "new" organisms. As brewers we need to pay farmers a fair price so that they are willing to grow barley varieties that are suitable for brewing and that can compete in profitability with other crops in order to make a compelling argument that we don't need genetic modification of malting barley.

Barley, though important to brewers, has become such a minor crop worldwide that research and licensing currently doesn't justify the development of genetically modified varieties. Wheat, a much larger domestic and global crop, will probably see the influx of genetic modification in the near future. Some feel that genetically modified barley won't be too far behind if genetically modified wheat is accepted in the marketplace. Some industry observers suggest that it's probably only a matter of time before economics drives the development of genetically modified barley, but others feel strongly that with so many other methods now at our fingertips to assist conventional plant breeding, a nongenetically modified solution is achievable. The public outcry over the genetic manipulation of our food supply isn't universal. Brewers around the world have historically been a conservative bunch when it comes to altering traditional ingredients, but sentiments seem to have started to change with global consolidation and the drive towards efficiency and cost cutting. Many breweries are now run by accountants, and financial decisions trump quality and tradition. The brewing industry needs smart financial people, but they shouldn't be dictating how we brew or what goes in our beer.

14

DOING THE RIGHT THING

Beer . . . a high and mighty liquor.

—Julius Caesar

Most of Sierra Nevada's very early energy efficiency projects were driven by economics, but as our production grew, I started to pay more attention to the fact that we, like all breweries, are a large consumer of resources in the forms of gas, electricity, and water. In addition to my general sensibility about saving resources, we had the opportunity to save precious dollars as well.

One major benefit of growing the business to a sustainable and profitable size was that there was sufficient cash flow to invest in projects and explore concepts that would have been difficult to justify when we were so strapped for cash and counted on every penny to help us brew enough beer to satisfy our customers. For years I explored pushing the boundaries of conventional business models in a wide range of areas. But even now, some of the ideas I pursue don't make sense using the cost-benefit analysis taught in business school and used by most corporations to justify expenditures. Making money is important because it allows us to prosper as a company, but it also allows us to be leaders and show that businesses can be successful doing the right thing.

When I built my first brewing kettle, I had the romantic, and perhaps silly, notion of trying to heat it utilizing the local orchard wood that was in abundance. I had built the kettle out of a surplus tank. Initially I hadn't come up with a way to heat the kettle, but I considered building a wood-fired burner and using almond wood as the fuel source. I gave up on the idea when it became apparent that controlling the intensity of the fire and dealing with stoking a fire during the boil would have been nearly impossible.

Even though that first attempt at alternative energy wasn't successful, I was later able to incorporate other progressive and energy- and money-saving technologies into the original Gilman Way brewery. In my scrounging I came across a used ice storage system that had been used in a large dairy to provide chilled water for milk cooling. Because cows are milked twice a day at roughly 12-hour intervals, the need for refrigeration has two distinct peaks during a 24-hour period. An ice storage system builds a large quantity of ice with a small refrigeration system that then can provide large quantities of chilled water quickly to circulate through a heat exchanger. I was able to incorporate that same concept for cooling hot wort out of the brew kettle and take advantage of energy savings because with this system I could build ice at night when power is cheaper[1] and more abundant and then quickly cool wort during the day with the stored ice.

When I designed and built the 20th Street brewery, I had the ability to incorporate even more energy-saving concepts into the new brewery, but I was still limited by our financial situation. Although some efficiency technologies came with a high cost, many small, inexpensive innovations were easily introduced. Additional insulation, energy-efficient lighting, and high-efficiency motors contributed to our energy- and money-saving efforts without driving up construction

---

[1]In California we have tiered energy rates based on the time of day and time of year. Electricity costs less at nonpeak periods at night and during the cooler months.

costs adversely. Being in California, there were many programs and rebates available to help cover the cost of some of these upgrades. Those incentives coupled with power costs that were roughly 50 percent higher than the national average certainly helped motivate me to accept slightly higher upfront costs.

Over the past 10 years, I've had the ability and resources to explore many fun tangents to the business that were not possible during those early scrappy years. Few of these projects make sense on a strictly return on investment (ROI) basis. Even for me the justification for some of my pet projects is often slightly intangible, but they feel like the right thing to pursue. Although not all of my projects have worked as anticipated, on the whole the decisions I have made have moved us in the right direction, both in terms of technology and of our philosophy as a company.

FINDING ALTERNATIVE POWER

As we had grown and modernized, many of the systems that controlled everything from grain handling to refrigeration contained some sort of sophisticated electronics. Partly fueled by the Y2K doomsday debate and the uncertainty of an uninterrupted power supply, I decided to make plans for the potential of an external or internal system failure at the utility or at the brewery. It would be a disaster to lose power, have a disruption to our natural gas delivery, or be unable to get water for any length of time. I started researching what steps we could take to make the brewery totally self-sufficient and operate essentially off the grid. I gathered information about which of our systems would be vulnerable and then made sure we had back-up plans in case they faltered.

I also started determining how to have enough back-up generators to run the entire plant. I had installed a 1,100-horsepower Caterpillar generator in 1998 as part of the big expansion. In the years prior, we had lost several batches of beer when we lost power because of natural disasters; mishaps, such as when a squirrel made its last leap between the wrong wires at a Pacific Gas and Electric Company substation (which seems to happen a lot in Chico, and several have been vaporized this way over the years); wildfires that downed high-voltage distribution lines; or brownouts the overloaded California power grid succumbed to during hot summers. It doesn't take long without electricity during the middle of a brew to create problems. A 30-minute delay at several critical steps in the brewing cycle would damage or alter the beer quality to the point that it is probably not worth the risk to continue, so the prudent thing is to dump the batch, and in some cases several batches, that are in progress. In the case of an even more prolonged outage, lack of refrigeration at the crucial height of fermentation can also cause irreversible damage to many batches of beer. We had borne the cost of dumping batches many times. With our current brew size, that can mean up to 12,000 pounds of wasted malt along with all the hops, energy, and labor that went into the beer up to that point.

I initially decided to install enough generator capacity and automated switchgear that in the case of a grid failure, the generator would fire up in about 15 seconds and provide enough power to finish the batches in process and keep half of the refrigeration systems running. We didn't have enough power to run the bottling or kegging lines during an outage, but if those processes failed, we would lose only a very small percentage of the batch. Our utility company had a program that gave a discount on our annual power bill if we had the capability to shed load during power shortages that helped us justify the purchase of the back-up generator. That savings alone paid for the generator and other equipment in a matter of years.

I then began looking at alternatives to generate enough power to run the entire plant. I started looking at power generation equipment that could be utilized on a more continuous basis and visited many facilities, such as hospitals and businesses, that were self-generating electricity with small co-generation plants. The most successful installations utilized in some productive fashion both the electricity and waste heat that was produced. I finally decided to purchase a second generator to provide emergency power for the entire plant. This one utilizing the most advanced particulate and air pollution control equipment available to give us enough generation to operate almost every aspect of our business, including the Pub, while disconnected from the electrical grid.

Next I tackled a back-up supply of natural gas. Because I was going down the path of the worst-case scenario, I decided that I might as well go all the way. I figured that even if the world collapsed around me, there would still be a need for beer, and I might as well be the one providing it. I found a supplier that made a system that could blend propane with a small amount of air to match the British thermal unit (BTU) content of natural gas. It could be switched on in minutes without the need to modify any of our equipment. I installed it for the worst case scenario and never ended up needing it for over 13 years. I also met with the local water company several times. They assured me that their newly installed back-up generators would be able to provide an uninterrupted water supply.

On December 31, 1999, I waited for midnight at the brewery, and as we had anticipated, nothing of consequence happened when the clock hit 12:01 AM. Of course it was a relief, and I now knew we were prepared for almost any disaster that might disrupt our operations. Since then the generators have come in handy many times and have allowed us to ride out many outages when the troubled California grid has gone down. If we hadn't made the investment, the brewery would have been out of power for several hours numerous times and would have lost a significant amount of beer over the years since then. Since the Pub is also on our back-up system, on stormy nights when the rest of the town is plunged into darkness, the brewery becomes a place people can meet and wait out the storm or power outage.

FUEL CELLS

My quest for energy independence continued after the turn of the millennium, and I started looking at self-generation again. I still believed that we could produce energy more efficiently than what was provided from the grid because brewery operations could easily utilize the heat by-product, therefore nearly doubling the efficiency of conventionally produced power.

I researched various alternative energy sources, including fuel cells, microturbines, and conventional generators, but I settled on a European-made generator with an engine fired by natural gas that would generate the majority of our power and provide a significant amount of our hot water as well. I went through the permitting process because, like any industrial use of natural gas, it required approval from the California Air Resources Board, which prompted a public forum. I started having second thoughts about the emissions and before signing the contract revisited the much cleaner fuel cell.

The manufacturer of the fuel cells, Fuel Cell Energy (FCE), had fewer than 50 units in operation in 2005, and most were outside of the United States. As an early adopter, I knew I was assuming some risk, and I wanted to mitigate as much of it as I could. Our four fuel cells were going to be the largest private installation in the world at the time and would supply the majority of our electrical power needs and a portion of our steam requirements. Installing the fuel cells was a significant project and would cost nearly $5 million. It also required a significant investment to upgrade our power distribution and site infrastructure. Because the technology held a lot of future promise, there were utility and tax incentive programs, and we received several million dollars in credits and rebates. With them, the overall cost of the project came in at just under $2 million. Theoretically, the payback was supposed to be five years, but because we were using natural gas as the source of hydrogen, the payback time was not guaranteed. We had secured a natural gas contract but only for one year. Natural gas prices had been volatile and were deemed above market; the expectation was that they would stabilize and then decline, so we were reluctant to contract out any further into the future as gas prices rose. The project went smoothly and FCE did their best to leverage the public relations, so much so that the kickoff celebration included a visit and speech by then-governor Arnold Schwarzenegger.

For several years the system, which comprised four 250-kilowatt (kW) units capable of generating 1 megawatt (MW) of electricity, operated as intended, but over time we experienced increasing maintenance issues and downtime that cut into our ability to make enough electricity to meet our needs. The stacks in the fuel cells convert natural gas into hydrogen and then into electricity and usable heat. FCE's technology was one of the most efficient methods of doing that, but in order to achieve such high overall output, the cells operate at temperatures exceeding 1,000 degrees Fahrenheit. The cell components were projected to last over three years in operation, with the promise that the company would develop advanced materials in the near future to increase the life to five years or longer. Unfortunately, that breakthrough never materialized, and we had more performance issues than anticipated. Over the next few years, we saw greater volatility in natural gas prices and huge spikes that at one point more than tripled the cost, resulting in power production costs that were almost equivalent to the cost of purchasing power from the utility. The gas markets stabilized, the input costs have been mitigated, and currently the maintenance issues have moderated and we now often generate more power than we can use and sell it back to the utility.

SOLAR POWER

Shortly after I installed the fuel cells, I decided that the addition of solar photovoltaic panels would also benefit our overall energy strategy because we use most of our power during the day when we could take advantage of the sun to generate the balance of energy that the fuel cells couldn't produce. In 2007, I started a project to install a large array of solar panels above our parking lot that would produce 500 kW of direct current power, or about 400 kW of usable alternating current power. We designed the array as a covered parking structure with a tracking system; the panels shift to follow the sun during the day, thus increasing output 20 percent over a fixed, flat panel installation. As an added benefit, the panel structure provides shade for employee and customer parking.

After the success of the first solar project, I looked at where we could add additional panels to meet a greater percentage of our daily peak electrical needs. I calculated that with our ability to cover our base load at night with the fuel cells and solar panels to make up the balance of our needs during the day, we could produce nearly all the electricity we'd need. In 2008, we set about installing thousands of panels on top of brewery buildings. It didn't take long to use up all of the available energy credits and tax credits that initially helped get the project's cost down to a somewhat reasonable payback of around seven years. As new structures went up around the brewery, I continued adding additional panels, so we now have over 2.7 MW of solar capacity and have installed over 10,000 panels.

The ROI on the last several projects was in the neighborhood of 13 years. The longer payback period didn't bother me at the time—it was the right thing to do, and I was investing for the long haul. During our peak year in 2009, we produced more than 80 percent of our own electricity with the fuel cells and solar panels. With the current consistent good production of the fuel cells, even with our growing production, we have again exceeded 80 percent on-site generation, but we're still actively working on reducing our power consumption. We just finished a major upgrade to our cooling plant, the most energy intense component of our operation, that we expect to provide a significant decrease in electrical consumption and put us closer to our goal of 100 percent on-site electricity generation.

KEEPING TRACK

Sierra Nevada has implemented a focused, company-wide effort to analyze our operations to find ways to improve what we do. Al Spinelli, my plant manager, and his assistant, Melissa Cafferata, put together a comprehensive Key Performance Indicator (KPI) program across the whole of the company. They worked with every department to develop metrics to monitor efficiencies in every aspect of our operation. Our KPIs run the gamut from water, electrical, and natural gas usage to safety, raw material consumption, and productivity. We track every call or comment we receive about our beer to determine if there is something we could do better to get the best tasting and best packaged beer into our customer's hands. The sustainability department performs trash audits and monitors how much material we send to the landfill every month. We set goals for everything we can control in each department and then see how we can improve year over year. Even if it's only a fraction of a percent, there is always room for improvement. We post the monthly KPIs on several interactive screens around the brewery to allow all employees to see our results.

Although there are industry benchmarks for some of the areas we track, our business is unique, so I find it best to focus on what we do and how to improve it. It's like the cliché: you are only competing against yourself. Sure, I often look at what my peers do and where the rest of the industry stands, but much about brewing is art and philosophy. How can you compare what we do with an operation that embraces completely different sensibilities toward the products they produce? Our company's values are different than other brewers' values; I don't necessarily think that makes us any better, but we have to keep what we hold dear in the forefront of our day-to-day operations. There are dozens of ways we could make beer more cheaply and easily than what we currently do, but my brewing philosophy is about quality and not about trying to cut corners in the process or using inferior ingredients to save costs. I believe in balance, choice, and judgment.

No different from when we started, Sierra Nevada continues to use only whole-cone hops. We shun the practice of high-gravity brewing (brewing a higher alcohol content beer and then diluting it with water before bottling). We capture our own carbon dioxide from the fermentation process for reuse, which adds to our energy consumption but offsets the environmental impact required to obtain it from another source. Sierra Nevada utilizes many processes in our operations that make us unique. Ironically, many of them stem from an early lack of funds but have become the hallmark of our dedication to the craft of brewing, quality, and sustainability.

15

GOOD IS NOT GOOD ENOUGH

They who drink beer will think beer.

—Washington Irving

A big factor in our continuous success and sustained growth is that we have never been satisfied with the status quo. Being good was just not good enough. I have always approached our beer and our company with the thought that no single process or system is perfect; there are always things that can be improved, whether it's reducing how much power or water it takes to make a barrel of beer or hitting the alcohol or color specification target on every batch.

We try to stay focused on what we are doing and how to improve it, not what others are doing. Continuous improvement is an ongoing learning exercise for all of us as we drill down to understand the aspects of our business that we can control. This is a journey; there is no definite end point, and we will continue to strive to create great products. As we grew over the years, we continued to make infrastructure and process improvements and tried to buy the best equipment available. On top of that, I had a strong conviction that we needed to be on a continuous quest to study and refine our knowledge about brewing.

Some of you may be wondering why we would want to continue to tinker with what had been by every measure a very successful and popular brand. It wasn't that I didn't think we were making great beer at the time, and it wasn't that I wanted to change the recipes or the flavor profiles of what had been very well-received beers. I was keenly aware that there are always slight differences caused by variations in barley or hops or from one yeast generation to another, let alone what happens in the marketplace with heat, light, agitation, and age. My quest wasn't to change Sierra Nevada's beer but to make exactly the same beer time and time again to provide consumers exactly the same experience, whether they drink it in Chico in July or in New York in January a few months after it's bottled. For years we were confident that we had some of the best quality control in the industry, but product quality is one area that I firmly believe everyone can always do better in—good is not good enough.

Our inability to do small-scale experimental brewing became a major obstacle to implementing what we were learning. We were frustrated by our inability to validate the suspicions and hunches that we were starting to develop as we gathered the increasingly puzzling data from our various beers, but it didn't make sense to brew (and potentially waste) 100 barrels to test our theories.

Although people have been brewing for more than 7,000 years, scientists still have not unraveled all of the mysteries and nuances of the process. Flavor stability has long been an area of science that brewers have been trying understand and improve on for years, but a lot remains unknown; no one has discovered a way to stop beer from aging. Hundreds of chemical reactions take place as beer sits on a shelf, and light and agitation increase the damage.

Even more complicated is the fact that not all beers age the same way, and raw materials and the fermentation process play a role in how beer evolves over time. Although there are no hard and fast rules, most lager beers develop a cardboard character from the formation of a compound called trans-2-nonenal as they age. Hoppy beers lose much of their fresh aroma as they age, and malty beers start to take on sherry- and wine-like notes. As some beers age they may still be fine to drink, and some styles, such as barley wine, may even develop desirable traits with age.

In my early days I would spend hours poring over texts and periodicals from the University of California, Davis. Over the years since then, I continued to spend my evenings reading brewing books, scientific periodicals, and industry trade publications. The demands of the brewery meant that I spent more time behind a desk, overseeing and directing the growth, trajectory, and culture of the business, but what I've always enjoyed the most is the science and engineering of brewing. Although a little more than 20 years after I started I was running a larger and more successful business than I had ever imagined with more than 300 employees, my passion was still driven by the alchemy of brewing and the equipment and skills necessary to control it.

As part of my quest, I've tried to understand and learn about everything going on in the industry, even if only at a high level. I read about and keep up with barley and hop breeding, advances in refrigeration efficiency, the latest technology for bottle filling, and everything in between. Staying abreast of industry and technological advancements allowed me to lead the company in the right long-term direction, focusing on the beer first. If we got the product right, the other aspects of running the company would come together more easily. I don't view myself as an expert in any one discipline, but I can generally understand and converse about any area of the brewing industry with people who are experts. When I deem it vital to the business or if something particularly intrigues me, I dig in deeper.

The growth we experienced over the years allowed us to embrace and afford improved technology for minimizing oxygen pickup during the brewing process. Much research has shown that contact with air or oxygen other than what is necessary to feed the yeast in the beginning of the fermentation process is generally bad for beer. Bottle filling, in particular, has seen major strides in technology, making the primitive equipment I started out with obsolete. Modern filling equipment does a much better job at reducing oxygen pickup to help preserve beer's freshness as well as being significantly more hygienic and easier to clean. We have continually upgraded our packaging lines to the best technology available, but even eliminating oxygen and keeping beer cold won't stop it from aging after it's packaged. To some degree our bottle conditioning process helps minimize the negative effects of oxygen that's always present when filling any container because active yeast takes advantage of any oxygen for growth, minimizing the degradation to the beer. Still, I had become enthralled with analytical equipment that had the potential to uncover the holy grail of the effects of oxidation on beer.

FRESH BEER IS BEST

We became a national brand around the year 2000, and even though our beers we weren't available everywhere in every market, we were selling beer in almost every state. As we began brewing larger batches to fulfill the increasing demand for our beer, we had to focus on ensuring that it would maintain the same flavors and aromas, even if it would be in storage or on shelves months before being bought.

I began to research and experiment with concepts to prolong freshness in our beers. Not added preservatives, mind you, but improvements that could be had by honing our skills to be better brewers. Well-made beer is a great source of natural anti-oxidant compounds that help limit the effects of free radical formation that contributes to the staling reactions that degrade beer, but process factors in the production or handling of the raw materials and brewing process may have the opposite effect. Many of these naturally occurring beneficial compounds are found in malt and hops, as well as produced by yeast. The challenge is keeping these compounds as intact as is practical without affecting the clarity or other aspects of beer quality. Because much of this science is still being unraveled, it's not easy to discern how variations in malt variety, kilning and roasting of the malt, or fermentation temperature might add or subtract a few days, or even as much as a week, to beer's shelf life.

Maintaining a consistently cool storage temperature is probably the single most controllable factor affecting beer quality once it is packaged. Cooler storage temperatures help slow almost all flavor-changing reactions. Years ago we made the commitment to transport all of our beer in refrigerated trucks if it takes more than a few hours to arrive at a warehouse, which we also require to be refrigerated. Heat damages all beer; although lightly flavored beers will certainly stale and not retain their fresh flavor as they age, very flavorful beers have a lot more compounds to react and stale, and in general will age worse.

We continue to do research in many areas, but for years our focus has been on hop aroma and new hop variety development. We have one of the most sophisticated gas chromatographs available for aroma analysis and have worked with several researchers and hop breeders on brewing trials. For years we have also done extensive research on bottle cap liner material. This seemingly insignificant packaging material has a major influence on beer quality because liner materials scalp, or absorb, many desirable aroma compounds. Also, although counter-intuitive, the physics of gas law allows the damaging ingress of oxygen to occur even when the cap is sealed and holding CO_2 pressure. We've done a lot of work on various liner materials and bottle designs to ensure the best possible seal and minimal scalping. The pace at which projects and firm discoveries unfold can be frustrating, but it's great to see employees get caught up in the same questions that keep me interested and driven as a brewer.

THE SEARCH FOR THE HOLY GRAIL

Although attempting to control the temperatures at which our beers are stored and transported goes a long way to helping drive freshness, I still wanted to understand what reactions or chemical and biological changes could affect the flavor of our beers. I read several papers that touted the benefits of a research tool called an Electron Paramagnetic Resonance (EPR) or Electron Spin Resonance (ESR) to help predict and uncover factors that might help improve beer flavor stability.

These spectrometers are complicated devices used for research in a variety of high-level university and research centers. They are used in a variety of capacities from cancer research to dating anthropological finds, such as prehistoric fossils, but for my purposes, they could be used to measure and potentially track sources of pro-oxidants that accelerate beer staling and may be present in raw materials or in iron- or copper-containing equipment. They could also help in looking at our process and maybe finding ways to preserve antioxidants naturally found in malt and hops.

I called Charlie Bamforth, who had recently become brewing chair at the University of California, Davis, to get his opinion on the value of the instrument and research. He wasn't convinced that it would lead me to the holy grail of flavor stability improvements and thought other less sophisticated instruments could provide similar keys to flavor stability. I was undeterred, though, and made the decision that if we were serious about producing the best beer possible, then we should invest in all the tools that might help in that pursuit. The instrument cost nearly $200,000 and would require quite a bit of training just to operate, let alone to grasp the highly technical principles of the underlying science. We purchased the instrument in 2002 and began to analyze our beer.

I hoped an EPR would help in our quest to preserve the flavor of our beers because it supposedly had the ability to quantify the level of the natural antioxidants and provide a deeper look into every phase of our beer production to help minimize the influence of pro-oxidants. Previous research done with this type of instrument was done on lager beer and had little relevance to the data we generated. Lager yeast produces low levels of the powerful antioxidant sulfur dioxide, which the EPR readily quantified, but because ale yeasts don't produce much of this fermentation by-product, our data wasn't at all similar to what other researchers had found. Although we had some support from the equipment supplier and other researchers in brewing laboratories at research centers around the world, we were pretty much on our own to understand the data we were collecting.

BACK TO MY ROOTS

Now that we had the technology to test beers and experiment with different possible improvements that would help us create a more consistent end product, I needed a way to be able to create batches of beer on which we could do trials and run tests. I had been contemplating building a small research brewery for some time, and now the need seemed that much more pressing. I started to work on the design and specifications for a 10-barrel brewery (if you're counting, the fourth brewhouse I built) that would incorporate all of the new ideas and technologies that I had been researching in the years since I built my first brewery.

After we had moved our operation into our beautiful 100-barrel copper brewhouse back in 1989, we sold the original 10-barrel system we started Sierra Nevada on to an old friend and aspiring craft brewer in northern California.[1] It didn't make any sense to keep it once we had moved production over to a more versatile and efficient German-engineered brewhouse. Once we added another 200-barrel German brewhouse in 1998, our expansions left us with a very well-engineered state-of-the-art brewery that could produce great, consistent beers. The downside was that given the larger batch size, we lacked the ability to do small-scale experimental brewing and were limited in our ability to make small, one-off brews for our pub without risking having to dump more than 3,000 gallons of beer if it didn't meet our expectations.

While planning what would come to be known as the Pilot Brewery, I designed a brewery that would allow the validation of technology as well as match our existing brewing system as closely as possible. We knew we needed to replicate our existing brews seamlessly in order for the brewhouse to be of the most value, particularly for developing new recipes. If we couldn't match what we did every day, then we would have trouble quantifying the value of any process change or creating a new recipe we could produce on a larger scale in the main brewery.

I went to several equipment manufacturers both in Europe and the United States to build the Pilot Brewery. Most of the suppliers were challenged by my desire to incorporate the wide range of design ideas and technologies I envisioned. I finally settled on a US supplier that

---

[1]Amazingly, given its cobbled together nature and years of hard use, it is still in use today at the same brewery almost 35 years after I pieced it together from cast-off scrap.

was open to building my dream pilot brewery. It aligned with my vision of consistently trying to improve the quality of our beer. I decided to take the research quest another step further and build a laboratory attached to the Pilot Brewery that was outfitted with the latest tools and instrumentation[2] to further our pursuit of brewing science and support our mission of trying to get the best beer into our consumers' hands.

Even though we now had the latest and greatest instrumentation, the human nose and a well-trained taste panel are still two of the most sensitive and valuable analytical tools available. Even if a beer passes every analytical test, it fails if it doesn't taste right. With those principles in mind, I also outfitted the lab with a state-of-the-art sensory area to allow for more rigorous taste panel training and human threshold validation. Our sensory center includes two workstations, a table for panel discussions, a galley with six tap handles, and five specially built booths that isolate tasters to allow them to focus on the beer in front of them. Our quality assurance department has established several panels, from those that participate in weekly triangle tests that support research projects to a quality panel that tastes every beer prior to release.

By the time it was finished, we had invested over $5 million in the research facility. We built an amazing compact brewery that could produce almost any conceivable beer style. Today it remains virtually unmatched in its design and capabilities compared with any pilot or 10-barrel brewery anywhere in the world. Since we built it, we've made a lot of discoveries and produced amazing beers, some as test runs for full-scale production and others for release only in our Pub. Some of our talented scientists' and brewers' discoveries have made only minor gains for better flavor stability and consistency, but others have been

---

[2]For the science geeks, who may be the only ones still reading this: We bought a state-of-the-art gas chromatograph to assist in hop aroma research, a high-performance liquid chromatograph for analyzing a wide of beer components from the naturally bitter resins of the hops to the essence of the malt sugars, and an inductively coupled plasma optical emission spectrometer that could detect metals in water or finished beer down into the low part-per-billion ranges. (Both copper and iron are detrimental to beer flavor stability.)

significant, such as a procedure we developed to remove free iron from new stainless steel beer kegs. We continue to work with bottle cap suppliers to try to develop an improved liner material; earlier research led to the change from twist-off crowns to a much improved pry-off crown that decreased the convenience for some drinkers but greatly improved the flavor stability and security of the package.

SHARING WHAT WE LEARNED

Over the years, as we met with the store owners and distributors who delivered our product to the consumer, it was very apparent that many of the people involved with distributing and selling Sierra Nevada beer didn't know a lot about the product. Most distributors, store owners, and bar and restaurant owners really didn't understand the brewing process, and even fewer knew how the basic raw materials were cultivated and utilized in the beer-making process. But the tremendous growth of craft beer had bred legions of beer geeks who were extremely knowledgeable about beer, and they expected the people they bought their beer from to have the same degree of expertise. Because we already had a great research and training facility, we decided to open our facility to others in the industry. We came up with the concept of Beer Camp and invite people in the beer industry for an intensive, hands-on, two-day course in brewing. Those who enroll in Beer Camp learn about beer and the brewing process by making and developing a new brand of beer, from recipe formulation to the development of a brand name.

We've had nearly 100 camps since we started the program in 2008 and have hosted a wide range of campers from salesmen, barley farmers, chefs, pub and store owners, and established brewers from around the world. We don't just let the 10 to 12 campers loose to play in our brewery. My brother, Steve, along with long-term employee, Terence Sullivan, act as camp counselors, taking them through an educational process that helps them grasp how all of the raw materials are combined to create a unique beer. Then our Pilot Brewery staff carefully guides them as they put together a recipe. After some education and much discussion, the campers decide on a concept and style for the beer, and then our brewers work with them to produce a practical recipe (sometimes campers go a little overboard with the creativity) that everyone hopes will produce an amazing, one-of-a-kind beer.

Beer Camp has been an incredible learning exercise both for brewery staff and for the more than 1,000 people who have attended. Letters from happy campers and articles that journalists have written about their experiences almost always mention the gracious and welcoming attitude of our employees. I'm glad that my employees are proud of what they do and where they work and are happy to show off our amazing campus and equipment.

Until 2011, Beer Camp was an invitation-only affair. However, after word got out about the camp, and we began receiving overwhelming interest from people who wanted to sign up for it, we wanted to give our loyal fans a chance to participate; the marketing department came up with the Beer Camp Contest in 2011. We asked consumers to submit videos that demonstrated their dedication to beer and awarded "golden tickets" to attend Beer Camp to the makers of the top 20 videos. In 2011, we hosted two successful consumer Beer Camps, in addition to over 40 other Beer Camps that resulted in a host of interesting, sometimes off-the-wall, and unique beers. In the years that we've run this contest, we've received some truly creative (and more than a few over-the-top) entries that we also screened for employees.

Besides giving fans and fellow brewers a behind-the-scenes peek at our operations, there were some unexpected benefits from Beer Camp. The collaborations between our brewers, homebrewers, and craft beer aficionados inspired many out-of-the box concepts. They help challenge our brewers to create beers outside our normal portfolio and do so in a way that still meets our high standards for quality and flavor. After several years of the program, we had some real winners and wanted to go a step further and package them for the public. In 2011, Sierra Nevada produced its first-ever variety pack composed of four Beer Camp creations that proved that we can still be innovators and leaders in the field based on our beer alone. The feedback was overwhelmingly positive, so we repeated the Beer Camp variety packs in 2012, with four different beers.

COLLABORATIONS

Our collaboration with other brewers extends beyond craft and homebrewers who visit Sierra Nevada. The craft brewing industry is unlike any other business in the world because of the sense of camaraderie that's become a hallmark of the craft movement. Brewers have a long history of helping each other out by supplying malt or hops to another brewer in a pinch, loaning a critical machine part, and even supplying yeast to a fellow brewer whose culture may have been compromised. When I first opened Sierra Nevada, I received a warm reception from the smallest to the largest brewers in the country. As we've grown, we've always tried to repay some of the generosity that was afforded to us. Historically this willingness to help has crossed all segments, and in many instances craft brewers large and small have come to each other's aid in a wide variety of ways. I sincerely doubt that the largest global players are as keen to lend a helping hand to their peers these days, though.

The newer generation of craft brewers has taken the idea of cooperation even further with collaborative brewing, when two or more brewers work together to develop a recipe and jointly produce and market a beer. Most collaborations are one-off projects done in the spirit of fun and innovation, and ideally, all of the brewers share equally in both the creative and production direction of the beer. Besides providing the opportunity to work with breweries that have expertise in different styles, another outcome of collaborations is the ability to get them into new markets where one of the breweries may not have had distribution or exposure. We've had fun and learned a lot doing a few collaborations with a handful of breweries that we admire and brewers whom we've been friends with for many years. They've all brought different creative insight and challenges to work through, and every one of them has broadened our knowledge and stretched our comfort zone. Hopefully, we've had the same positive effect on our partners.

In 2009, we worked with Sam Calagione, of Dogfish Head Craft Brewery, to create Life & Limb®, a very personal expression of our two brewing philosophies. Sam sums up collaborative brews with the 1970s advertising premise about the great success of the accidental mixing of chocolate and peanut butter—who knew they'd taste so good together? His approach to brewing is decidedly experimental and pushes the boundaries of beer in every sense. The creation of Life & Limb expanded our use of exotic sugars, including maple syrup from Sam's family farm and birch syrup from Alaskan birch trees. For a taste of Chico, we used some of Sierra Nevada's estate barley to produce dark, malty-style brown ale. Sam was involved in the development of the beer from day one and came with his wife, Mariah, to Sierra Nevada for the inaugural brew. I spent a rare and enjoyable day in the brew-house and was pleased with the results. Even the packaging artwork reflected Dogfish Head's off-centered sensibilities as well as our pre-disposition for nature. Life & Limb was such a hit that we came together again in 2011 to produce Life & Limb 2.

To celebrate our 30th anniversary, we had the idea to collaborate with the pioneers of the industry and pay homage to the way they helped pave for us and so many others. Working with Fritz Maytag, Jack McAuliffe, Fred Eckhardt, and Charlie Papazian, we created three beers that reflected what each of them contributed to Sierra Nevada. We kicked off 2010 with Fritz's visit to brew our beer, which we launched at a beer dinner at Anchor Brewery. A few months later Jack came to Chico; I hadn't seen him since the early 1980s because he left the business when New Albion closed. The last time he'd seen Sierra Nevada was when we were still on Gilman Way. Finally, Fred and Charlie lent their experience to the third beer in the series. We fol-lowed up the stout, ale, and bock with a grand cru that contained a blend of Pale Ale, Bigfoot Ale, and Celebration Ale, which seemed like a fitting trio to round out 2010.

In 2011, we embarked on another collaboration, but it was so long in the works that it didn't make an appearance until mid-2012. My son, Brian, along with Vinnie Cilurzo and his wife, Natalie, of Russian River Brewing Company, had been good friends for several years. Vinnie is one of the most accomplished and talented brewers in the country, having perfected a wide range of styles including a lot of sours and other funky beers and several outstanding IPAs. Many of the yeasts and bacteria that he uses in his brewing are generally the bane of most breweries because in careless or unskilled hands, they cause off flavors and unwanted consequences. Brian had always loved drinking Russian River's sour beers and approached Vinnie and me about collaborating on a Belgian-inspired beer using a very distinct strain of yeast called *Brettanomyces bruxellensis* that can produce a range of unique, and what some would call funky, flavors reminiscent of a horse blanket, leather, tobacco, or a wet dog. Its flavor evokes a wide range of reactions, from love to hate and everything in between. Under the right control and with careful balance, *Brett*, as it's called, can create very intriguing and interesting flavors in beers. Because of its tenacious nature, it can live for months or years in the bottle, working its magic and thinning out the body as it consumes complex sugars, which means that a beer brewed using *Brett* yeast continues to evolve even years after it has been bottled.

Initially, I had serious reservations about introducing *Brett* into the brewery. It is one of the thousands of yeast strains found lurking everywhere, but brewers typically want only their pure proven strains to be introduced into their breweries to minimize the risk of contaminating other beers. *Brett* is more insidious than most wild yeasts because it can linger for months or even years and then work its magic, or in some cases its evil, in beers that aren't intended to taste funky. In an early discussion about the collaboration, one of our managers commented with a heavy dose of incredulity, "It's the one thing brewers are fanatical about keeping *out* of their brewery, and we're going to bring it in?" In general the wine industry also fears this yeast because it can establish itself in wooden barrels and wreak havoc years later. Many high-end, classic European wines have a touch of *Brett*, which can live in wooden barrels and slowly infect its host and is often at such low levels that it is undetected at bottling but shows its funky self years later. Before I agreed to incorporate *Brett* into our brewing, we did quite a bit of work in our laboratory to assess the protocol necessary to kill it to get a good sense of what steps would be required to contain the culture. We determined that it would be less of a challenge than I thought because it was actually fairly easy to kill and manage—as long as we kept it isolated to the small packaging line where we handle only specialty products and exercised a high degree of diligence and careful sanitizing steps when handling the little critters.

I reluctantly agreed to proceeding with the collaboration, but I wanted to keep *Brett* out of contact with the internal valves and rubber parts that comprised the bottle filler. Thus, the *Brett* would have to be added to the brew after the bottles had already been filled but just before the corks were inserted. I started working on a plan that included a small, precision dosing unit normally used to fill pharmaceutical vials that I could mount on the filler and directly couple to a small keg containing the yeast culture. Nicknamed The Inseminator, my device allowed us to dose and domesticate the yeast safely. The result of months of planning and preparation, the new creation, Brux, took its name from the yeast we successfully tamed, with Vinnie on the brewing end and Sierra Nevada on the mechanical end, and earned the tagline, "domesticated wild ale."

In 2012, we worked on a fun, limited-run, barrel-aged beer for Savor, an annual Washington, DC, event produced by the Brewers Association. The Association asked us to brew the title collaboration with our friends and brewers at Boulevard Brewing Company in Kansas City, Missouri. I had been friends with John McDonald (the owner of Boulevard Brewing) for years, so we were happy to say yes to the collaboration. Our head brewers, Steve Dresler and Steven Pauwels are also friends and were excited about the project. Inspired by the California Trail, used in the 1840s and 1850s by hundreds of thousands of Americans migrating west from Missouri to Northern California, we decided to call the brew Terra Incognita. The beer traversed that same route in reverse, starting in Chico with some of our estate-grown malt and ending in Kansas City, where it was treated with *Brett* and aged in Missouri oak barrels. The beer was a big hit at the event (the only place it was available), and because it has *Brett*, the fans who have the patience to hold onto the unique brew may be in for a pleasant surprise when they open it. The beer will continue to evolve for years, going through phases of evolution in flavor and aroma that are hard to predict, which is part of the charm of beers like these.

COLLABORATING FOR A CAUSE

In 2010, we were approached by one of the founding monks of the Abbey of New Clairvaux, a local Cistercian monastery, to help them raise funds for a historic restoration project at their abbey, located in the small town of Vina just off Highway 99, 15 miles north of Chico. The property had an interesting history, having been originally owned and developed by Leland Stanford of Stanford University fame in the 1880s. During that time, it became one of the largest wineries in the world. Even though he invested great sums of money in the land and the vineyards, the unfavorable climate and his lack of knowledge about winemaking ultimately doomed the winery. In the 1940s it was purchased by the father of one of my friends, who farmed more sustainable and suitable crops on the property until 1955. He had been approached by a group from the Trappist order that wanted to establish a monastery in the fertile northern Sacramento valley region. The Trappist charter emphasizes work and prayer, and manual labor and self-sufficiency are characteristic of the order. Cistercian monasteries around the world often have agricultural pursuits that support their mission, and the peaceful property in Vina was an ideal place for them to establish a California sanctuary called the Abbey of New Clairvaux.

In 1955, Father Thomas Davis, then a young man, left the Trappist monastery in the Midwest, where he had lived, to help establish this new outpost in Vina, California. On his way to his new home, he detoured through San Francisco, where he was told he could find the remains of a twelfth-century Spanish monastery, the Abbey of Santa Maria de Ovila, that was once one of the monasteries of his church's ancestors. In 1931 William Randolph Hearst had purchased parts of it and other Spanish abbeys with the intention of moving the stones from La Mancha, Spain, and using them as the basis for an opulent home called Wyntoon he intended to build in California near Mount Shasta along the McCloud River. The Great Depression forced Hearst to change his plans, and the stones ended up scattered in San Francisco's Golden Gate Park, where Father Thomas found them. He vowed to bring the sacred stones to the site of the new abbey in Vina and 30 years after he first discovered them was able to convince the city of San Francisco to part with them.

In 1985, Father Thomas was finally able to embark on the process of rebuilding the chapter house on the grounds of the monastery in Vina using the stones from the Abbey of Santa Maria de Ovila. The project was much more involved than he ever could have imagined, and the cost of reassembling a twelfth-century building mounted. Although the monks were well along with their fundraising for the project, they still needed additional funds to complete their mission. After 25 years of slow but determined progress, Father Thomas and the current abbot, Father Paul Mark, approached Sierra Nevada with the idea of developing a beer in conjunction with the monastery as a way to help raise funds for the project.

The collaboration made complete sense. For thousands of years there's been a connection between wine and beer and many religious orders that utilize the libations both for nourishment and enjoyment for their members, as well as to generate income for the order through off-site sales. Trappist orders in particular have a long and revered brewing tradition, and today there are eight monasteries that produce a range of spectacular and distinctive beers.[3] Trappist products have a great reputation for quality, and the order has tried hard to maintain the Trappist brand, so to speak. Only beer brewed at a Trappist monastery either by or under the direction of the monks can be labeled a Trappist beer and bear the symbol of a Trappist product.

---

[3]Many of the monasteries are struggling to maintain their operations with a dwindling monk population and are relying on the support of several of the larger Trappist beer brands, such as Orval, Chimay, and Rochefert, which, although limited, have export sales that provide necessary income to themselves and the other 170 monasteries around the world.

The project started with a trip to Belgium, where Father Thomas, our brewers, and I visited a number of Trappist breweries for inspiration and education. Because we were going to produce the beer in our Chico facility and not on the monastery grounds, it would be referred to as an abbey beer. The tradition of brewing beers in conjunction with or in support of a monastery also has a long tradition in Europe, and many brands still bear the name of the order they supported. We thought it would be a great way to help their cause and created a brand of beer called Ovila® in homage to the original Spanish monastery. Since then we've hosted the monks of New Clairvaux at the brewery and developed several types of beer under the Ovila label. With the support of the community, they've made tremendous progress toward rebuilding the chapter house with the sacred stones. We've enjoyed working with a different part of our community, and their project gave us the opportunity to introduce new beer styles to our portfolio.

16

THE FUTURE

It is my design to die in the brew-house; let ale be placed to my mouth when I am expiring, that when the choirs of angels come, they may say, 'Be God propitious to this drinker.'

—Saint Columbanus, 612 CE

As this next chapter unfolds for our company and our family, I can't help but be amazed looking back at what Sierra Nevada has accomplished in a little over 30 years. At the same time, thinking about what lies ahead is at once terrifying and exciting. What has happened since we opened our first brewery in 1980 has been nothing short of a revolution in a time-honored craft that was near the brink of monopolization and industrialization. Not that consolidation and globalization haven't dramatically changed the dynamics of the players at the top tier, but the explosion and success of the previously non-existent grass roots brewing community has shocked even the most ardent supporters and participants. Few people, whether involved in the industry or watching from the sidelines, could have imagined or predicted what has happened to beer and the brewing industry in America. Craft brewing in the United States and around the world continues to show accelerating growth and relevance in an age-old and mature industry, and as I write this, the excitement and momentum don't show any signs of abating. In 2013 alone, nearly 1,000 breweries are purported to be in the planning stages in the US. Aspiring entrants are cobbling together business plans with a range of business models from homebrewing-sized operations, to some seemingly well-funded ventures with incredibly ambitious plans of becoming the next regional or national brand.

Almost without exception, in the highly developed craft markets, such as Portland, Seattle, San Diego, and the San Francisco Bay Area, craft beer sales make up 25 percent or more of the market share and are in almost all cases still growing. Although other less progressive regions may never reach those levels, there are still plenty of parts of this country with only a few percent market share for craft beer with plenty of room to grow. As the craft market has evolved so have the consumer, retailer, and distributor. Understanding how this dynamic market is evolving and staying relevant with the consumer will make or break many existing and newly minted breweries. I will be the first to acknowledge that this is an exciting and fun time to be in the beer business (at least for the majority of independent craft brewers), but the reality is that the brewing business is really difficult. Not everyone will succeed; there will plenty of fallout in the years to come. The next generation of brewers has their work cut out for them, whether it's the day-to-day challenges of making great consistent beer—to do it right is not as easy as many believe—or getting and maintaining good distribution in a highly competitive marketplace, where tap handles and shelf space are increasingly congested and loyalty can be fleeting.

My family, hopefully the next generation to take over the company, has embraced Sierra Nevada in different ways, and their interest and engagement also continue to evolve. My kids and wife have all lived with a father and husband who has been driven by, and at times obsessed and overwhelmed with, the brewery. I was gone a lot: Running a brewery is hard; running a brewery well is all encompassing. They have all suffered from a lack of attention and my availability for over 30 years; they have seen the time commitment and challenges firsthand that an operation and business as complex as our brewery is can have. Even so, they still want to be the guiding force in taking Sierra Nevada into the future.

After I had worked so hard to build my first little brewery, failing wasn't an option. I had to face every crisis and challenge head on, no matter how much time and energy it took. I have never pushed my kids into the brewery, at least not intentionally, although the idea of not having the family involved with the company I started probably weighs on them heavily. My oldest daughter, Sierra, like all my kids, worked in and was exposed to the brewery at a young age. She worked in various capacities in the Pub and later directly in the brewery in areas as varied as the maintenance shop and reception. In college she went into the health field and after graduating worked in a local clinic. She got the urge to find a role back at the brewery and jumped in with both feet, getting involved with sales and marketing. Most recently she took on the ambitious role of the director of customer experience, a job with new challenges and mounting responsibilities. Sierra also has been one of my copy editors and my voice of reason for many parts of this book. Having been born a few years before I started the company, she has lived through much of this story firsthand. Like Sierra, my middle child, Carrie, held various jobs at the brewery, working in the lab during high school and later college before she moved to Portland to get her master's in social work. She returned to Chico a few years later when she was starting her family and worked at the brewery part-time. Although she currently is not working at the brewery and hasn't decided if working with her siblings is what she wants to do, the opportunity is always available. My youngest child and son, Brian, like his older sisters, held a variety of summer jobs before and during college. The entire family, including my wife and me, attended Butte Community College and later Chico State. While at Butte, Brian pursued a degree in law enforcement but just before graduation had a change of heart and went for a business degree at Chico State. After graduation he came back to the brewery full-time. Brian has taken a very active role in brewery management, getting exposure in everything from sales and distribution to customer experience, including a brief stint managing the Pub. He recently made the huge commitment to help lead the next phase of Sierra Nevada's growth.

Would I love for one or all of them to one day take the reins? Of course! But I also know the challenges and sacrifices I made and don't want to set them up for either failure or taking on the all-encompassing role that I had. Having built the company from scratch and been involved in nearly every decision and aspect of the operation, my current role is one that can't and shouldn't be replaced. It's not realistic to expect anyone to step into my role and try to manage or be involved in the same fashion with everything that I have lived through and experienced.

I have a lot of friends in the brewing business, and almost without exception the ones who are the most successful are highly engaged and somewhat consumed by their companies. That is not to say that you have to be on 24/7 to be successful. I haven't always done the best job delegating roles and responsibilities; some of my friends have at least outwardly done a better job than I have at balancing family, work, and play, but when the company demands it, they are on 100 percent.

The past few years our management team has been focusing on putting together a plan for succession and working to get the right people in place to help lead the company when we individually decide or are forced to step away. Are we there yet? No, not completely. We have hired some great talent but still have several key spots to fill. The past few years I have been searching for a strong technical and yet practical brewer to assist me in both technical matters and overall vision and innovation for the future. After searching for months I wasn't able to come up with what I felt was someone with the industry experience, passion, practicality, and leadership skills, and the last thing I wanted was someone in that role who could alter or derail what we had built. As the company has evolved the last few years my vision for that person has also evolved and I'm still looking. I'm confident I'll know I've found the right person when I meet him or her.

NO END IN SIGHT TO SALES INCREASES

As we continued to see sales increases over the years, we regularly bumped up against capacity constraints in Chico. For the short term I had no choice but to continue adding necessary equipment and infrastructure in Chico, solving production bottlenecks where practical with additional fermentation tanks and small improvements to eke out a little capacity, in order to not short our customers or be forced to pull out of existing markets, neither of which was acceptable to me. Sierra Nevada's 20th Street brewery had been expanded far past the original 60,000 barrels that it had been designed to produce, and even with the addition of the second brewhouse in 1998, we were still well above my original sales projections. In 2007, I did one last review of potential production bottlenecks and did what I thought was my last significant project to maximize the Chico plant. We spent over $5 million to add 14 German-built 800-barrel fermentation tanks. With the extra capacity, we could theoretically brew and ferment 1 million barrels per year, but we didn't have a plan to allow us to grow past that.

In 2008, we sold 600,070 barrels of beer, far in excess of what I had ever envisioned possible, and our sales growth was starting to accelerate. In 2009, sales were up almost 8 percent, and by 2010 they were up 9 percent, which translated to annual production of nearly 800,000 barrels. Now it looked like we were on track to exceed our growth projections, and I started to feel some urgency about the company's future and next steps. With our increasing rate of growth, our timeline for making a decision accelerated. I knew it didn't make much sense to add a lot of capacity to Chico (and, frankly, we don't have much room left). We thought it prudent to do projections to compare an expansion scenario with a greenfield plant and to weigh those options against doing nothing and effectively maximizing our current brewery and then either rationing beer or pulling out of markets when we hit capacity. But we did have another alternative: A second Sierra Nevada brewery.

I have always viewed myself as cautious and somewhat fiscally conservative, at least when it came to making big financial bets. Not that I haven't put it all on the line before; I have many times. But I like to make sure the odds are well stacked in my favor before placing the bet. Building a completely new second brewery on the East Coast would be a big bet; we are well capitalized and have sufficient demand to justify the brewery, even if we miss our targeted growth. But I continue to ask myself, when is the marketplace going to get saturated? Is it already there? How many Pale Ales or IPAs can the marketplace support? Where is the shelf space going to come from to support all these aspiring brands?

We got to the point that we had to make a decision—make concrete plans for future growth or put the brakes on? After much thought, discussion with company managers, and debate among my family, I decided that sitting still wasn't an option for Sierra Nevada. We'd worked too hard to build our company and brand and weren't willing to sit on the sidelines as the craft industry continued to grow and evolve. I opted for growth, putting us on a new path for the future, and we chose North Carolina as the site of our second brewery; it couldn't be done soon enough.

Our rate of sales started to accelerate, and we projected a fairly ambitious 8 percent growth rate for 2012. After seeing good momentum by the end of 2011, ending up 7.6 percent, we felt that 8 percent might be a slight stretch but achievable if the segment continued its overall strength. We were in the third year of an overall declining beer market, but craft was still holding steady at nearly 10 percent growth. I felt I had to pull the trigger on the new brewery, or we would most likely experience shortages. It was a tough decision. I agonized over it long enough, but based on our 8 percent growth rate, I had just two years to get beer out the door of a new facility. January sales shocked us by being up 23 percent. It's hard to gauge trends or make predictions on one month's sales, but we were caught a little off guard. We hadn't shipped nearly that much beer, so the distributors' inventories had supplied the balance. February was up again with an 18 percent increase in sales, which was obviously great, but we started to get more concerned. We had been brewing around the clock at our main brewhouse for some time but hadn't yet added weekends to our 100-barrel brewhouse. We staffed up and went into overdrive in both brewhouses to try to meet demand, which we hadn't anticipated needing to do for another year. I felt like Captain Kirk saying, "Gimme all you got, Scottie." By that point we were playing catch-up and could barely make enough beer. March was up 10.5%, but because we had shorted some of our distributors, we may not have fulfilled all of our orders. April was up only 12.7 percent, and again we were dealing with low distributor inventories. May was up 21.4 percent, and these trends looked like they were here to stay. The new brewery was still at least a year-and-a-half away.

I am either lucky or unlucky, but I now have the luxury or challenge to build what will be my fifth brewhouse, if I include Sierra Nevada's pilot plant. I am often asked if I had any idea or plan when I started my brewery that it would grow to where it is today. The truthful answer is no, not a clue. It has been an adventure that continues to captivate and amaze me. I never expected (nor wanted) to be building another brewery, but I find myself just as involved and consumed by it as I was 35 years ago. Hopefully it never stops.

INDEX